D0769003

TECHNOLOGY AND ORGANIZATION: ESSAYS IN HONOUR OF JOAN WOODWARD

RESEARCH IN THE SOCIOLOGY OF ORGANIZATIONS

Series Editor: Michael Lounsbury

Recent Volumes

Volume 15:	Deviance in and of Organizations
Volume 16:	Networks in and around Organizations
Volume 17:	Organizational Politics
Volume 18:	Social Capital of Organizations
Volume 19:	Social Structure and Organizations Revisited
Volume 20:	The Governance of Relations in Markets and Organizations
Volume 21:	Postmodernism and Management: Pros, Cons and the Alternative
Volume 22:	Legitimacy Processes in Organizations
Volume 23:	Transformation in Cultural Industries
Volume 24:	Professional Service Firms
Volume 25:	The Sociology of Entrepreneurship
Volume 26:	Studying Differences between Organizations: Comparative Approaches to Organizational Research
Volume 27:	Institutions and Ideology
Volume 28:	Stanford's Organization Theory Renaissance, 1970–2000

RESEARCH IN THE SOCIOLOGY OF ORGANIZATIONS
VOLUME 29

TECHNOLOGY AND ORGANIZATION: ESSAYS IN HONOUR OF JOAN WOODWARD

EDITED BY

NELSON PHILLIPS
Imperial College Business School, London, UK

GRAHAM SEWELL
University of Melbourne, Australia

DOROTHY GRIFFITHS
Imperial College Business School, London, UK

United Kingdom – North America – Japan
India – Malaysia – China

Emerald Group Publishing Limited
Howard House, Wagon Lane, Bingley BD16 1WA, UK

First edition 2010

Reprints and permission service
Contact: booksandseries@emeraldinsight.com

British Library Cataloguing in Publication Data
A catalogue record for this book is available from the British Library

ISBN: 978-1-84950-984-8
ISSN: 0733-558X (Series)

CONTENTS

SECTION 4 – SHORT ESSAYS IN TECHNOLOGY AND ORGANIZATION

LIST OF CONTRIBUTORS

Shahzad Ansari — Judge Business School, University of Cambridge, Cambridge, UK

Adam J. Bock — Imperial College Business School, London, UK

Anna Canato — IÉSEG School of Management Lille, La Defense, France

Andrew Davies — Imperial College Business School, London, UK

Sandra Dawson — Cambridge Judge Business School and Sidney Sussex College, University of Cambridge, Cambridge, UK

Graham Dover — Simon Fraser University, Vancouver, BC, Canada

Lars Frederiksen — Imperial College Business School, London, UK

Annabelle Gawer — Imperial College Business School, London, UK

Gerard George — Imperial College Business School, London, UK

Royston Greenwood — University of Alberta, Edmonton, AB, Canada

Dorothy Griffiths — Imperial College Business School, London, UK

Cynthia Hardy — University of Melbourne, Parkville, VIC, Australia

C. R. (Bob) Hinings	University of Alberta, Edmonton, AB, Canada
P. Devereaux Jennings	University of Alberta, Edmonton, AB, Canada
Sarah Kaplan	Rotman School, University of Toronto, Toronto, Canada
Lisl Klein	The Bayswater Institute, London, UK
Thomas B. Lawrence	Simon Fraser University, Vancouver, BC, Canada
Michael Lounsbury	University of Alberta, Edmonton, AB, Canada
Kamal Munir	Judge Business School, Cambridge University, Cambridge, UK
Fiona Murray	MIT Sloan School of Management, Cambridge, MA, USA
Wanda J. Orlikowski	MIT Sloan School of Management, Cambridge, MA, USA
Markus Perkmann	Imperial College Business School, London, UK
Charles Perrow	Yale University, New Haven, CT, USA
Nelson Phillips	Imperial College Business School, London, UK
Davide Ravasi	Università Bocconi, Milan, Italy
Graham Sewell	Department of Management and Marketing, University of Melbourne, Melbourne, VIC, Australia
André Spicer	Warwick Business School, University of Warwick, Coventry, UK
Jennifer Whyte	University of Reading, Reading, UK
Tyler Wry	University of Alberta, Edmonton, AB, Canada

ADVISORY BOARD

PREFACE

When Joan Woodward died in 1971 at the age of 54, she left behind an enormous professional and personal legacy. This volume is a tribute to her work and life, to the profound effect she had on those she worked with, and to the important impact her work has had on how we think about organizations. It is also a tribute to a woman who succeeded in what was, at the time, overwhelmingly a man's world. That she was only the second woman appointed as a full professor at Imperial College London provides ample evidence of her success in the unlikely and very masculine setting of post-war Britain.

To reflect on both her life and her work, we have brought together a diverse group of contributors. Some, such Sandra Dawson and Lisle Klein, knew and worked with her in 1960s; others, such as Charles Perrow and Bob Hinings, were involved in the same streams of research and in the development of what we now know of as contingency theory; whereas others, such as Sandra Kaplan and Wanda Orlikowski, continue to push ahead with the research agenda focusing on links between technology and organization pioneered by Joan.

The idea for this volume arose out of one of Joan's many legacies at Imperial College. Shortly after her death, the friends and colleagues of Joan Woodward established a fund to bring scholars of international renown to Imperial to give a biannual lecture on some topic related to technology and organization studies. The Joan Woodward Lecture has been given by many eminent scholars over the past 30 years and, while at a dinner following the most recent lecture given by Steve Barley, Dot Griffiths brought up the idea of commemorating Joan's profound impact on our thinking about organizations. This would involve contributions by people who knew her personally and worked with her directly combined with the reflections of eminent scholars whose own work has been deeply influenced by Joan's watershed studies. The general response to the idea was overwhelmingly positive, and after an animated discussion and several glasses of wine at a South Kensington restaurant, the idea of this volume was born.

The idea went through a number of iterations before the current format was decided upon. The volume contains four sections. It begins with an introduction in which we provide some background on Joan's life and summarize the main themes in her work. We have written this as an overview to explain her contribution and also give some sense of how impressive her contribution was given the context in which she worked. In the second section, a number of people who worked with her provide very personal reflections and describe the time they worked with her. These reflections are fascinating, both in understanding Joan as a person and also in providing compelling pictures of organization theory research at that time. In the third section, we bring together a set of chapters that build on Joan's work. These chapters are all original contributions by leading scholars that continue her legacy of considering the connection between technology and organization. Finally, in the fourth section, we have included a number of essays discussing trends and future themes in technology and organization. Combined, the four sections provide an overview of Joan's work and life, exemplary work extending her legacy, and some ideas of where the field is headed in the future.

As always with projects of this sort, a number of people have been of tremendous help in putting together this volume. First of all, we thank all the authors who put so much time and energy into their chapters. Without their enthusiasm, hard work, and patience, the volume would not have been possible. Second, we thank Michael Lounsbury, the series editor, for all his help and support. He was very enthusiastic about the idea from the beginning, and his assistance as an editor and an author is much appreciated. Third, we thank our editor at Emerald, Rebecca Forster, for all her help in guiding us through the process. Finally, we thank Donna Sutherland-Smith for all her help in proofreading chapters, managing permissions forms, and all the other things she did to keep the process running and get the chapters in shape. Her help was essential to the successful completion and final quality of this volume.

Putting this volume together was an incredible experience for us. Revisiting Joan's life and work through her contemporaries was moving and poignant. But coming to understand her achievements as a scholar and her impact on our understanding of organizations and the importance of technology was also hugely inspiring. Joan was, above all, a scholar, and understanding her approach and contribution highlighted the possibilities and importance and innovative scholarship about organizations. We hope you will find this volume interesting and trust that it will help to inspire future generations of organizational theorists to continue to develop our understanding of technology and organizations.

Nelson Phillips
Graham Sewell
Dorothy Griffiths
Editors

SECTION 1 – INTRODUCTION

INTRODUCTION: JOAN WOODWARD AND THE STUDY OF ORGANIZATIONS

Graham Sewell and Nelson Phillips

> The problem of welding an enterprise into an integrated whole varies with the amount and kinds of differentiation of its parts and with the kinds of relationship which the technological process requires; that is, different kinds of heterogeneity call for different ways of homogenizing. The technology appropriate to a particular purpose not only determines in an important way the extent and type of differentiation but also determines the amount of coordination and cooperation required and the locus of responsibility for these.
>
> – Thompson and Bates (1957, p. 338)

It is fitting to commence a volume dedicated to the legacy of Joan Woodward with a theoretical proposition that, by the time James Thompson and Frederick Bates were writing in 1957, she had already worked through systematically in an empirical setting. The initial findings of Joan's famous study of the organizational structure of manufacturing firms in South East Essex were contained in a modest 40-page pamphlet, *Management and Technology*, published in 1958 by the UK's Department of Scientific and Industrial Research. This amply demonstrates how advanced her thinking was in global terms at a time when "administrative science" was in its infancy in the United Kingdom.[1]

Although she is now best remembered for the 1965 book, *Industrial Organization: Theory and Practice*, this 1958 volume had already exerted a

Technology and Organization: Essays in Honour of Joan Woodward
Research in the Sociology of Organizations, Volume 29, 3–20

ISSN: 0733-558X/doi:10.1108/S0733-558X(2010)0000029005

considerable influence on key US scholars by the time *Industrial Organization* appeared. In an era where research is widely available almost at the moment it is written, we can all too easily underestimate the rapidity with which ideas were exchanged in the 1950s but, even with this caveat, it seems remarkable that such an apparently parochial report (South East Essex hardly being the powerhouse of the mid-twentieth-century industrialized world!) should reach such a select and influential audience so quickly. Charles Perrow's fascinating personal recollections in this volume recalling how he came into contact with Joan sheds some light on how this influence spread, but this introductory chapter is less concerned with such path dependencies and more concerned with the "What?" and "Why?" of her legacy.

The first thing we should remember when considering Joan's career is how limited the opportunities were for those who wished to work in the British university sector in the immediate post-war period. Long before the Robbins report of 1963 had recommended the massive expansion of the sector, higher education was an exclusive pursuit for a small number of (usually male) students and academics. Despite this exclusivity, Joan secured an academic post at the University of Liverpool between 1948 and 1953 where, as a member of the Department of Social Science, she conducted research on employment relations in various settings such as hospitals, docks, and shops. As Charles Perrow notes in his personal reflection, this was an unusual change in direction for someone who was previously a classics scholar! Nevertheless, this early research resulted in a number of publications that have been overshadowed by her subsequent work, although her 1960 book, *The Saleswoman*, is a pioneering but neglected study of employment in the service sector. At Liverpool she also came into contact with industrial relations scholars like Tom Lupton who were conducting their own ground-breaking work on the shopfloor effects of technical change, and this explicitly influenced her thinking in her later study of South East Essex (Woodward, 1965).

After Liverpool she moved on to the South East Essex Technical College where she headed the Human Relations Research Unit from 1953 to 1957. We return to her activities in Essex in the next section, as these form the crucial period of data gathering and analysis that later became so influential. For now we simply note that this was a staging post in a career that ended with a chair in industrial sociology at Imperial College of Science and Technology (then part of the University of London, although it has recently received its own Royal Charter as an independent degree awarding institution). In the late 1950s Imperial College was, demographically speaking, overwhelmingly male and Joan was only the second woman to hold a chair at this prestigious institution. While at Imperial College, Joan also lectured at the Oxford University Delegacy for Social Administration – a delegacy being a vehicle used by Oxford to incorporate new activities and emerging disciplines in a sort of "semi-detached" way until they were able to command wider acceptance by the university's more conservative elements.

The personal recollections of Joan's life and work contained in this volume all speak of the great loss felt among her friends and colleagues as she succumbed to illness in 1971. Talking to these people, even now there is still a palpable sense of collective bereavement. However, in this volume we wish to celebrate Joan's life and work; a legacy that lives on as each subsequent generation of organizational sociologist learns of her influence for the first time (we note that she is still included – along with people of the stature of Frederick W. Taylor, Max Weber, Elton Mayo, and Herbert Simon – in the most recent edition of Derek Pugh and David Hickson's *Great Writers on Organizations*). To be sure, not everything that Joan originally propounded back in the 1950s as part of the turn to the "technological imperative" in organizational sociology has stood the test of time (see Harvey, 1968; Mohr, 1971; Child & Mansfield, 1972). But, as we and the other authors in this volume argue, there is still much to be gained from a critical engagement with her work.

Thus, in the rest of this chapter, we set out our case for the continued relevance of Joan's work. We begin by looking at the initial reception of *Industrial Organization: Theory and Practice* before going on to examine how the main findings of that book were empirically tested by others, most notable by members of the "Aston School." We then look beyond the narrow focus on the relationship between technology and organizational structure for which Joan is best remembered to rehabilitate her reputation as a scholar of the politics of technological and organizational change before concluding by reflecting on the contributions of the other chapters in this volume.

THE INITIAL RECEPTION OF INDUSTRIAL ORGANIZATION: THEORY AND PRACTICE

Joan undertook the ground-breaking project originally reported in the 1958 pamphlet, *Management and Technology*, not at one of Britain's great universities, but at the unfashionable address of the South East Essex Technical College (then in the county of Essex but now part of the London Borough of Barking and Dagenham). The Human Relations Research Unit had been set up at the college, which is now part of the University of East London, in 1953 with support from a number of agencies including funding ultimately derived from the Marshall Plan. Its express purpose was to enhance the performance of industry and commerce through the application of social science. Those readers familiar with the area will know that, at the time, it was economically and culturally dominated by the Ford assembly plant in nearby Dagenham, but it was also home to a diverse range of small- and medium-sized industrial workshops that were typical of the pre-war Greater London economy (Woodward, 1965; Massey & Meegan, 1982). It was into this diverse industrial milieu that Joan and her research team ventured (Fig. 1), completing their main study in 1958.

As we noted earlier, the preliminary results were published by the British Government's Department of Scientific and Industrial Research (Woodward, 1958) and, according to Joan herself, the most important finding the research team revealed was

> … that similar administrative expedients could lead to wide variations in results. Firms in which organizational structure reflected an implicit acceptance of what has come to be known as classical management theory were not always the most successful from a commercial point of view. This theory did not therefore appear to be adequate as a practical guide to those responsible for the organization of industry. (Woodward, 1965, p. vi)

This observation – that successful manufacturing organizations did not always conform to the prescriptions offered by the management textbooks of the day but rather responded to the demands of their unique operating circumstances – became popularized through its role as a foundational assumption of "Contingency Theory" (Klein, 2006). Of course, ideas that seem so obvious today can be remarkably radical when they are proposed for Joan was challenging the fundamental orthodoxy of the time: that "classical management theory" derived from Frederick Winslow Taylor, Henri Fayol, or Mary Parker Follett did indeed offer a universal set of principles that would lead to a convergence of organizational structures and practices, be they to be found in Detroit, the Soviet Union (Lenin and other Bolsheviks were famously attracted to the "scientific" aspects of Taylor's ideas), or in an unprepossessing East London suburb bypassed by the A13 arterial road.

According to Joan, by applying these principles, we ought to find three characteristic configurations of authority relations: (1) line organization where authority flows directly from the chief executive to subordinate managers and onto employees in a traditional bureaucratic manner; (2) functional organization where individual employees were directed by a

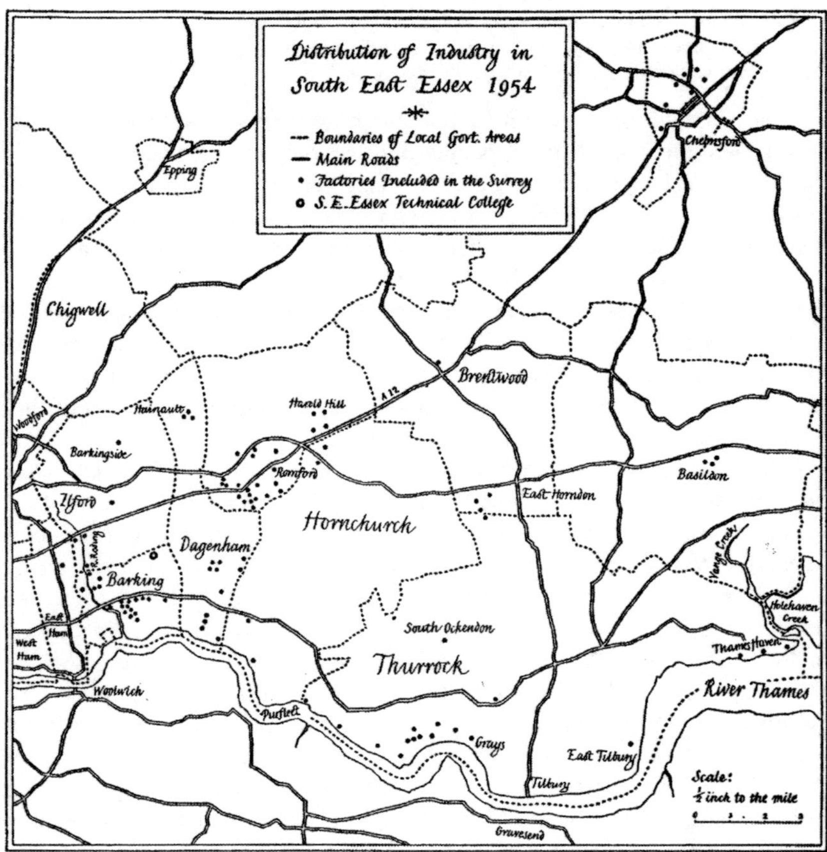

Fig. 1. Location of Woodward's Original Study Firms. *Source:* Woodward (1958).

number of specialist supervisors; and (3) hybrid line-staff organization where a direct line of authority is retained by senior managers as employees are assigned to functionally specialized departments. Little advice was ever offered, however, by advocates of these respective organizational structures about how a manager should go about choosing which one would best guarantee their organization's success. After first wrestling with the problem of defining success, the consternation felt by the team is palpable when it reported that, of the 100 manufacturing firms studied:

> No relationship of any kind had been established between organizational and other characteristics, and to a research team based on a College that spent so much time and

> effort on the teaching of management subjects, the lack of any inter-relationship between business success and what is generally regarded as sound organization structure was particularly disconcerting. (Woodward, 1965, p. 34)

Thus, the finding for which Joan's research is best remembered – that the way a manufacturing firm is socially and technically organized depends on the nature of its production process – can be seen as a serendipitous by-product of an original objective to determine what makes an organization successful or not in terms of its structure. Indeed, Klein (2006) indicates that it was something of an afterthought to classify the study's firms according to the complexity of their production system – the now familiar typology of unit and small batch, large batch and mass, and continuous process production (Fig. 2).[2] This reordering of the data revealed that the most successful firms of each type shared something in common in terms of their planning and control of production.

Reading contemporary North American reviews of *Industrial Organization: Theory and Practice*, one is struck by how perplexed many of the reviewers are to discover that such a seemingly atheoretical and inductive research enterprise (an enterprise that, according to some sociologists, lacked methodological rigor to boot!) could yield such profound and influential results. Sympathetic reviewers (people of the stature of Arthur Stinchcombe in the *Journal of Business*, Terence Hopkins in the *Administrative Science Quarterly*, or Charles Perrow in the *American Sociological Review* – see Stinchcombe, 1965; Hopkins, 1965; Perrow, 1967a) had the perspicacity to see Joan's work as a rough diamond with an intrinsic value that shone through despite its flaws. Interestingly, the original methodological objections have paled as case studies and data collection using interviews have become acceptable features of a more ecumenical approach to research in organizational sociology. Even the problem of the atheoretical and inductive nature of the research is rarely mentioned. We suspect that this is due, at least in part, to the fact that most people learn about Joan's research second hand as undergraduates and would be surprised to discover that a central feature of the curriculum had such apparently lowly conceptual origins.

The accusation that has endured, however, is Joan's sin of "technological determinism" (Perrow, 1967a). Of course, to be deterministic about anything at all is frowned upon in sociological circles these days and all the chapters in this volume confront this problem directly or indirectly. Nevertheless, in addressing this criticism, we would be well served to remember the kind of economic and intellectual climate from which Joan's South Essex project emerged. Before we go on to do this, however, we wish to spend some time considering the role played by *Industrial*

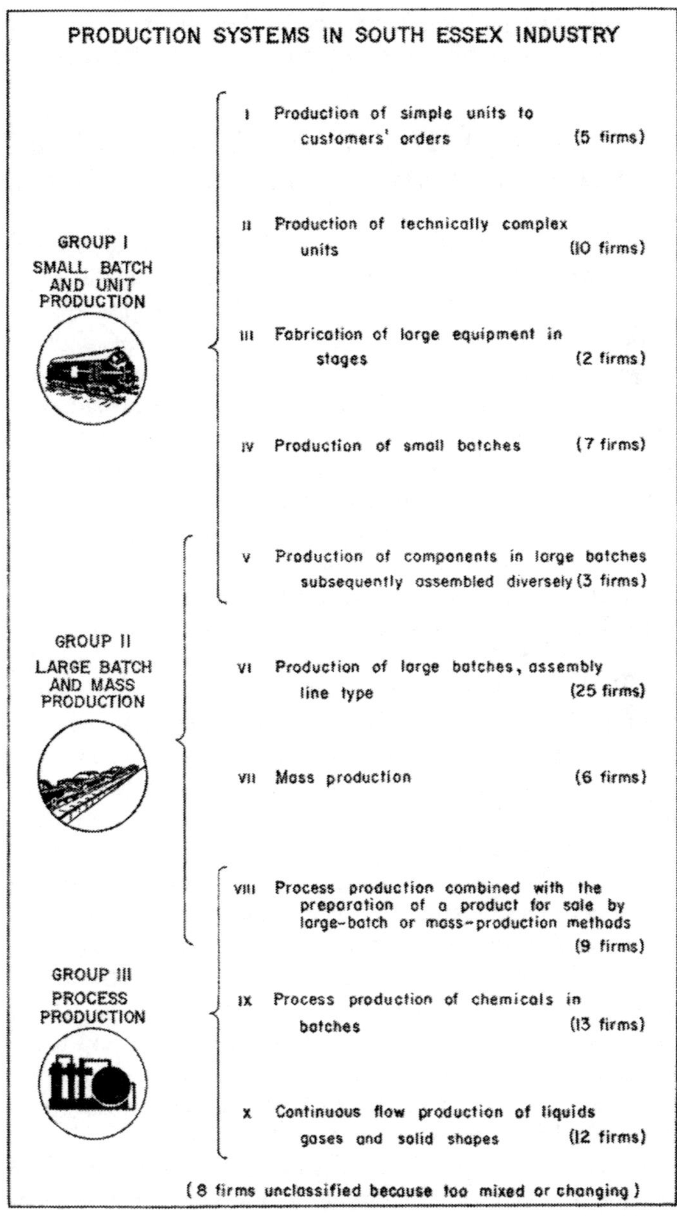

Fig. 2. Woodward's Original Typology of Production Systems. *Source:* Woodward (1958).

Organization: Theory and Practice in establishing a research program that considered the relationship between technology and organizational structure.

JOAN WOODWARD AND THE TECHNOLOGICAL IMPERATIVE IN ORGANIZATIONAL SOCIOLOGY

Looking back on *Industrial Organization: Theory and Practice* five years after its publication, Joan noted that "patient and detailed exploration of what really happens inside industrial firms was a prerequisite to the development of an organization theory comprehensive enough to provide managers with a reliable basis for their decisions and actions" (Woodward, 1970, p. 234). In these days of "evidence-based" policy making this may seem to be a statement of the obvious, but we would do well to remember that Joan saw her principal achievement as debunking the ideological basis of much of what passed for twentieth-century management theory; ideology that made it "impossible for managers to be detached and impersonal enough to be conscious of the nature of their own achievements" (Woodward 1965, p. 256). In this sense, her championing of an empirically based research program stands alongside her inspiration of the "technological turn" as a major aspect of her legacy.

It is something of an irony then that one of the earliest and most influential interpretations of Joan's work was Charles Perrow's framework for the comparative analysis of organizations (Perrow, 1967b). Like Joan's three-way typology of technology, Perrow's division of the organizational world into four ideal types (based on whether work is standardized or involves many exceptions and whether those exceptions can be analyzed systematically or whether intuition, experience, and guesswork must be used) is still a staple of management textbooks. In his seminal article, Perrow draws the distinction between three main functions of management. The first he calls "Area One," which includes the design and planning function. "Area Two" involves the *technical control* of and support for production and marketing, and "Area Three" involves the *supervision* of production and marketing.

According to Perrow, the rationale for making the distinction between control and supervision of production and marketing – thereby setting apart Areas Two and Three – was developed by "Joan Woodward in her brilliant study, *Industrial Organization*" (Perrow, 1967b, p. 199n). Later, however, he goes on to add a note of caution about the usefulness of Joan's framework, stating that production technology is a useful predictor of the way that productive tasks are done in organizations but warning against taking production technology and productive tasks together as predictor of social structures such as authority relations. Thus, Perrow's (1967b) framework can simultaneously be seen as one of the first major applications of Joan's work and also one of the first to point out its analytical limitations. It was not until the emergence of the Aston School, however, that her work was to be subjected to its first major empirical test.

David Hickson (1996) and David Pugh (1996) – key figures in the development of the Aston School – each provide fascinating insights into the kind of intellectual climate in which, along with Joan, they were operating in the United Kingdom during the 1960s. Both Hickson and Pugh were involved in a detailed empirical study (Hickson, Pugh, & Pheysey, 1969) that appeared to confirm Perrow's (1967b) proposition that productive technology only affects those structural variables directly related to the organization of work. In other words, although we can draw conclusions about the degree to which a production system is integrated from the intrinsic nature of a product and the way it must be put together, there was little evidence to suggest that "technological imperative" also led to characteristic patterns in things like the extent of hierarchy or the span of control.

They arrived at this conclusion by applying Joan's original fine-grained typology of production systems (Fig. 2) to the 31 manufacturing firms in their sample taken from the West Midlands region of the United Kingdom. They found that none of the relationships between an organization's social structure and its technology of the kind observed by Joan in South East Essex were repeated in their study. Nevertheless, Hickson et al. (1969) do not go as far as repudiating Joan's core thesis, preferring to represent it as important contribution with inevitable limitations. This high level of regard is later reflected in the Aston School's "strategic contingencies theory of intra-organizational power" (Hickson, Hinings, Lee, Schneck, & Pennings, 1971). Here Joan's observation that you could explain a firm's success by the status and influence it afforded to its "critical function" (be it design, marketing, or production – Woodward, 1965) is taken as a foundational assumption of a sophisticated model that links the power of a subunit with its centrality in the workflow in the organization.

Other important studies that focus on the variation of technology and task-specific characteristics as independent variables affecting management processes and organizational structures include Mahoney and Weitzel (1969), Grimes, Klein, and Shull (1970), Kynaston Reeves and Turner (1972), Grimes and Klein (1973), Blau, Falbe, McKinley, and Tracy (1976), McMahon and Ivancevich (1976), Billings, Klimoski, and Breaugh (1977), and Reimann (1980). All these works not only cite Joan's work (usually on the first page if not the first paragraph) but also use it as a foundational component of their contingency approach (cf. Lawrence & Lorsch, 1967) that includes technology as an operationalized concept in an empirical study. Most notable among these, insofar as it represents a direct continuation of Joan's project by members of her team at Imperial College, is Tom Kynaston Reeves and Barry Turner's decision to focus exclusively on batch production to determine the relationship between centralized control and planning on the one hand and complexity and uncertainty on the other (cf. Thompson, 1967). Their rationale for this focus was Joan's observation that, of the three main types of manufacturing organization, batch producers were least constrained by their technology in terms of the authority relations they could adopt (Woodward, 1965). Adopting Glaser and Strauss's (1967) grounded theory approach, Kynaston Reeves and Turner conducted three case studies that indeed showed how batch producers developed flexible and localized strategies to deal with complexity and uncertainty in ways that made it possible to regulate the flow of work without the need to for central planning and control.

By the early 1980s, after Reimann (1980) published one of the last major articles that can be broadly described as being directly inspired by Joan's original study, her work started to become less central to organizational theory. To a large extent, this could be explained as a result of changing fashion. The 1970s were the heyday of theoretical approaches that concerned themselves with macro-level features like the determinants of organizational structure, but the emergence of institutional theory (Meyer & Rowan, 1977; DiMaggio & Powell, 1983), and the turn to culture and cognition it signaled, along with a growing interest in things like leadership and entrepreneurial activity, were indicative of a shift in emphasis toward interpretive approaches and methodological individualism in organizational sociology.

Interestingly, it was not until researchers such as Orlikowski (1992), Barley and Tolbert (1997), and Orlikowski and Barley (2001) began to reengage with matters of both structure *and* agency using Anthony Giddens' "structuration" approach that Joan's work began to gain recognition among a new generation of researchers interested in technology and organizations, albeit through a critique of the "technological imperative." For example, Orlikowski (1992, p. 400) considers Joan's to be representative of a view that "largely ignores the action of humans in developing, appropriating, and changing technology." To be sure, *Management and Organization* and *Industrial Organization: Theory and Practice* are today remembered for their claims about the way in which technology appears to be an independent variable that predicts human behavior or organizational properties but, in considering Joan's continuing legacy, we would be well served to look back to the intellectual and cultural influences that shaped her research. We argue that reconnecting with these influences allows us to reconsider her contribution, not just as a technological determinist, but as a prescient observer of the impact that technological change has on organizational power structures.

THE INTELLECTUAL AND CULTURAL ANTECEDENTS OF WOODWARD'S WORK

Given that the Human Relations Research Unit at South East Essex Technical College was charged with providing a social science dividend for an economy struggling to emerge from the ravages of war, it should come as no surprise that Joan drew heavily on the European and North American sociological mainstreams, mentioning authors such as Max Weber, Thorstein Veblen, and Philip Selznick as sources of intellectual inspiration. Some reviewers of Joan's later collaborative work (Woodward, 1970) accused her of being ignorant of the more technical and quantitative traditions in North American organizational sociology (e.g., Magnusen, 1970), but the title of the Unit undoubtedly reflected the strong influence exerted on her by the Human Relations School of Elton Mayo and his acolytes such as Fritz Roethlisberger. This influence was, however, moderated by the work of the nascent Tavistock Institute (founded in 1946), which was developing a distinctly post-imperial British take on the challenges of organizational design (Trist & Bamforth, 1951; Rice, 1953).

From Mayo (1940), Joan took an approach to studying authority relations in the workplace that rejected a priori theoretical abstractions in favor of a close examination of specific local conditions at the level of the firm. From very early on Mayo had been interested in legitimating a technocratic style of management (and, ultimately, a style of capitalism) where workplace conflict, employee dissent, and resistance to change were seen as irrational responses that had their basis in managers' failures to understand what employees really valued. In other words, he advocated a paternalistic approach to management that could, by turning its attentions to the social needs of the workforce, promote the interests of all in the organization, if only managers were sufficiently enlightened.

Thus, in Mayo's (1946, 1949) classic statements on what has become known as "unitarism" (Fox, 1971), there is the belief that the division of labor between managers and the managed is part of the natural order of things because only a few people have the necessary abilities to be managerial experts (cf. Landes, 1986). Here Mayo shared much in common with Frederick Winslow Taylor who thought that employees would eventually come around to seeing that managers were working just as hard as anyone to achieve an organization's shared goals. Of course, such views were congenial to a political ideology that saw the United States as the bastion of freedom and liberty; a place where anyone could make it if they wanted to without let or hindrance from the effects of an ossified class system.

The genius of the British Human Relations School that set it apart from its US variant was that it disabused the reader of the conceit that managers were really acting in the best interests of everyone in the organization. Thus, although it was eventually also a technocratic approach (i.e., organizations could become more effective if managers understood social processes better), it dispensed with the US version's dubious normative position that employees ought to be grateful that management used their superior knowledge to attend to the broad social needs of everyone. Taking Trist and Bamforth's (1951) classic study of the UK coal mining industry in support of the assumption that technical change has a profound effect on social relationships (see also Scott, Banks, Halsey, & Lupton, 1956; Dubin, 1959), Joan went on to show that some conflict in the workplace was unlikely ever to be resolved. This was especially the case in large batch/mass production where the technical ends of organization (i.e., having employee control and coordination systems embedded in a highly rationalized manufacturing process – Edwards, 1979) were at odds with its social ends (i.e., the desire to foster a cooperative workforce who enjoyed a highly quality of working life and who also identified closely with the strategic objectives of their employer). In this way Joan was prefiguring more radical authors (e.g., Friedman, 1977; Burawoy, 1979) who focused on how organizations attempted to obscure this fault line at the heart of the employment relationship by allowing employees to participate in low-level decision-making activities. Joan's now largely forgotten great insight was that whoever had ultimate control over the inception, design, and operation of new technical systems exerted a great deal of subsequent influence over employees' activities regardless of whether those employees were consulted about (or even participated in) the change process itself.

For us, this interest in technical change and its relationship to the social relations of work is the most enduring aspect of Joan's work. Indeed, it is still recognizable in all the essays collected here. Although her position may now be considered to be unduly unidirectional and deterministic – that is, understanding the details of technical systems of production provides us with the key to unlock the secrets of the social organization of work – we should also remember the intellectual, economic, and social milieu in which Joan operated.

This is not some hackneyed apologia for her along the lines that she should be excused as a woman trapped in the thinking of her time. Rather, we should remember that after the Second World War there was a genuine belief that technology and social science could be wielded as morally neutral tools in a progressive project that would rebuild society (Beniger, 1986). This could be seen in the rise of the technocratic consciousness beyond something so prosaic as technical change in manufacturing industry; it took in housing, health care, and the decision-making apparatus of government. It was even believed that war itself could be put on a rational and calculative footing (witness the RAND Corporation's application of game theory to the Cold War and other regional conflicts). Given the social and economic conditions of the immediate post-war period such optimism is understandable.

Indeed, it appears that this post-war optimism was sufficient to offset the effect of previous warnings from the likes of Lewis Mumford (1934) and Siegfried Giedion (1948) that technology involved moral choices (as well as purely technical choices) that were manifested in characteristic social arrangements such as the master and servant and, later, the manager and the employee. Thus, her perceived technological determinism aside, we believe we can be justifiable proud that, well before people like Herbert Marcuse (1964) were reconnecting with Munford and Giedion's earlier warnings, Joan was providing us with a framework for understanding the interaction of the technical and social aspects of work that did not pretend that managers were benign and disinterested servants of everyone in the organization. That she did it from the unglamorous setting of South East Essex rather than from the heartland of the intellectual elite makes this achievement all the more impressive.

A VOLUME ON JOAN WOODWARD

In putting together this volume, we had four objectives. First, we wanted to provide an accessible and concise overview of Joan's work as well as provide readers with some idea of the intellectual and social context in which it appeared. This chapter is intended to provide just this sort of introduction to her work. We hope that the above discussion provides not only a clear overview of her ideas but also some indication of how important and original her work was, especially given its context of time and place.

Second, we wanted to provide some idea of Joan as a person. Despite the 40 years that have passed since her untimely death, there are still many people who remember her fondly as a friend, mentor, and scholar. We have therefore included essays by Dorothy Griffiths, Sandra Dawson, Lisl Klien, Charles Perrow, and Bob Hinings reflecting on their memories of her. These essays are fascinating, both as a way to understand Joan as a person and also in providing compelling pictures of organization theory research at that time.

In the third section, we bring together a set of chapters that build more or less directly on Joan's work. These chapters are all original contributions by leading scholars that continue her legacy of considering the connection between technology and organization. These chapters range widely across organizational theory, but all owe some debt to the early work of Joan. In the first chapter, Anna Canato and Davide Ravasi discuss the connection between technology and organizational identity. Shahzad Ansari and Kamal Munir then examine user-generated content and its ramifications for organizations. In the third chapter, Sarah Kaplan and Fiona Murray examine the construction of value in technological entrepreneurship drawing on new perspectives from French social theory. Tyler Wry, Royston Greenwood, Dev Jennings, and Michael Lounsbury then examine the role of community in the production of knowledge in nanotechnology. In the fifth contribution, Andy Davies and Lars Fredriksen build directly on Joan's work by exploring innovation in project-based organization. Finally, Jennifer Whyte presents a framework for understanding technology and organizations through an examination of digital visualization technologies. The contributions in this section provide a sense of how far research in technology and organization have come, and how much more potential remains for expanding our understanding of various aspects of organizing.

Finally, in the fourth section, we have included a number of short essays discussing trends and future themes in technology and organization. We asked a number of leading scholars to think about what they see as interesting areas of future research that connect with the theme of technology and organization. The result is a set of essays by Wanda Orlikowski, Cynthia Hardy, Graham Dover and Tom Lawrence, Markus Perkmann and Andre Spicer, Gerry George and Adam Bock, and Annabelle Gawer exploring this critical intersection from a range of theoretical and methodological directions. We hope these fascinating essays will spark ideas for readers in terms of new areas for their own research.

Combined, the four sections provide an overview of Joan's work and life, exemplary work extending her legacy, and some ideas of the where the field might be headed in the future. The intersection of technology and organization that Joan first highlighted remains a fruitful and critically important area of study. It is an area that, despite the large existing literature, continues to attract the attention of a large group of scholars working from a diverse range of perspectives. We hope that readers find this volume an interesting, engaging, and inspiring contribution to this important stream of literature.

NOTES

1. An indication of this is given by the fact that *Management and Technology* was appended to a 1987 facsimile reprint of *Comparative Studies in Administration* (Thompson, Hammond, Hawkes, Junker, & Tuden, 1959). This was an edited collection that contained a reprint of James Thompson and Frederick Bates' *Administrative Science Quarterly* article, "Technology, Organization, and Administration."

2. This stance shares something in common with Burns and Stalker's (1961) analysis insofar as they were interested in the market orientation of the firms they studied which, through things like product volume and degree of product standardization, feeds back into production organization (Klein, 2006).

REFERENCES

Barley, S., & Tolbert, P. (1997). Institutionalization and structuration: Studying the links between action and institution. *Organization Studies, 18*, 93–117.

Beniger, J. R. (1986). *The control revolution: Technological and economic origins of the Information Society*. Cambridge, MA: Harvard University Press.

Billings, R. S., Klimoski, R. J., & Breaugh, J. A. (1977). The impact of a change in technology on job characteristics: A quasi-experiment. *Administrative Science Quarterly, 22*, 318–339.

Blau, P. M., Falbe, C. M., McKinley, W., & Tracy, P. K. (1976). Technology and organization in manufacturing. *Administrative Science Quarterly, 21*, 20–40.

Burawoy, M. (1979). *Manufacturing consent: Changes in the labor process under monopoly capitalism*. Chicago: University of Chicago Press.

Burns, T., & Stalker, G. M. (1961). *The management of innovation*. London: Tavistock Publications.

Child, J., & Mansfield, R. (1972). Technology, size, and organizational structure. *Sociology, 6*, 369–393.

DiMaggio, P. J., & Powell, W. (1983). The iron cage revisited: Institutional isomorphism and collective rationality in organizational fields. *American Sociological Review, 48*, 147–160.

Dubin, R. (1959). *The sociology of industrial relations*. Englewood Cliff, NJ: Prentice-Hall.

Edwards, R. (1979). *Contested Terrain: The transformation of the workplace in the twentieth century*. New York: Basic Books.

Fox, A. (1971). *A sociology of work in industry*. London: Collier-Macmillan.

Friedman, A. (1977). *Industry and labour: Class struggle of work and monopoly capitalism*. London: Macmillan.

Giedion, S. (1948). *Mechanization takes command: A contribution to anonymous history*. Oxford: University of Oxford Press.

Glaser, B. G., & Strauss, A. L. (1967). *The discovery of grounded theory: Strategies for qualitative research*. Chicago: Aldine Publishing Company.

Grimes, A. J., & Klein, S. M. (1973). The technological imperative: The relative impact of task unit, modal technology, and hierarchy on structure. *Academy of Management Journal*, *16*, 583–597.

Grimes, A. J., Klein, S. M., & Shull, F. A. (1970). Matrix model: A selective empirical test. *Academy of Management Journal*, *13*, 9–31.

Harvey, E. (1968). Technology and the structure of organizations. *American Sociological Review*, *33*, 247–259.

Hickson, D. (1996). Reminiscences of the ivory tower in the basement. In: T. Clark & G. Mallory (Eds), *Advancement in organizational behaviour*. Aldershot: Dartmouth.

Hickson, D. J., Hinings, C. R., Lee, C. A., Schneck, R. E., & Pennings, J. M. (1971). A strategic contingencies' theory of intraorganizational power. *Administrative Science Quarterly*, *16*, 216–229.

Hickson, D. J., Pugh, D. S., & Pheysey, D. C. (1969). *Administrative Science Quarterly*, *14*, 378–397.

Hopkins, T. K. (1965). Review of industrial organization: Theory and practice by Joan Woodward, 1965. *Administrative Science Quarterly*, *11*, 284–289.

Klein, L. (2006). Joan Woodward memorial lecture – Applied social science: Is it just common sense? *Human Relations*, *59*, 1155–1172.

Kynaston Reeves, T., & Turner, B. A. (1972). A theory of organization and behavior in batch production factories. *Administrative Science Quarterly*, *17*, 81–98.

Landes, D. (1986). What do bosses really do? *Journal of Economic History*, *46*, 585–623.

Lawrence, P. R., & Lorsch, J. W. (1967). *Organization and environment: Managing differentiation and integration*. Boston: Harvard University Press.

Magnusen, K. (1970). Review of industrial organization: Behaviour and control edited by Joan Woodward, 1970. *Industrial and Labor Relations Review*, *24*, 644–645.

Mahoney, T., & Weitzel, W. (1969). Managerial models of organizational effectiveness. *Administrative Science Quarterly*, *14*, 357–365.

Marcuse, H. (1964). *One-dimensional man*. Boston, MA: Beacon Press.

Massey, D., & Meegan, R. (1982). *The anatomy of job loss: The how, why, and where of employment decline*. London: Methuen.

Mayo, E. (1940). Industrial research. *Harvard Business School Alumni Bulletin*, *16*, 97.

Mayo, E. (1946). *The human problems of an industrial civilization*. Cambridge, MA: Harvard Graduate School of Business Administration.

Mayo, E. (1949). *The social problems of an industrial civilization (with an appendix on the political problem)*. London: Routledge & Keegan Paul.

McMahon, J. T., & Ivancevich, J. M. (1976). A study of control in a manufacturing organization: Managers and nonmanagers. *Administrative Science Quarterly*, *21*, 66–83.

Meyer, J. W., & Rowan, B. (1977). Institutional organizations: Formal structure as myth and ceremony. *American Journal of Sociology*, *83*, 340–363.

Mohr, L. B. (1971). Organizational technology and organizational structure. *Administrative Science Quarterly*, *16*, 444–459.

Mumford, L. (1934). *Technics and civilization*. New York: Harcourt, Brace & Co.

Orlikowski, W. J. (1992). The duality of technology: Rethinking the concept of technology in organizations. *Organization Science*, *3*, 398–427.
Orlikowski, W. J., & Barley, S. R. (2001). Technology and institutions: What can research on information technology and research on organizations learn from each other? *MIS Quarterly*, *25*, 145–165.
Perrow, C. (1967a). Review of industrial organization: Theory and practice by Joan Woodward, 1965. *American Sociological Review*, *32*, 313–315.
Perrow, C. (1967b). A framework for the comparative analysis of organizations. *American Sociological Review*, *32*, 194–208.
Pugh, D. S. (1996). Derek Pugh: A taste for innovation. In: A. G. Bedian (Ed.), *Management laureates* (Vol. 4). Greenwich, CT: JAI Press.
Reimann, B. C. (1980). Organization structure and technology in manufacturing: System versus work flow level perspectives. *Academy of Management Journal*, *23*, 61–77.
Rice, A. K. (1953). Productivity and social organization in an Indian weaving shed: An examination of the socio-technical system of an experimental automatic loomshed. *Human Relations*, *6*, 297–329.
Scott, W. H., Banks, J. A., Halsey, A. H., & Lupton, T. (1956). *Technical change and industrial relations*. Liverpool: University of Liverpool Press.
Stinchcombe, A. L. (1965). Review of industrial organization: Theory and practice by Joan Woodward, 1965. *Journal of Business*, *40*, 92–93.
Thompson, J. D. (1967). *Organizations in action*. New York: McGraw-Hill.
Thompson, J. D., & Bates, F. L. (1957). Technology, organization, and administration. *Administrative Science Quarterly*, *2*, 325–343.
Thompson, J. D., Hammond, P. B., Hawkes, R. W., Junker, B. H., & Tuden, A. (Eds). (1959). *Comparative studies in administration*. Pittsburgh: University of Pittsburgh Press.
Trist, E., & Bamforth, W. (1951). Some social and psychological consequences of the long wall method of coal-getting. *Human Relations*, *4*, 3–38.
Woodward, J. (1958). *Management and technology: Problems and progress in technology 3*. London: HMSO.
Woodward, J. (1965). *Industrial organization: Theory and practice*. Oxford: Oxford University Press.
Woodward, J. (Ed.) (1970). *Industrial organization: Behaviour and control*. Oxford: Oxford University Press.

A BIBLIOGRAPHY OF WORKS BY JOAN WOODWARD

Major Works

Woodward, J. (1950). *Employment relations in a group of hospitals: A report of a survey by Joan Woodward*. London: Institute of Hospital Administrators.
Woodward, J. (1958). *Management and technology: Problems and progress in technology 3*. London: HMSO.
Woodward, J. (1960). *The saleswoman: A study of attitudes and behaviour in retail distribution, etc*. London: Isaac Pitman & Sons.
Woodward, J. (1965). *Industrial organization: Theory and practice*. Oxford: Oxford University Press.

Selected Works with Major Contributions by Joan Woodward

Flanders, A., Pomeranz, R., & Woodward, J., assisted by Rees, B. J. (1968). *Experiments in industrial democracy: A study of the John Lewis Partnership*. London: Faber.

University of Liverpool Department of Social Science. (1954). *The Dock worker: An analysis of conditions of employment in the port of Manchester*. Liverpool: University of Liverpool Press.

Selected Articles and Chapters

Rackham, J., & Woodward, J. (1970). The measurement of technical variables. In: J. Woodward (Ed.), *Industrial organization: Behaviour and control*. Oxford: Oxford University Press.

Kynaston Reeves, T., Turner, B. A., & Woodward, J. (1970). Technology and organizational behaviour. In: J. Woodward (Ed.), *Industrial organization: Behaviour and control*. Oxford: Oxford University Press.

Kynaston Reeves, T., & Woodward, J. (1970). The study of managerial control. In: J. Woodward (Ed.), *Industrial organization: Behaviour and control*. Oxford: Oxford University Press.

Woodward, J. (1966). Right management. *New Society*, *8*(208), 441–443.

Woodward, J. (1968). Resistance to change. *Management International Review*, *8*, 137–143.

Woodward, J. (1969). How the prices and incomes board should work. *New Society*, *13*(331), 168–169.

Woodward, J. (1970a). In: *Industrial organization: Behaviour and control*. Oxford: Oxford University Press.

Woodward, J. (1970b). Technology, material control and organizational behavior. In: A. R. Negandhi & J. P. Schwitter (Eds), *Organizational behavior models*. Kent, OH: Kent State University Press.

Selected Book Reviews

Woodward, J. (1965). Review of Tom Lupton, industrial behaviour and personnel management (London: Institute of Personnel Management, 1964). *British Journal of Industrial Relations*, *3*, 263–265.

Woodward, J. (1968). Review of John H. Goldthorpe, David Lockwood, Frank Bechhofer, & Jennifer Platt, *The affluent worker: Industrial attitudes and behaviour* (Cambridge: Cambridge University Press, 1968). *New Society*, *12*(304), 132–133.

Woodward, J. (1969). Review of Anne Crichton, personnel management in context (London: B. T. Batsford, 1968). *Sociological Review*, *17*, 133–135.

SECTION 2 – PERSONAL REFLECTIONS ON JOAN WOODWARD

JOAN WOODWARD: A PERSONAL MEMORY

Dorothy Griffiths

Joan interviewed me for my first job in 1969. Little did I realize what an opportunity I was about to be given. I was about to be offered a post with one of – if not the – United Kingdom's most eminent industrial sociologist (as we were called then) and to join the most exciting and dynamic group of young researchers in the subject at the time; a group that have all gone on to make their mark in various ways. I was recruited because I was interested in the organization and management of industrial research and development, and Joan wanted to test her ideas outside traditional manufacturing environments.

Others in this volume will speak more eloquently than I can about her work. I want to focus on the person. She created an extraordinarily supportive and trusting intellectual culture. We were encouraged to develop our own ideas, to work independently and given what might now seem to be responsibility beyond our years. She always had time for us despite the challenges of her increasingly fragile health. I am sure that every member of the group has a memory of traveling to an organization with Joan, watching them hang onto her every word and then discussing what we had seen, heard and observed. She allowed us to feel – or me to feel anyway – that my untutored, inexperienced self could produce meaningful insights into organizations.

When Joan worked with organizations, it was always a two-way process: she gave back as much as she got. Organizations sought out Joan. While others in the field struggled to find organizations in which they could do research, Joan had organizations asking her to use them as a research site.

Technology and Organization: Essays in Honour of Joan Woodward
Research in the Sociology of Organizations, Volume 29, 23–24

ISSN: 0733-558X/doi:10.1108/S0733-558X(2010)0000029006

From Joan, I learned how to make teaching rich in examples and stories from real organizations to bring our subject alive: not that I had many stories of my own at the time!

Joan was only the second woman to be awarded a Chair at Imperial College. She arrived at the College in 1957 in a part-time role. She became full time in 1962 and was awarded her Chair in 1969. Her Chair was all the more impressive as she was a social scientist in a College of science and technology (medicine joined much later). The academic world was very male, particularly at the senior level in the 1960s and 1970s. Joan was an exception and exceptional. She was one of the very few UK social scientists whose work and reputation reached the United States where she was regarded as a major contributor. She was a very successful woman in two very male worlds: academia and industry. I can think of no other woman of her generation who so successfully straddled these two worlds.

And then she died.

For me, as a young member of her team, her death was unexpected. We knew she was ill and that her cancer had spread; indeed, she discussed it with me at one point. She had explicitly appointed a Director of Research to carry the work on should anything happen to her. I, anyway, did not expect her death at that moment. She worked to the end. Her death was a terrible shock and a deeply felt loss. Our team had lost its leader. Her intellectual charisma and her persona were the glue that bound us all together. For a while, we behaved as organizations do when they lose a charismatic leader, and we recognized ourselves behaving as such. Her funeral and the later memorial service were attended by a roll call of UK plc such was her impact and such was her persona. I do not remember much about the funeral except that it was overwhelmingly sad and a beautiful sunny day.

We raised an endowment to remember Joan and her work. This still funds the Joan Woodward lecture and undergraduate and postgraduate prizes.

As I look back on my own career and the things that have influenced it, I feel very fortunate to have worked with Joan. She taught me lessons that I have never forgotten, not just about how to bring our subject to life in the classroom, but above all about courage and humanity.

I am delighted that we have produced this volume. What greater testament can there be to Joan's work and to her insights that they can still generate debate 50 years later. Joan, who was always very modest, would be both surprized and delighted.

FROM MEDIEVAL HISTORY TO SMASHING THE MEDIEVAL ACCOUNT OF ORGANIZATIONS

Charles Perrow

I may get my account of Joan Woodward wrong because I am relying on my memory of decades-old events, and others may be more accurate. Joan was, I believe, teaching at a technical university when she was asked to do a survey of a number of Midland firms in terms of industrial policy. It was an odd choice for a female professor with an Oxford degree in medieval history, with no background in industrial policy let alone organizational theory. This may have been her advantage. She came to the task without the medieval theories of organizations that reigned. She looked at these firms in a way that no one in organizational theory had before. She wrote a preliminary report that said that because they use different technologies, they had different structures; the most successful matched their structures to their technologies – routine processes allowed centralized control, nonroutine ones required decentralization, to put it crudely.

Before this and for several years after her 1965 publication *Industrial Organization: Theory and Practice*, organizations were classified in terms of their goals. All manufacturing firms should be alike, because their goal is production of goods. All hospitals should be alike because their goal is health care and so on through other types. When Talcott Parsons was asked to write an article for the first issue of *Administrative Science Quarterly*, he followed

Technology and Organization: Essays in Honour of Joan Woodward
Research in the Sociology of Organizations, Volume 29, 25–28

ISSN: 0733-558X/doi:10.1108/S0733-558X(2010)0000029007

the prevailing convention of distinguishing organizations on the basis of their goal – profit-making, healthcare, education, and so on.

The closest thing to a contrary perspective was an important book by Tom Burns and G. Stalker, *The Management of Innovation* (1961), where they distinguished organic from routine production but did not otherwise address the issue of organizational types. I do not believe that Joan was acquainted with that book when she was doing her work. Though preliminary compared to her work, it was a significant break with the century-old tradition of looking for the one best way of organizing every organization. Most of the work on organizations in the United States was concerned with making organizations more efficient, and in the early 1960s, the most popular theory was that of Rensis Likert, who had found in his "system five" scheme the best way to organize all organizations, public and private. "Leadership" was the key along with "fundamental organizing principles," which were vacuous injunctions by and large. This may explain why Joan's insight remained so obscure for so long; the few theories of industrial organizations were heavily leadership-oriented, normative, and hortatory. She was not, I believe, aware of what she had written. Not until 1967 was her break with this tradition to be explicitly recognized.

Around 1964, I had just formulated an idea that had first arisen from work I have done on a survey of six juvenile correctional institutions with three colleagues. I theorized that the structure and practices of the six correctional institutions had much less to do with leadership (punitive vs. therapeutic) as my co-authors believed (although that remained the central focus of our joint publication, over my strong objections), than with the way the executives viewed their "raw material" – that is, the boys. If they saw them as lacking in discipline, they organized their institution in a way to provide the discipline they needed. (We labeled it punitive but they did not.) If they thought the children lacked ego strength, they organized their institution to provide psychiatric help. Given these different perceptions of the inmates (the raw materials), they used different techniques (or technologies) that require different structures (centralized, authoritarian, vs. decentralized and collegial).

I formulated my ideas about the relationship of technology (the kind of techniques used to process the raw materials) to organizational structure in a study of 13 industrial firms in two states and drafted a theoretical piece that appeared in 1967. In 1965, before that was published, I made some comments about my ideas about technology and structure at an American Sociological Association meeting. In the audience, fortuitously, were Paul Lawrence, a prominent Harvard Business School professor, and his student Jay Lorsch. After the session ended, they came up, introduced themselves, and said we must talk, because they were thinking along the same line.

By then I had just come across the first inkling of Joan's work, in a reference to a short technical report on her survey in a paper by a sociologist Robert Dubin, then at the University of Oregon. I mentioned Joan's technical report, and Lawrence, sensing an important convergence of theories, arranged a meeting that brought Joan Woodward over from England and included two or three other academics who were interested, including Gerald Bell of the University of North Carolina, who was also working along these lines. It was in the air.

We were all very excited, particularly to find that Joan had just published her *Industrial Organization: Theory and Practice*, a monograph on her work. (Much later, I asked Joan how she managed to get Oxford University Press in London to publish their first book concerned with either organizations or industrial policy. She described a report she got from someone at the editorial meeting: "I don't know what this book is about, but she is an excellent scholar of medieval history so it must be worth something.") Paul Lawrence arranged a meeting for the next spring, which was dubbed the "Connamasset Conference" for the name of the resort on Cape Cod where we met. Joan, Paul Lawrence and Jay Lorsh, Gerald Bell, I, and perhaps two others delivered our papers with high expectations that we had changed the course of organizational theory and research for ever. In the audience were 15 or 20 scholars from MIT, Harvard, Chicago, and elsewhere, most of them economists from business schools. I am sure that they were not as overwhelmed as we were by this convergence, these independent inventions, but that is not important. The notion of "contingency theory," as Lawrence and Lorsch fruitfully dubbed it, would have a substantial impact.

The next year, 1967, saw the publication of my piece, "*A Framework for Comparative Organizational Analysis*" and *Organizations and Environments* by Lawrence and Lorsch. Their book took a broader view than my article did, linking technology to the environment. But Joan was there first two years before with this remarkable breakthrough by a medieval scholar.

Some years later, I was asked to reflect upon my "comparative framework" piece and thus the fate of contingency theory. I concluded that it forever put to rest the idea that goals dictated structures and processes, because, as I had observed in 1967, some schools are run like prisons and some prisons are run like schools. Contingency theory established a strong link between technology and structure (or as Lawrence and Lorsh would put it, between environment, technology, and structure). But I acknowledged that the world was more messy and contingent than our contingency theories allowed.

In my own research on 13 industrial organizations, concluded after my 1967 publication, I found significant exceptions. A firm that should have had a routine technology scored high on the nonroutine variables because of the interests of the vice president in maintaining close personal control and keeping the president uninformed. It had no clear structure and few routines and appeared quite inefficient. Conversely, a semiconductor firm that should have been decentralized and flexible because of the uncertainties of their front-line, innovative technology was forced to run as if production were routine because of dictates by the parent organization. (They believed there was one best way to run all their divisions.) Because the market was very favorable for both of these firms, they were very profitable, despite their inefficiencies. The interests of top executives were sufficient to trump any dictates of technology.

As there was nothing resembling a "power theory" of organizations around at the time, I feel I do not need to apologize for my innocence. In a personal communication Joan said she was not surprised; there were significant variations related to power in her own sample, but not enough to destroy the overall findings. Just so, I feel; technology is prior, but not fully determinate.

Finally, some months before she died, we met for lunch, in New York City as I recall, and she told me she only had months to live because of her advanced cancer. I was stunned and openly cried for her pain and fate. I was also shaken by another thought. She was only 53 or 54, eagerly building a research team in England that promised to be very influential; it was far too soon for her to go. To my surprise (and honour), she asked me if I would allow her to put my name forward as her replacement as the head of the Industrial Sociology unit at Imperial College, where she had collected an impressive group of teachers and graduate students. I was very flattered, but had to decline.

In 1972, a year after her death, I accepted a year's appointment at the London Graduate School of Business Studies. Dorothy Wedderburn had replaced Joan as the head of the unit at Imperial College and invited me to moonlight one day a week at the unit. The sadness of her departure was still palpable in the unit. But Dorothy Wedderburn seemed to be doing a remarkable job of continuing to build the unit, the quality of the faculty and students was excellent, and my one day a week visit was the best day of the week for me for the academic year.

The unit was a tribute to this remarkable woman, who not only was the first to lay out a plausible theory but was also able to confirm it with empirical data from a large sample of organizations, something the much larger organizational research establishments in the United States took a much longer time to do.

JOAN WOODWARD: A STYLE FIT FOR THE TASK

Sandra Dawson

Imperial College in 1969 looked like a man's world; it was certainly difficult to locate a ladies' room which was not apparently hastily constructed in a tight space as an afterthought to a great design. Yet I joined a powerhouse of women. Joan Woodward had already tempted Dorothy Wedderburn from Cambridge and together they had secured large sums of research monies from the Research Councils, Fords, Pilkingtons, ICI, the Post Office, the Coal Board, government departments, and other supporters who were each captivated by the promise of the work and rare combination of intellectual strength and practical concerns of its leader. With research funds flowing in abundance, driving passions to explore further the relationship between structure, technology, and performance, and very few specific commitments, Joan and Dorothy set about recruiting what was to be one of the largest groups of young researchers in the United Kingdom in the late 1960s.

Sitting as a raw recruit in what was then the Government Social Survey, working on employment practices in a group charged to develop plans for implementing the recommendations of the White Paper "In Place of Strife,"[1] I was intrigued by glimpses of industrial life and management practice, and yet irritated by the ponderous pace of work. Joan Woodward was a name, the author of a celebrated book (Woodward, 1965) I had read when at Keele University for a paper on Industrial Sociology. I chanced upon an advertisement for temporary research assistants to join Woodward at Imperial on one year contracts to gather data in various settings. The aim

Technology and Organization: Essays in Honour of Joan Woodward
Research in the Sociology of Organizations, Volume 29, 29–34

ISSN: 0733-558X/doi:10.1108/S0733-558X(2010)0000029008

was to expand and deepen robust testing of Joan's thesis: that industrial organizations which design their structures to fit the implicit requirements of their production technologies are likely to be more commercially successful than those who either try to conform to some conventional wisdom of unified managerial practice or think that management is common sense and thus need give it no further thought (Woodward, 1965). Joan had chosen to locate her work at Imperial College to be alongside engineers who would help her to understand the nature of technology, and in return she would bring the sociological imagination into the mix. Both Woodward and the engineers were brave to embrace the other.

Giving no thought to security and status, and running in the face of advice from my seniors in the Civil Service, I submitted my application, and so I had my first meeting with Joan. It was more a conversation than an interview. She did not care much for formal experience or qualifications; she wanted people to join her team who shared her preoccupation to reveal the challenges and opportunities of life on the shop floor, or hidden in layers of middle management, or in smoke-filled board rooms. She wanted us to be her eyes and ears in as many work places as possible. She expected us to be as interested in "what was really going on" as she was; to have the capacity to empathize and engage so that there would be few who would refuse to talk to us; and to share a desire to create sense through synthetic analysis. Our job was to unfold layers of understanding which would convince both theorists and practitioners that "there was no one best way to manage" and provide practical advice about how to increase productivity and effectiveness.

We were devoted to her, we believed in her approach, but we did not all think that the path to the holy grail had (yet) been as clearly mapped out as did she, and of course although all part of "Joan's group," we did not all think alike. But for the moment, when in the summer and autumn of 1969 Dorothy Griffiths, Robin Fincham, and I joined Celia Davies, Arthur Francis, Graham Lister, Don Harper, Peter Combey, Tom Kynaston Reeves, and Barry Turner in a huge room on the north side of Princes Gardens, South Kensington, we could be certain only of one thing: we were there because Joan believed that by working with the Imperial engineers across Exhibition Road, we would become a genuine multi-disciplinary group who would strive to understand, even measure, dimensions of technology, structure, and performance in many different sectors.

The throw of the dice placed me in a study of communications in the Post Office, and within a week of joining Imperial I was on my first field trip with Joan: an overnight stay in the station hotel (or so I remember it) in Cardiff. Sorting offices were always so conveniently placed for the station. Sitting on first class seats over dinner on the train (in itself a novel experience for me), Joan explained how we would conduct the interview. Once again, in the inimitable Woodward style, I learned it was to be more like a conversation. We needed to understand the position of the Head Postmaster and to do so we needed to cover key topics. We would begin with how he (inevitably a man) managed his discretion over structure and his thoughts on any changes which could conceivably improve performance, even though we knew from prior work that concepts of performance measurement or improvement were embryonic at best in this combined postal and telephone nationalized industry. We would cover relations upwards to the regions and national center (largely paper driven and highly bureaucratic), any peer contact (largely seen as irrelevant unless there was a crisis in the distribution network), and relations with the unions and especially the shop stewards, who in "I'm Alright Jack"[2] caricatures, were asserting that only they could communicate directly with their members. All this would, she knew from previous work, be much as we would expect, but what was changing and where we should probe as the impetus and fascination for the study – was the technology. Automation was being introduced into sorting offices and here was to be a study of technology and organization in real time. How were managers adapting to the changes, even taking advantage of them, to develop new organization structures and processes that would lead to improved performance? What role did technology play? Did it lead to organizational change? Did it determine or facilitate or inhibit change? Would the productivity promise of the technology only be unlocked by action when managers really understood the nature of the opportunities and constraints that Joan saw as inherent in, but not determined by, the technology?

The morning's discussion went according to plan; there was a de-brief on the return journey, I proudly presented the handwritten write-up the following morning and without any formality or even comment that I can recall, it was agreed that my apprenticeship had been served, the post office mantle passed to me and the study of the management practices of 30 or so Head Postmasters became my job, and I got on with it. In her group, Joan gave authentic reality to the thesis that management style should fit the nature of the work. Research for her was driven by curiosity, sharp thinking, and data. It was a process of revelation, best conducted by articulate, good communicating, self-directed people, who therefore needed little direct guidance. Working with her on the Post Office and then on the organization of work in prisons (Dawson, 1975) was a wonderful entry into management research. We had an overarching framework constructed to test the thesis developed from Woodward's classic study of 100 or so firms in South East

Essex (Woodward, 1958, 1965), but beyond that there was little constraint and great encouragement to be curious; a style that built confidence and capacity.

In that very research process were seeds for its development in ways which while being warmly welcomed by Joan, would also engender tension and challenge. Although she demonstrated that there was "no one best way" to manage, she did think there was one best framework for its analysis, and it was hers. Her certainty found fertile ground in contemporary work in the USA where Perrow (1970), Thompson (1967), and Lawrence and Lorsch (1967) were writing in similar vein under an emerging banner of contingency theory. We did indeed discover a great deal in our UK studies that was to chime with a contingency theory of organization structure and design, but we also became increasingly seized in different ways with the need to push back any explanation that smacked even slightly of technological determinism, and to give more foreground to management action, power, and interests in explaining the role of technology (Davies, Dawson, & Francis, 1973).

Joan was sympathetic to these arguments – but only to a certain degree. She had led the movement from large-scale surveys to case studies, from generalizations to fragmentary specifics, but in doing so she wanted to keep hold of the certainty which could be found in survey results, and which could be packaged in readily accessible forms for discussions with business leaders and government officials who were always eager to sit at her table and seek her advice. Coincidentally, however, our encounters with the data and contemporary currents in sociological discussion created paths to tables at which Joan was less at home. When we were not collecting, analyzing, and writing up the case studies, seeking to understand the intricate imperatives of different technologies or presenting findings to our sponsors, we were sitting in cafes around The London School of Economics (LSE), often before or after the Industrial Sociology Group meetings of the British Sociological Association, arguing over Habermas and critical theory (Habermas, 1968), Goffman and symbolic interactionism (Goffman, 1969), Silverman's new book (Silverman, 1970), and the three dimensions of power being elucidated by Lukes (1974). How could we reconcile the weight of contingency with a fundamental acknowledgment of power and knowledge, of choice and resources, or technical imperatives and values, in short, of structure and action? I did not then fully appreciate that these fault lines were as old as the human condition and would carry forward for decades of debate. This is of course no surprise as in a sense they speak to the nature of organized human activity that transcends particular contexts and requires one's own resolution of the structure–action conundrum.

Joan was intrigued and I think mostly delighted that her group was intellectually engaged on a broad field, but she remained of the view that our new friends as she saw them were the friends of the young without responsibilities. Fundamentally, we could, she felt, enrich her framework, but not reconstruct it; for the pragmatic concerns of deriving use and relevance would in the end have to outweigh the niceties of social theorizing. In an evaluation of the significance of her work written with Dorothy Wedderburn (Dawson & Wedderburn, 1980), we detail Joan's contribution to theory and comment that while this represents a justifiable source of pride, her greater passion was her contribution to practice. As she said in her inaugural lecture at Imperial College she saw the ultimate objective of her research to be to "enable those concerned with industrial organisations, at whatever level they may be working, to refine their models and to deal in a more sophisticated way with the problems of organisation structure and behaviour they encounter" (Woodward, 1970). All this was of course in the prehistory of British Business Schools, long before the articulation of the double hurdle (Pettigrew, 1997) of rigor and relevance, at a time when Imperial, Oxford, and Cambridge had each turned their backs on the prospect of hosting one of the two pioneering foundations which had subsequently gone to London and Manchester.

We never had the chance to really press our points with Joan for as the urgency for a critical reflective slant became felt more acutely, so Joan's illness advanced. She died. We arranged our car shares and set off to Kent. It rained. We walked in the beautiful garden which she and her husband Leslie Blakeman created around the medieval fishponds that gave their house its name. The list of mourners was a roll call of bosses of nationalized industry, business magnates, industrial relations negotiators, and senior civil servants. Lord Penny, then Rector of Imperial College, headed the contingent from South Kensington. I recall a special sadness, a hunger for more conversation, and a profound gratitude that a window had been opened into the world of industry, business, and work which I felt I was unlikely ever to want to shut.

NOTES

1. *In Place of Strife* (Cmnd 3888) was published in 1969 as a UK Government White Paper on industrial relations policies.
2. *I'm Alright Jack* is a british satirical film about industrial relations directed and produced by John and Roy Boulting, released in 1959.

REFERENCES

Davies, C., Dawson, S., & Francis, A. (1973). Technology and other variables. In: M. Warner (Ed.), *Sociology of the workplace*. London: Allen and Unwin.

Dawson, S. (1975). Power and influence in prison workshops. In: P. Abell (Ed.), *Organisations as bargaining and influence systems*. London: Heinemann.

Dawson, S., & Wedderburn, D. (1980). Joan Woodward and the development of organisation theory. In: J. Woodward (Ed.), *Industrial organisation: Theory and practice* (2nd ed.). Oxford: Oxford University Press.

Goffman, E. (1969). *Strategic interaction*. Philadelphia: University of Pennsylvania Press.

Habermas, J. (1968). *Knowledge and human interests*. Cambridge: Polity Press.

Lawrence, P. R., & Lorsch, J. (1967). *Organization and environment*. Boston: Harvard University.

Lukes, S. (1974). *Power: A radical view*. London: Macmillan.

Perrow, C. (1970). A framework for the comparative analysis of organizations. *American Sociological Review*, *32*(2), 194–208.

Pettigrew, A. M. (1997). The double hurdles for management research. *Advancement in Organizational Behaviour*. Ashgate: Aldershot.

Silverman, D. (1970). *The theory of organisations*. London: Heinemann.

Thompson, J. D. (1967). *Organizations in action*. New York: McGraw Hill.

Woodward, J. (1958). *Management and technology*. London: HMSO.

Woodward, J. (1965). *Industrial organisation: Theory and practice*. Oxford: Oxford University Press.

Woodward, J. (1970). *Behaviour in organizations*. Inaugural Lecture, Imperial College of Science and Technology, 3 March, p. 122.

WORKING WITH JOAN WOODWARD

Lisl Klein

To understand what goes on in the social sciences, you need to look at where the funding is coming from. The 1950s were the time of the Marshall Plan. As part of the Marshall Plan, under the so-called Conditional Aid Scheme, funds were made available for industrial social research, and there began the first major broad-based program of industrial social science in this country. The essential feature of the scheme was that the problems being tackled should have some bearing on productivity and that the research carried out should produce practical results.

Already in 1947, the Attlee government had set up a Committee on Industrial Productivity to advise on the application of science to the problems of industry. The same idealism that led to social security legislation and the creation of the National Health Service lay behind the wish to use science in the service of problem-solving. The Committee had included a "Human Factors Panel" chaired by Sir George Schuster (the "Schuster Panel"), which had sponsored some psychological and sociological investigations into industrial problems. When the Committee decided to dissolve itself in 1950, the Department of Scientific and Industrial Research and the Medical Research Council were working out a scheme to cover the national needs for research in this field. They had divided it into three areas: industrial health, individual efficiency, and human relations in industry; and they had set up committees to look after each. With the coming of the Conditional Aid funds, these committees now had bigger resources to spend.

Technology and Organization: Essays in Honour of Joan Woodward
Research in the Sociology of Organizations, Volume 29, 35–39

ISSN: 0733-558X/doi:10.1108/S0733-558X(2010)0000029009

The members were academics and top-level industrialists and trade unionists. The program was administered by the DSIR; the secretary of the Human Relations Committee was Ronald Stansfield, a senior scientist in the DSIR, who had been involved in Operational Research during the war.

Joan Woodward's research looking at industrial organization, and eventually linking success with organizing according to the production technology in use, was part of that program. So was a project on the human implications of work study, in which I was a junior research assistant. Until then, the DSIR had been responsible for research in the physical and engineering sciences only. Administering social science research was new to them, and to understand better what the particular issues involved might be, they had decided to locate one of the Conditional Aid projects in their own headquarters. It was the work study project, and Stansfield was responsible for that as well as for the administration of the Human Relations Programme.

The researchers at that time on the whole knew each other and each other's work, and Joan took an interest in our study. We had carried out two case studies, one in a firm where work study was being newly introduced, and one where it had been established for a long time. By the time the fieldwork for the second study was finished, the other members of the team had moved on, and I was left to write it up. Joan offered to supervise me – I had no social science qualifications and had come to the research from working as a factory personnel manager – and I joined her at Imperial College, although still on the payroll of DSIR, to write my first book (Klein, 1964).

The work study project and, perhaps more importantly, the fact that it was carried out from within the DSIR, has had a lasting effect on my thinking and on everything I have done since then, in two ways: first, I met, saw the work of, and listened to the discussions about researchers coming from a wide spectrum of disciplines, from psychoanalysis to ergonomics through industrial psychology, social psychology, anthropology, industrial sociology, and I saw the contributions these different disciplines could make. Ever since then I have wondered why everyone else does not see it that way. And second, it was how I came to work with Joan Woodward.

A background in personnel management was one of the things we shared; another was being grounded in domestic realities. When I bought my first, very small, flat Joan contributed ideas about how to make the most of the storage space. At one point, we went to Brussels to some international conference. It was for me the first such experience, and I was very excited. (The academic discussions over lunch were a terrible anticlimax: "If you invite me to yours in Rome in the summer, I'll get you invited to ours in

Copenhagen. But let me know in time so that I can organise the family's holiday.") But when I suggested we should stay an extra day and look round Brussels, she said no, she had to be home in time to put the Sunday joint in the oven. Joan and her husband Leslie Blakeman had bought an old farmhouse in the country and were refurbishing it, with Joan passionately developing the garden.

Leslie Blakeman was Industrial Relations Director of Fords in Dagenham, at a time when the car industry was torn by unrest and mainly unofficial strikes. Joan's way of introducing production engineering students at Imperial College to industrial relations was to get shop stewards from Fords to come and talk to the students about their problems. Shop stewards had problems too? Wow. What a revelation for students who only knew what they read in the newspapers.

Her supervision of me was quite stringent: I have a liking for anecdotes to illustrate a point, and she would say, "You're not supposed to be a journalist!" But she liked the analysis and involved me in planning her next major research, which was to be about control systems. (She also passed on some consulting assignments, which is how I came to study all 23 flax mills in Northern Ireland.) The technology research had shown that, at the two ends of the scale of complexity of production technology, that is unit production and process production, you could predict a great deal from the technology to behavior. In the middle area of the scale, around batch production, you could not, and she hypothesized that here the control system was likely to be the intervening variable. So, while I took a year off to finally get some formal qualifications, Joan developed the grant application and the plans for a study of the behavioral effects of control systems. When I rejoined her for that study – this time on the staff of Imperial College – two other researchers had been taken on. The three of us, Peter Combey, Jeff Rackham, and I, each took a product or batch of products and traced them through what happened to them, from the decision to make them till they left the factory gates, to analyze the control systems that impinged on them. There were methodological problems, and much debate about how to define the degree of detail we should collect to make the cases comparable. I remember Joan, at the end of such a session, saying with some exasperation, "Oh, get as much as you can!"

That study is not nearly as well known as the one on technology; in fact, it is hardly known at all. And yet I believe it to have both greater theoretical importance and greater practical usefulness – Joan liked to quote Kurt Lewin's dictum that there is nothing as useful as a good theory. Technology changes and information technology have changed the manufacturing process beyond earlier analytic models. But the reality of control systems and their consequences is a constant. If that study had been better known, it is inconceivable that we would now be suffering from a railway system in which the operation of trains is under separate ownership and control from the maintenance of the infrastructure.

The importance of the technology study is that it opened the way to a contingency approach to organization. But a contingency approach is not just about technology. That finding has led to my looking for any fact of structure in a situation – that is, any feature that is unalterable, at least in the short run, and that therefore affects behavior and organization: the ownership structure of an organization, the type of market it is in, the legal system, the geography, and the size. In a study of hospital anesthetists, a major fact of structure was that patients come into hospital for an operation, not for an anesthetic. It is undeniable, and its impact on behavior, relationships, and organization was wondrous to trace. That is where the contingency approach takes you.

But it has been – and continues to be – hard to assert, in the face of all the fads and fashions that were to come. Among them, the "human relations movement" not only continued, it also seemed to grow stronger. During the 1960s, a growing wave of OD consultants began to come to Europe, usually through Britain where they did not have language problems. I remember Charles Perrow practically yelling at me – I had become Social Sciences Adviser in Esso Petroleum by then, and he was on a visit to Joan – "Why do you people buy all this crap from us?" And within the social sciences here, the very success and popularity of Joan's research generated envy. I can think of several developments in the social sciences which I think had some of their roots in envy of Joan Woodward.

I am struck by the arbitrariness of things. In the first wave of the Conditional Aid Programme, the DSIR commissioned short versions of the researches they had funded. Sometimes journalists wrote them, but Joan wrote her own (Woodward, 1958). The full account of the research came later (Woodward, 1965) and gave the scientific underpinning to the short one, but it was the short one that had the public impact: it was clear, short, and well written in normal language. By contrast, the book about the control systems research, which was published in 1970, is a collection of rather diverse papers by diverse authors – not to say something of a mishmash. The central message gets lost unless you look for it quite hard; Joan was merely the editor (Woodward, 1970).

But by then she was ill. In early 1968, I had discovered a small breast lump. It was benign, but it had to be removed. When Joan came to see me in hospital, she said that my situation had prompted her to examine herself and she, too, had found a lump. Only hers was not benign, and there began the cruel cat-and-mouse game that is breast cancer. Just as you are beginning to think you are OK, it recurs somewhere else. On the day after her first operation, she was sitting up in bed marking exam papers. She asked, "If you thought you might only have two years to live, what would you do? Teach? Write a book?" Well, she had more than two years, and the answer was that she carried on doing what she had been doing before. The last time I saw her was in her office at Imperial College, where I had dropped in for a cup of tea. Joan looked small and frail, sitting behind a desk that seemed to have grown in size, while waiting for Leslie to collect her and take her home. I asked, "Do you want to talk shop, or shall we gossip?".

With a sweet, tired smile, she said "Oh, let's just gossip". That was how I realized how weak she had become, because talking shop was always the greatest of pleasures. She died five days later.

REFERENCES

Klein, L. (1964). *Multiproducts Ltd. A case study in the social effects of rationalised production.* London: HMSO.

Woodward, J. (1958). *Management and technology*. London: HMSO.

Woodward, J. (1965). *Industrial organization: Theory and practice*. Oxford: Oxford University Press.

Woodward, J. (1970). *Industrial organization: Behaviour and control*. Oxford: Oxford University Press.

THE CONTRIBUTION OF JOAN WOODWARD: A PERSONAL REFLECTION

C. R. (Bob) Hinings

I first met Joan Woodward in 1962 when she visited the "Aston" group as we were working on our theoretical and methodological approach to understanding organizational structure and context. We were a brash, young group (the oldest member of the team was 30) working at what was then the Birmingham College of Advanced Technology (CAT). The Birmingham CAT did not have university status and it was not until 1966 that it became the University of Aston. Both what we were doing and where we were located were intriguing to Joan; after all, her famous book on technology and organization had been carried out at the South-East Essex Technical College, another nonuniversity, and, in the status order of the times, "below" Birmingham CAT! Both Joan's work and that of the Aston group illustrate how innovation often comes from the margins of the academic world!

It was, of course, vital for the Aston team to meet with Joan because she had become one of the two most influential researchers on organizations in the United Kingdom (the other being Tom Burns who also visited us to talk about his work on the management of innovation). It is important to remember that the world of organization theorists in the United Kingdom at the beginning of the 1960s was extremely small. In fact, none of the members of the Aston team were trained in the study of organization structure and

Technology and Organization: Essays in Honour of Joan Woodward
Research in the Sociology of Organizations, Volume 29, 41–45

ISSN: 0733-558X/doi:10.1108/S0733-558X(2010)0000029010

context per se so to hear from those who were was very necessary; that's how we obtained our training.

Recapping ideas that are, in Joan Woodward's case, more than 50 years old can produce a response of "isn't that obvious." And the answer in 2008 is "yes, of course," because of the work of pioneers like Joan. Putting such ideas into their historical context is an attempt to show how groundbreaking they were at the time; how they reoriented a field that was trying to establish itself. In their book, *Writers on Organization*, Derek Pugh and David Hickson have what they see as a defining quote from Joan Woodward, namely, "the danger lies in the tendency to teach the principles of administration as though they were scientific laws, when they are really little more than administrative expedients found to work well in certain circumstances but never tested in any systematic way." Today's academic reaction is "of course," after all, we know about contingency theory, population ecology, institutional theory, and so on. However, one could argue that there are still management gurus who, without saying directly that there is one best way of organizing, of managing change, of doing continuous improvement, actually operate as though there is one best way.

At the time of her meeting with the Aston group, Joan Woodward had made two very important contributions to the study of organizations. The first was to challenge the work of management theorists such as Urwick and Brech, by suggesting that effective organizational design was a matter of contingency. The second was to establish the importance of technology as one of those contingencies. The impact of both of these, at the time, cannot be overstated. So many management approaches were about searching for the Holy Grail of organizing and discovering that grail in over-generalized reflections from senior managers coupled with isolated case studies. Joan Woodward was interested in a strong, empirical base for statements about organizations. In terms of the first challenge that she issued to the management thinking of her day, as Pugh and Hickson put it, "she forces thinking away from the abstract elaboration of principles of administration to an examination of the constraints placed on organisation structure and management practice by differing technologies and their associated control systems." She argued that principles of effective management change from one technological context to another. Indeed, one might argue that she showed, convincingly, that the principles of the classical management theories are only relevant in mass production firms.

It is, of course, for the second contribution, the importance of technology to understanding organizations, that Joan Woodward is most remembered. It is not uncommon to see her work still cited as an "historic" reference that laid the groundwork for later approaches. Joan produced a sophisticated, nine-category approach to technology in manufacturing organizations, and she suggested that these categories formed a scale from the least to the most complex technologies, a scale of production continuity. At the heart of her approach was the idea that it is only possible to understand structures and practices if one truly examined what organizations actually do. Structures are about organizing work and work is embedded in technologies. Her technological categories were a scale of the embedment of work, the extent to which the worker had some degrees of freedom in carrying out the work. It was because of this insistence on the importance of work that, after Joan's visit, the Aston team were clear that in the organizations they studied the first imperative was to understand the workflow. In manufacturing organizations, in particular, this meant starting the research with a tour of the plant. But inservice organizations such as an education system, it was also necessary to start with descriptions of what the organization actually did.

Lex Donaldson (2001, p. 52), who has almost singlehandedly kept the contingency theory of organizations alive and well, describes Woodward's work as "another path-breaking contingency theory study … ." He goes on to say that her work "has become an exemplar of contingency theory research at the macro-level." One of the indicators of the importance of Woodward's research lies in the amount of work that it generated. The 1960s and the 1970s were a time of great focus on technology as exemplified by, inter alia, the work of Perrow, Thompson, and Burns and Stalker, three "greats" in the study of organizations. A debate developed about "the technology imperative" and a great deal of work was done that attempted to establish the relationship between technology and elements of organization structure in particular. In all of this research, the work by Woodward was central and every writer had to deal with both her conceptualization of technology and her strong empirical findings. Indeed, between 1970 and 2008, there have been more than 2,000 citations to her work which attest to its importance. So, all the time, in her work, Joan directs us to an understanding of *work* and how that is organized, to the idea that the principle raison d'etre of organization is to produce goods and services.

I believe that if Joan Woodward examined much of contemporary organizational research, she would feel that it had lost its way because of a lack of concern with what organizations actually do. She would argue that organization theory needs to bring work back in. Again, as Pugh and Hickson put it, "the basic assumption and conclusion of Woodward's work is that meaningful explanations of differences in organization and behaviour can be found in the work situation itself." Organizational theory has developed in a number of ways that take us away from studying technology and work. One of these has been to study large populations of organizations over time, for example, institutional theory and population ecology. Another has been to be concerned with culture, meaning, and discourse. A further development is related to the changing nature of Western economies with increasing emphasis on knowledge. None of these necessarily take us away from a concern with technology, but I believe that they have done so.

Indeed there are two books produced by Joan Woodward that underpin her arguments about technology. One was *The Dock Worker* and the other *The Saleswoman*. Interestingly, neither of these made it on to the organization theory "hit parade," unlike her work on technology and control systems. But what they both show is a concern with the nature of work in organizations *as exemplified by front-line workers*. For Joan, the only possible way to arrive at any kind of abstract theory was to actually understand the work that was being done in an organization. The design of organization structures and systems is about the management and control of work. So, for her, whether studying organizations through the lens of knowledge workers, or ecological developments or in their institutional framing, the starting point would have to be "what do these organisations do" because only in that way would it be possible to understand how they are managed, how they change, how they respond to external events, and so on.

There are also methodological implications of her work, which are not necessarily seen in much contemporary organization theory, primarily, that one has to collect information through direct contact with the organization, even when carrying out a survey. Part of Joan's advice to the Aston group in 1962 was "get to know the organizations that you are studying." Visit them, talk to employees, attend meetings, and have lunch in the cafeterias. Only in this way would it be possible to bring a scientific approach together with meaning; only in this way could we truly understand the importance (or not) of the information we were collecting. Only in this way would it be possible to develop sensible, meaningful scales. Partly as a result of this advice, all of the information collected by the Aston team that eventually became the various scales of specialization, standardization, formalization, centralization, technology, ownership, and so on was through site visits and interviews. The scales were then developed from the interview materials; at no point was any kind of survey used. This kind of approach was also central to Joan's work on technology and control systems. Derek Pugh, who initially came from an experimental psychology background, described it as "handling your own rat!." I am sure that Joan Woodward would believe that many (most?) contemporary organization theorists are too far removed from the organizations that they study.

These observations bring me back to what was the central issue in Joan Woodward's work, namely, to understand management organization and practice and, as a result, to improve it. That improvement was to come from comparative studies of organizations so that generalizations about management could be securely based and the limits of theories established. In the 1950s and 1960s, samples of 50–100 organizations were large. And a major reason for that was the methods of data collection and the strong relationship between the researchers and the organizations they were studying. For example, in the Aston studies, collecting data on 46 organizations by intensive, semistructured interviews and then constructing and proving the subsequent scales took four people two years. But only this way, believed Joan (and the Aston researchers and Lawrence and Lorsch), could the necessary contingency thinking be based in a true understanding of organizations. And the starting point has to be the work that organizations do, the goods and services that they produce and the methods that they use to produce those goods and services.

REFERENCES

Donaldson, L. (2001). *The contingency theory of organizations.* Thousand Oaks: Sage Publications.

SECTION 3 – STUDIES IN TECHNOLOGY AND ORGANIZATION

WE ARE WHAT WE DO (AND HOW WE DO IT): ORGANIZATIONAL TECHNOLOGIES AND THE CONSTRUCTION OF ORGANIZATIONAL IDENTITY

Davide Ravasi and Anna Canato

ABSTRACT

Past research has highlighted multiple interrelations between technology and social cognition. In this chapter, building on past studies, as well as on our own research, we advance propositions about the conditions under which technological features are likely to serve as cues for the construction of organizational identity and about the consequences of this fact for the enduringness of these features. In doing so, our emerging framework may contribute to increase more general understanding of how organizational features come to be perceived as part of organizational identity.

Technology and Organization: Essays in Honour of Joan Woodward
Research in the Sociology of Organizations, Volume 29, 49–78

ISSN: 0733-558X/doi:10.1108/S0733-558X(2010)0000029011

1. INTRODUCTION

Technology – broadly understood as tools, machines, and techniques for instrumental actions, as well as the beliefs and principles they embody (Woodward, 1965; Dosi, 1982; Barley, 1990; Griffith, 1999) – is considered a central element for understanding organizations, as it affects both the way they are organized and the pattern of evolution of internal structures and processes (Woodward, 1965, Patel & Pavitt, 2000).

Past research on the influence of technology on organizational life has highlighted the interaction between technologies, technological features, and the social structure of organizations (e.g. Barley, 1986; Orlikowski, 1992; D'Adderio, 2003), as well as the reciprocal influence between technology and managers' mental models (e.g. Garud & Rappa, 1994; Tripsas & Gavetti, 2000; Kaplan, Murray, & Henderson, 2003). Collectively, these studies suggest that technology shapes how organizational members make sense of and organize their social reality. In this chapter, we focus on a specific aspect of organizational sensemaking, that is how members develop and preserve a collective sense of what their organization is and stands for – or, in other words, of their organizational identity (Albert & Whetten, 1985; Brown, Dacin, Pratt, & Whetten, 2006).

Past research has highlighted the influence of organizational identity on strategic processes (Dutton & Dukerich, 1991; Gioia & Thomas, 1996; Ravasi & Schultz, 2006) as well as internal social dynamics (Golden-Biddle & Rao, 1997; Glynn, 2000; Humphreys & Brown, 2002). Some studies have pointed at the role of leaders in shaping identity beliefs and understandings (Gioia & Thomas, 1996; Fiol, 2002). However, how certain specific features of the organization – values, practices, symbols, or else – become part of what members perceive as their organization's identity is still unclear.

In this chapter, building on past literature on organizational identity, as well as on our own research, we develop a framework for understanding under what circumstances technological features embedded in organizational products or processes are likely to be perceived as constitutive elements of the identity of the organization, and how this fact influences organizational decisions and actions. In Section 2, we account for the main constructs and notions concerning organizational identity research and technology sensemaking. In Section 3, we propose some antecedents of technology as identity referents, and we illustrate our arguments with reference to our own as well as published research. In Section 4, we discuss the potential consequences of the inclusion of technological features among identity referents. We conclude by discussing implications of our proposed interpretations for research on organizational technologies and organizational identities.

2. LITERATURE REVIEW

2.1. Organizational Identity

Organizational identity was initially defined by Albert and Whetten (1985) as a set of features perceived by members to be central, enduring, and distinctive of their organization. According to David Whetten, these features – or *identity referents* – contribute to craft a self-referencing narrative that help members construct a collective sense of self and that satisfies organizational and individual needs for continuity, coherence, and distinctiveness (Whetten & Mackey, 2002; Whetten, 2006). In this view, organizational identities are conceived as emotionally laden, stable, and enduring self-descriptions or characterizations of an organization (Ashforth & Mael, 1996), underpinning deeply held beliefs, embodied in formal claims, which tend to change only rarely and never easily (Whetten & Mackey, 2002).

Empirical evidence of changing interpretations about the identity of organizations, however, has led other scholars to observe how members' beliefs about central and distinctive characters of their organization may indeed evolve in the face of internal and external stimuli (Dutton & Dukerich, 1991; Gioia & Thomas, 1996). In their view, organizational identities reside in shared interpretive schemes that members collectively construct to provide meaning to their experience (Gioia, 1998). These shared schemes may, or may not, correspond to the official narrative (Ashforth & Mael, 1996). Scholars embracing this perspective observe how substantial organizational changes generally require alterations in the way members interpret what is central and distinctive about their organization. In other words, substantial changes require members to "make new sense"– that is to develop new interpretations – of what their organization is about (Fiol, 1991; Gioia & Chittipeddi, 1991).

Recent research suggests that these apparently conflicting perspectives may emphasize different aspects of the construction of organizational identities (Ravasi & Schultz, 2006). Together, they suggest how organizational identities arise from processes of sensemaking and sensegiving, through which members periodically re-construct shared understandings and revise formal claims of what the organization is and stands for.

2.2. Constructing Organizational Identities

Even if organizational identity scholars may disagree on where organizational identities mainly reside – members' beliefs, claims, or even fleeting images – or on whether they are more or less prone to change, most researchers tend to agree on the idea that organizational identities are the product of social construction (Corley et al., 2006). How organizational identities are constructed – or, in other words, how a certain feature or a categorical descriptor of the organization comes to be perceived as a self-defining attribute – however, is still unclear.

According to David Whetten, making sense of an organization is a process based largely on inter-organizational comparison. In other words, developing an understanding of what an organization is and stands for requires members to define how and to what extent it is different from and/or similar to other comparable organizations (Whetten & Mackey, 2002). Past research has shown how, on the one hand, members may draw on existing social categories – that is broadly accepted labels that are used to encompass a certain type of organization – to position their organization within a social space (e.g. Rao, Monin, & Durand, 2003). For organizations engaged in market competition, for instance, a particularly relevant subset of categories may be represented by clusters of competitors sharing similar strategies (firm scope, resource commitment, etc.) and a common "strategic group identity" (Peteraf & Shanley, 1997). In their respective industries, general categories such as "low cost carrier," "nouvelle cuisine restaurant," or "vertical retailer" are associated to a subset of strategic and structural choices that can be used not only to identify the organization within its market space but also as a template for organizing choices.

On the other hand, when members' attention shifts to issues of differentiation, they are more likely to search for cues inside the organization. Past research has shown, for instance, how members' interpretations of what their organization is and stands for may draw on various sources of cues such as collective practices (Pratt & Rafaeli, 1997), shared professional backgrounds (Glynn, 2000), organizational artifacts (Brunninge, 2007), or technology (Tripsas, 2009). In particular, past research has observed how organizational culture may serve as a powerful referent, helping organizational members substantiate their identity claims and express their perceived uniqueness in terms of collective values and their embodiment in practices, rituals, and artifacts (Albert & Whetten, 1985; Ravasi & Schultz, 2006).

It is generally understood that, as members invoke the identity of their organization or ask questions about it in different circumstances, they are likely to produce different answers (Albert & Whetten, 1985), as different claims and beliefs may be more or less salient (Ashforth & Johnson, 2001) to the issue that members are called to address. Although members of a given organization may share various identity referents – some based on social categories, others based on organizational features – only some of these referents may be perceived as relevant to a given issue. How a certain feature comes to be included – explicitly or implicitly – among the identity referents of an organization, however, is much less understood.

In this chapter, we focus on one potential referent – organizational technological features – and we develop a tentative framework for understanding how these attributes come to be perceived as part of the identity of an organization.

2.3. Technology and Social Cognition

Building on the seminal work of Joan Woodward (1965) on the relative appropriateness of different organizing principles for different production technologies, in the past few decades, research has investigated the influence of technology on organizational structures and processes and vice versa (De Sanctis & Scott Poole, 1994; Barley, 1986; Orlikowski, 2000, 2007). These studies have underlined the importance of considering technology both in its physical dimension (e.g. the structural features and properties of material artifacts such as machineries, products, or components of end products) and in its cognitive dimension (i.e. a set of goals and beliefs defining the appropriate way of accomplishing a task, designing, and/or using an object).

Past research has emphasized how, on the one hand, structural and cognitive features of a technology are the result of social processes occurring at organizational or institutional level (e.g. Bijker, Hughes, & Pinch, 1987; Garud & Rappa, 1994; Kaplan & Tripsas, 2008), whereas on the other hand they contribute to shape social interaction and the social order within which they are embedded (Barley, 1986; De Sanctis & Scott Poole, 1994; Tripsas & Gavetti, 2000). Garud and Rappa's (1994) study of the evolution of Cochlear implants, for instance, shows how the development of a technology within a social environment requires the interaction between the physical forms and functions of an artifact and the beliefs that engineers and managers hold concerning the logic of usage of the technology, its main characteristics and its evaluation metrics. Eventually, then, the establishment of a given technology in the market does not derive only from the physical and functional properties of technology itself but also from the institutionalized routines through which technological "improvements" are assessed.

Within organizations, defining technology as composed by physical and cognitive features highlights the interaction between tangible features and the mental models of organizational members (Weick, 1990; Griffith, 1999). Scholars who have studied technology adoption and usage, for instance, have investigated the way in which individuals and groups adapt and interact with new artifacts and technologies in organizations (e.g. Barley, 1986, 1990; Leonard-Barton, 1988; Dean, Yoon, & Susman, 1992; Orlikowski, 2007). On the basis of empirical findings, this stream of literature has progressively abandoned a deterministic view of technology, where machines and infrastructures are conceived as structures that dictate and shape individual and organizational responses, in favor of a more nuanced and interpretive perspective that stresses the relevance of the process of sensemaking and appropriation of new artifacts and their design logics (Weick, 1995; De Sanctis & Scott Poole, 1994). Empirical studies have focused mainly on the interaction between designers, artifacts and users and on the processes of sensemaking and appropriation that derive from the translation and adaptation of designers' cognitive logics, as embedded in technology artifacts, to users' cognitive domain (Orlikowski, 1992; De Sanctis & Scott Poole, 1994; Orlikowski, Yates, Okamura, & Fujimoto, 1995; D'Adderio, 2003).

Other scholars have addressed a similar research question at a higher level of analysis and investigated how technology dimensions can affect sensemaking at organizational level, that is how technology characteristics can affect the pattern of evolution and learning of organizations. For example, Leonard-Barton (1992) discussed how, thanks to the local nature of learning processes, extant technologies, and competencies limit the possibilities of future developments and constrain innovation opportunities. According to Leonard-Barton, such rigidity is linked not only to the cost of developing organizational knowledge in more than one direction but also to the specific beliefs and values that inspired the development of those competencies in first place. Later on, Tripsas and Gavetti (2000) extended this line of inquiry, by showing how entrenched managerial understandings of core organizational technologies tend to influence opportunity interpretation and future strategic decisions, therefore contributing to strategic inertia. More recently, Kaplan et al. (2003) have provided large-scale quantitative evidence of how mental models influence how a new technology is interpreted by senior managers, and therefore, how managers respond to technological opportunities.

These streams of research show the reciprocal influence of technology and sensemaking, at both individual and organizational level. However, although the influence of mental models on individual and organizational responses to new technologies has been investigated in the past, both conceptually (e.g. Griffith, 1999; Weick, 1995) and empirically (e.g. Tripsas & Gavetti, 2000; Kaplan et al., 2003), less is known about how *technological features* of an organization – for example the tools, machines, and techniques used in operational and administrative activities, as well as the design principles and technological attributes of its final products and services (i.e. their materials, components, functions, etc.) – become cognitive anchors, acting as either a source of stimuli or inertia in the face of environmental change.

In Section 3, we propose that one of the ways in which technological features may come to influence organizational members' cognitive processes is by becoming embedded in relatively shared beliefs and understandings about what the organization is and stands for – or in other words, by becoming identity referents.

3. TECHNOLOGY AS AN IDENTITY REFERENT

Despite the overall relevance of organizational technologies for organizational strategies, structures, and processes, we would expect organizations to vary in the degree of significance they ascribe to technology attributes. As previous research has shown, although organizations are periodically engaged in changes in their production systems, information systems, product technologies, and so on, occasionally, some of them display a tendency to resist the alteration of some of their technological features (e.g. Leonard-Barton, 1992; Tripsas & Gavetti, 2000).

Anecdotal evidence from research on organizational identity suggests a connection between *organizational technologies* – for example the core technical capabilities of an organization (Ravasi & Schultz, 2006; Fiol, 2002), the routines underlying how instrumental tasks are accomplished (Nag, Corley, & Gioia, 2007), the technological features of organizational products (Ravasi & Schultz, 2007; Brunninge, 2007; Tripsas, 2009) – and *organizational identity*. In this respect, organizational responses to external pressures for the alteration of some of its technological features might be explained by the emotional and cognitive reaction to the alteration of features that are perceived as part of the identity of the organization

(Reger, Gustafson, DeMarie, & Mullane, 1994). How technological features become part of members' identity beliefs in the first place, however, is still poorly understood.

Organizational-referencing discourse is frequently observed in organizations. However, according to David Whetten (2006), not all organizational descriptions (or self-descriptions) qualify as bona fide identity claims – or, in other words, would be highly emotionally laden and influential on organizational actions (Lerpold, Ravasi, Van Rekom, & Soenen, 2007). According to Whetten, only those attributes that "are manifested as an organisation's core programs, policies and procedures" (Whetten, 2006, p. 222), "have repeatedly demonstrated their value as distinguishing organisational features" (p. 221), and "have withstood the test of time" (p. 224), will act as legitimate identity referents. Whetten refers to these properties as centrality, distinctiveness, and enduringness (Albert & Whetten, 1985). He observes how only distinctive attributes effectively specify the way in which an organization is similar to or different from other comparable organizations. However, only attributes that are essential to the organization as it is known to its members, and to which members have shown deep commitment in the past, are likely to be considered distinguishing for the organization (Whetten, 2006).

In this chapter, we follow Whetten's arguments, and we argue that the likelihood that a certain organizational feature becomes an identity referent depends on the extent to which the focal feature is perceived by organizational members as central, distinctive, and enduring. In this section, we propose four potential factors increasing the likelihood that a given technological feature comes to be perceived as central and distinctive – hence to be considered as an identity referent. In the following section, we indicate some potential consequences of the inclusion of technological features among organizational identity referents, which may result in the increased enduringness of the feature (Fig. 1). In turn, as displayed by the feedback loop in the figure, we expect the long-lasting commitment to a given feature to further reinforce member's perception of it as a fundamental identity referent.

3.1. The Centrality of Technological Features

Centrality refers to the extent to which a certain feature is perceived by members as essential to the survival of the organization as it is, a feature without which the organization would no longer be or would become something different from what has been so far (Albert & Whetten, 1985). In

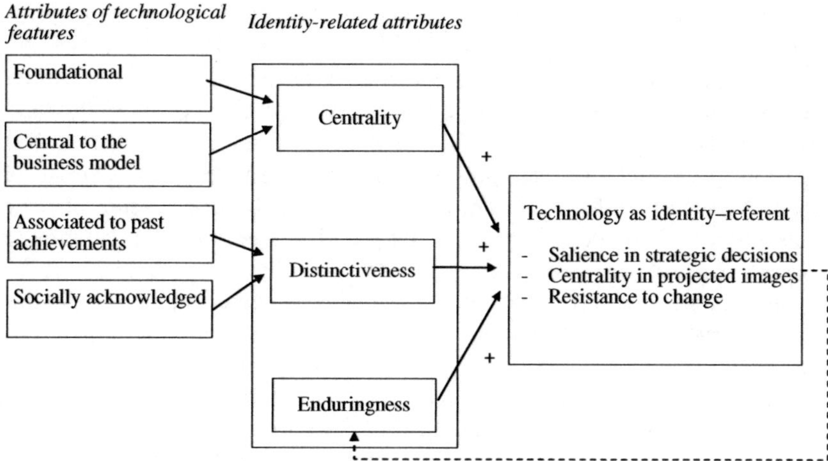

Fig. 1. Organizational Identity and Technology.

family-owned business firms, for example, the active participation of family members in the management and control of the organization is often reputed as essential for the organization to be considered a "family business." The decision of family members to relegate themselves to the role of pure investors may be resisted (or, conversely, be advocated) because of the changes in managerial philosophy, human resource policies, and in the overall atmosphere, which would result from changing perceptions of what the organization is (and, therefore, how it should be managed) that would follow the loss of family members' involvement, despite the de facto preservation of the "family-owned" condition.

An organizational feature, then, is defined as central when it is considered by its members as one of the fundamental attributes of the organization itself, shaping and conditioning decisions about more peripheral structural features and processes. In organizations, some features (such as, for instance, the corporate form or the mission of the organization) provide a sense of direction, or, as David Whetten (2006, p. 225) says, "constrain and give meaning" to lower level choices (such as human resource policies or pricing decisions). They provide a sort of a template against which potential courses of actions are evaluated and judged as "appropriate" or "inappropriate." Whenever actions and decisions are perceived as violating these features, emotional responses may arise in the organization, as members are likely to resist, debate, and challenge courses of action that contravene their need for coherence and continuity (Dutton & Dukerich, 1991; Golden-Biddle & Rao, 1997; Ravasi & Schultz, 2006).

Organizations, however, unlike individuals, have few, if any, "objective" identity referents such as gender, or ethnicity, that tend to naturally – and often implicitly – condition self-perception and influence other choices regarding personal lifestyle, professional career, or sentimental relationships. As social artifacts, organizations are by definition social constructions, subjected to continuous re-shaping and re-interpretation by internal and external actors, and there are few, if any, objective referents, such as industry or geographical location, that members cannot alter, should they really wish to do so (Whetten, 2003). Perceived or claimed constraints, therefore, should be looked for somewhere else. In particular, we argue that a given technology – or, more generally, a given feature – may come to be perceived as central to the organization to the extent that (i) it is historically associated with the founding of the organization, or with other major events in the life of the organization that are considered crucial in shaping the organization as it is currently known, and (ii) it underpins the pattern of activities and relationships which ensures the equilibrium of the organization in its environment – or, in other words, its "business model."

3.2. Foundational Features and Centrality

As social constructions, organizations are not "naturally" born with certain traits: their features – such as their legal form, their geographical location or their activity – are the result of more or less conscious and more or less deliberate choices of their founders. Once taken, however, these fundamental choices are likely to be taken as "given" and shape the identity of the organization in the following years (Whetten, 2003). In the future, alterations of "foundational" features may encounter emotional or cognitive resistance as they imply a change in what may be considered a "natural" characteristic of the organization (Reger et al., 1994). Eventually, the relative ease with which change occurs will depend also on the perceived distinctiveness (is the feature perceived as making the organization comparatively better than others?) and endurance (has the feature been around for a long time?) of the attribute (Whetten, 2006). We will return later on to the interrelations between centrality, distinctiveness, and enduringness.

If we accept this notion, a technology can be considered "foundational" if it is historically connected to the founding of the organization – its "birth" – or to other major events (or individuals) that deeply affected the organization as it is currently known by its members. Sometimes firms, for instance, are founded to exploit a specific technological innovation embodied in a new product or production process (Helfat & Lieberman, 2002). Their initial structures, strategies, and patterns of activities may be constructed around this technology. To the extent that these technological features are associated to corporate success, later on, corporate mythology may trace an explicit link between the founders – or other prominent members – and innovative technological features or innovations on which the fortunes of the organization were built. Eventually, this technology would become embedded in organizational self-referencing narratives and in members' beliefs as a central feature of the organization – a legacy of its past to be preserved, refined, and developed even when economic or commercial concern would suggest otherwise.

Take the case of Piaggio, an Italian manufacturer of motorcycles, scooters, and other light vehicles, currently one of the leading global competitors in the two-wheel business. Before the Second World War, Piaggio was one of the largest national producers of airplanes, trains, trams, and other means of transportation. During the war, production focused on war supplies. After the war, Piaggio had to quickly convert its production into something commercially viable. In the late 1940s and early 1950s, the rebirth of the company was linked to the development of what became the archetypal scooter, Vespa: a light motorcycle, whose frame – so the myth says – was obtained by legendary designer Corradino D'Ascanio from the steel plate of an airplane, bent to provide ample frontal protection for the legs and a comfortable footrest. Mr. D'Ascanio was an aeronautical engineer, and he did not like motorcycles; the new product, therefore, incorporated a number of features, from the gear change on the hand-grip to the bodywork completely covering the working parts, aimed at increasing comfort and simplicity of operation.

The quick commercial success and the immense popularity around the world in the years to come made Vespa a landmark for the entire organization. In the late 1970s and the early 1980s, the product seemed to gradually lose its appeal in the face of the multitude of smaller and cheaper scooters made available by the introduction of plastics – a technology mastered by Japanese manufacturers. The decline of Vespa seriously affected the financial conditions of the company. In the mid 1980s, therefore, the company's efforts focused on the expansion of its range with new models, different from Vespa and based on the less-expensive plastic technologies. Yet, the company refused to terminate the production of its flagship product, even if no really new Vespa models had been developed since the PX version in 1977. Only in the mid 1990s designers and engineers decided to re-propose the old Vespa scooter in an entirely revamped version. As the chief engineer at Piaggio told us:

> If we had insisted on proposing Vespa as our core product, clients might have doubted that we were able to produce anything else. We absolutely had to demonstrate that we were able to make good plastic scooters.... Once we did that, we could re-propose Vespa as our reference product.

Although the new model was vastly redesigned to include more modern technical solutions, some features were preserved even if they countered current trends in scooter designs. Among these was the metal body – by then, a unique feature that no other competing product sported anymore. As the head of the design centre remarked:

> Vespa has to be metallic: that's the bottom line.... Vespa has always had this rather maternal backside, very enveloping, and a somewhat slim, bony-looking front part rounded just right, but still made out of a single metal sheet with great industrial savvy.

According to a corporate historian, the decision, which substantially affected the industrial cost of the product, was profoundly linked with a collective sense of self that was re-captured in the design of the new product:

> [It] meant the revival of celebrated moulding factory, the nucleus around which production was centred until the eighties, when every two-wheeled Piaggio, from the PX to the mopeds, was in sheet metal.... There is said to be a certain amount of pride in those on the production line, who feel they are somehow involved in carrying on the special metal-working tradition...It's a question of collective identity, workmanship ability, professional updating and, at the same time, link with the past. (Mazzanti & Sessa, 2003, pp. 274–275)

As a Piaggio manager observed, touching Vespa "involves the very identity of the company." Eventually, a strong sense of what was central to the company and its core products – even from a technological point of view – had ensured the preservation of a unique identity on the market, embodied in its Vespa scooters, which was central in the late 1990s to the turnaround of the group.

Proposition 1. *The tighter the perceived connection between a technological feature and the founding of an organization – or other major turning point in its history – the higher the likelihood that it will come to be perceived as an identity referent.*

3.3. Organizational Business Model and Centrality

Although management scholars belonging to different schools of thought may differ in their focus of attention – the organization vs. the environment – they tend to agree that the survival of organizations depends on the interaction between environmental conditions and the pattern of resources and activities that characterizes an organization. According to Michael Porter (1996), successful organizational strategies rest on a few core concepts (such as cost minimization in the case of Southwest Airlines, or "design at low cost" for Ikea), which give sense, coherence, and direction to this pattern of resources and activities. In this respect, it has been argued that organizational identity and strategy perform similar functions (Ashforth & Mael, 1996), and several studies have shown multiple interrelations between organizational strategies and identity beliefs (Collins & Porras, 1996; Gioia & Thomas, 1996; Corley & Gioia, 2004; Ravasi & Schultz, 2006).

If we accept this notion, then it is not unreasonable to think that in organizations characterized by established models of interaction with the environment – in organizations engaged in market-competition we might refer to them as their "business models" – members come to consider as central those features that drive more general choices shaping the pattern of resources and activities. On the one hand, as central to the business model, these features are likely to be acknowledged as essential for the survival of the organization; challenging these features may be perceived as endangering the equilibrium on which survival rests and the very future of the organization. On the other hand, altering these features are likely to imply a further round of changes in the rest of the organization – its structures, its commercial policies, its reward systems, and so on – which may as well result in a profound transformation of the organization as members know it and understand it.

The case of Benetton, an Italian producer of fashion apparel operating on a global scale, is illustrative of the link between the configuration of resources and activities underpinning organizational advantage and the perceived centrality of a technological feature. Between the 1980s and 1990s, Benetton became a global leader in the apparel industry, thanks to a well-honed business model (see Stevenson, Martinez, & Jarillo, 1989; Camuffo, Romano, & Vinelli, 2001). Benetton's business model rested on a few innovative features – a network of independent franchisees providing frequent feedback about changing customers' preferences, a proprietary technology enabling it to dye finished wool products, a sophisticated automated warehouse reducing delivery time throughout the world, and colorful and provocative advertising campaigns supporting the slogan "United Colours of Benetton."

The combination of these features allowed Benetton to establish a dominant brand in the mass segment of the fashion industry, leveraging on its capacity to respond quickly and effectively to shifting customers' preferences. In the late 1990s and early 2000s, however, the sustainability of Benetton's model was seriously challenged by a new cohort of competitors, led by the Spanish group Inditex (better known for its Zara chain) and the Swedish retailer H&M, adopting a so-called fast fashion model, based on a tighter interaction between the retail outlets and the design centres at the headquarters, and on a more frequent, almost obsessive, renewal of the collections (Ferdows, Lewis, & Machuca, 2004).

Benetton's response was slow and, as one of its managers admitted later, conditioned by its technological heritage. Although in the managerial folklore Benetton had often been described as a flexible, light organization, embedded in a network of subcontractors and franchisees, the reality was different. The company was highly integrated upstream: around 60% of its sales were produced in-house. The company even owned large sheep farms around the world. On the one hand, for a mass-market global brand such as Benetton, vertical integration had ensured high efficiency of large-scale productions and tight control on the quality and timing of the process. On the other hand, the presence of the large plants constantly required intensive use of the productive capacity to cover the fixed costs (i.e. workforce). The industrial heritage of the organization, however, seemed to affect its responses to external changes in a more subtle way. As a manager put it:

> Of course sheep and workers are a constraint. But the real constraint is not material: it is a matter of identity.... Genetically, Benetton is a manufacturer: Zara and H&M have a history as retailers...The unanswered question now is: will Benetton become a retailer or not?

The difference was not purely semantic. The "manufacturing" identity and tradition, for instance, brought managers at Benetton to assess performance in terms of "sell-in" (items sold by the company to the network of franchisees), rather than "sell-out" (items sold in the shop to the customer). Pricing was determined as a mark-up on industrial cost. Product development followed the logic of seasonal collections (to be presented to the franchisees), rather than the logic of the in-shop assortment (to be proposed the final clients). Production was spread over 12 months to smooth down production peaks, rather than flexibly adjusting to market demands. Although these practices had worked well for several years, in a relatively stable and predictable environment, the arrival of fast fashion had changed the rule of the game. In the eye of its managers, effective response to the new challenge required substantial changes in the way sales were monitored, products were developed, production was planned, and so on. In turn, these changes seemed to imply a more profound revision of the widespread conceptualization of the organization, which underpinned its business model.

As the case of Benetton illustrates, an organization's business model rests on an internally coherent set of activities and resources, embedded in a web of cultural practices and schemes, and underpinned by a relatively shared organizational identity. Changing business models – changing "strategy" – therefore, often requires an alteration in the commonly, albeit tacitly, held beliefs about what the organization is (Gioia, Thomas, Clark, & Chittipeddi, 1994; Ashforth & Mael, 1996). In this respect, organizational technologies that are central to this pattern of activities may come to influence the very way in which organizational members understand their organization, potentially limiting their capacity to envision alternative models that would disrupt the equilibrium that is associated to those technological features. In summary:

Proposition 2. *The greater the centrality of a technology for the business model of an organization, the higher the likelihood that it will come to be perceived as an identity referent.*

3.4. The Distinctiveness of Technological Features

In the previous section, we have proposed that features that are perceived as "foundational" and central to the business model of an organization are more likely to be perceived as central to the organization, hence, to become part of its identity. However, not all features that characterize the organization at its inception and/or define its current business model are equally likely to be considered as identity referents. Individual and organizational identities satisfy both needs for coherence and continuity, *and* self-esteem (Ashforth & Mael, 1996; Whetten & Mackey, 2002). Organizational identity referents, therefore, should be perceived as both central *and* distinctive (Albert & Whetten, 1985; Whetten, 2006).

According to Whetten (2006), organizational attributes may satisfy members' needs for self-esteem to the extent that they make the organization positively different – or *distinguished* – from competitors and other comparable organizations. It is not sufficient that a certain feature makes the organization *different* from but also *better than* others: such difference, in other words, should be perceived as increasing the social status of the organization and therefore its members. In this respect, we argue that the likelihood that a technological feature comes to be perceived as an identity referent is related to (i) the extent to which the focal technology is related to past organizational achievements and (ii) the extent to which the focal technology has earned the organization widespread social acknowledgment. It is not unusual for these factors to coincide, as superior technologies and product design may not only let the organization succeed in competition but also earn the organization social recognition in the form of design awards, favorable press coverage, positive expert feedback, improved reputation, and so on.

3.5. Extraordinary Achievements and Distinctiveness

Many organizations are, occasionally or systematically, engaged in some forms of inter-organizational contests such as sport races for carmakers (Rao, 1994) or the annual competition for status that takes place among fine restaurants (Rao et al., 2003) or wine makers (Benjamin & Podolny, 1999). Success in these contests is usually perceived externally – but also internally – as a sign of superior capabilities (Rao, 1994). Other organizations may be silently engaged in more subtle contests, as they compete for the introduction of technological innovation, the establishment of industry standards, the pre-emption of distribution channels, the geographical expansion, the attention of the media, and so on. More generally, most business firms are involved in market competition and tend to gauge their performance in relative terms by comparing their turnover, growth rates, financial ratios, and market share with their competitors.

Organizational features that make an organization particularly successful in these contests may have a profound impact on members' collective imagery and sense of self. Even in "unofficial" competitive contests, extraordinary success may be marked by specific events (the introduction of a radically innovative product, the disclosure of outstanding results, etc.) that underlie the primacy of the organization over its competitors. As pride and enthusiasm for the organizational accomplishment spreads throughout the organization, merits are likely to be attributed to organizational features such as people, practices, products, technologies, and so on. Eventually, stories will diffuse and myths will arise, celebrating these features and shaping retrospective reconstruction of the causes of organizational success

(Boje, 1995; Lounsbury & Glynn, 2001). In turn, as members engage in a more or less explicit attempt to make sense of what distinguishes their organization from competitors, these "memories" encased in the organizational narrative may provide them with commonly accepted reference points to define how and why the organization is not just different, but *superior* to other comparable ones (Ravasi & Schultz, 2007).

In the early 1970s, for instance, managers at Bang & Olufsen, a Danish producer of high-quality and high-design audio video systems, engaged in a reflection on what made their company different from their competitors. The reflections were meant to reinforce commercial strategies aimed at countering the rising threat of Japanese producers, to provide guidelines for communication efforts and to imbue with meaning the new slogan: "We think differently." The obvious starting point for the company was the highly popular products that had reaped design awards in recent years. A review of the way successful products had been designed in the last 10 years brought to the identification of seven fundamental principles of product design, which were presented to the rest of the organization as the Seven Corporate Identity Components (CICs).

In the previous decade, attention to design and user experience had intensified under the leadership of product developer Jens Bang and chief designer Jacob Jensen. Design principles codified in the Seven CICs underpinned an approach to product design that, as one of our informants put it, unlike most of its competitors started from users and developed products around them rather than the other way around. Simplicity and essentiality had characterized the philosophy of the company and the design of its products since the very beginning (Bang & Palshøy, 2000). The influence of the Bauhaus movement in art and design was evident in early material expressions of the company: from the first B&O logo, dated 1932 and readopted in 1994, to products like the bakelite Beolit 39 radio. Later, the Seven CICs elaborated on the concept, observing how simplicity should inspire concept development (essentiality), the design of human–machine interfaces (domesticity and autovisuality), and even customer information (credibility). Over the years, the search for simplicity inspired such milestones as the Beomaster 1900 audio system, where user interfaces were designed to facilitate access to music reproduction, and the one-thumb integrated remote control, the Beolink 1000, connected to all the video and audio sources in a house (Bang & Palshøy, 2000).

Although their popularity waxed and waned throughout the years, in the following three decades, the Seven CICs represented a fundamental reference point for organization members. Although, later on, corporate mottos and espoused cultural values changed, reflecting the shifting focus of business strategies, the Seven CICs – an emblem of a golden age culminated in the exhibition of the company's products at the Museum of Modern Arts in New York in 1976 – were never forgotten and periodically reappeared in different forms in internal communication, training material, and corporate statements, to illustrate the unchanged principles that, in the eye of its members, have kept Bang & Olufsen viable – the only surviving European producer of a full range of audio-visual equipment – in an increasingly competitive market, dominated by a corporation whose yearly research budget exceeds the overall turnover of the Danish company (Ravasi & Schultz, 2007).

In summary:

Proposition 3. *The closer the relationship between a certain technological feature and an organization's extraordinary achievements, the higher the likelihood that it will be considered as an identity referent.*

3.6. Social Acknowledgment and Distinctiveness

A considerable body of research indicates that members' beliefs about the identity of the organization tend to be influenced also by how the organization itself is portrayed by external actors such as customers (Ravasi & Schultz, 2006), public opinion (Dutton & Dukerich, 1991), and the media (Elsbach & Kramer, 1996). Past research has shown how members' beliefs and understandings about their organization tend to mirror the feedback that they receive from external audiences (Dutton & Dukerich, 1991; Hatch & Schultz, 2002). As the seminal study by Dutton and Dukerich (1991) indicates, of all the potential identity referents of an organization, organizational leaders and members will emphasize those that seem to resonate with the impressions and expectations of the general public. If we accept this notion, then it is not unreasonable to expect that technological features that seemed to receive a broad social acknowledgment – hence contributing to cast the organization in a favorable light in the eyes of its external audiences – are more likely to be included among the identity referents of the organization.

At times, widespread social acknowledgment may be associated to triumph in the inter-organizational competitions mentioned earlier (Rao, 1994). Such is the case, for instance, of companies such as carmaker Alfa Romeo or motorcycle producer Ducati, whose members are proud to remind how few or no companies in their respective fields have won as many races as they have in their history. Similarly, at Bang & Olufsen, members' pride for the excellence of their design was reinforced by the numerous awards that their products were granted. Finally, it is not unreasonable to think that managers may be unwilling to abandon features that are celebrated in the management narrative as central and unique to their success.

Organizations, however, may not gain social recognition only for their successes. Organizations, for instance, are constantly evaluated by the media and the public on the conformity of their actions to social values and expectations (Meyer & Rowan, 1977). Although organizations may not be deliberately engaged in a competition for public goodwill, actions that are perceived as consistent with social concerns may earn a company a positive social acknowledgment in the form of favorable media coverage or supportive consumer advocacy (Fombrun, Gardberg, & Barnett, 2000).

Finally, but not less importantly, some organizations, their products or brands, may acquire a particular significance within society as they become more or less publicly associated with certain values, lifestyles, people, or objects (Ravasi & Rindova, 2008). In these cases, the organization and/or its product may come to affect the meaning of existing social categories (think for instance of how Apple, through its iPod, enriched the meaning of portable music players, or how Levi Strauss contributed to the diffusion – and characterization – of jeans pants around the world) or even foster the establishment of new ones (Kleenex and paper tissues, Xerox and copy machines, or Ryanair and low-cost flights in Europe). In some cases, the cultural significance of the organization is manifested in the spontaneous association between the organization and broader social categories, for instance in the use of its very name as a synonym for a certain category of products (Polaroid and instant photography), or people (the "iPod generation") and so on. The emergence and diffusion of these categories provides a powerful feedback to organizational members about what really identifies the organization in the eye of the broader public, and, to the extent that they do not possess negative connotations, what makes the organization distinguished. In addition, the fact that organizational features – often embodied in their products – become embedded in the cultural world may increase the commitment of members to preserve what has now become a social institution.[1]

Take for instance the case of Scania, a Swedish producer of trucks, buses, and engines (Brunninge, 2007). In 2005, Scania was the last European manufacturer to discontinue the production of bonneted cab trucks – the once dominant design, where the engine was placed under a bonnet in front of the driver's cab. The viability of bonneted cab trucks compared to the alternative design – the cab-over-engine trucks – had initially been questioned in the 1960s, when, in the face of rising European length restrictions, the higher comfort of bonneted cab trucks was offset by the lower transport capacity, as cargo space was sacrificed for the front "nose" of the truck. Consequently, most manufacturers soon abandoned the design, as the decreasing sales volumes would not cover the development costs of new products. At Scania, however, the decision to discontinue the development and production of bonneted cab trucks came much later and not without an intense debate (Brunninge, 2007).

As Brunninge's study shows, although other producers gradually abandoned bonneted cabs, Scania continued investing and developing new lines until eventually, in Europe, the name of Scania became strongly associated with bonneted cab trucks. Overtime, however, the market for bonneted cabs became smaller and smaller. Nevertheless, Scania kept producing bonneted cab trucks even when their share on the total turnover of the company became minimal and their profitability questionable. The first proposals to discontinue the production of bonneted cabs were met with "uproar," as organizational members refused to even consider such a decision – despite the apparent profit-orientation of the company.

The bonneted cab was perceived as representing "the essence of Scania" (Brunninge, 2007, p. 27). In fact, in 2000 an internal manual, defining design principles for Scania trucks, used mostly stories and examples from old trucks from the 1960s and 1970s, most of which were bonneted cabs. Externally, Scania managers found in the popular appeal of bonneted cab trucks arguments reinforcing their beliefs. In fact, among the general public, bonneted cab trucks were still popular, perhaps due to the anthropomorphic appearance that the bonnet conferred. Indeed, a common story at Scania observed how children, when asked to draw a truck, intuitively drew a bonneted cab: that was how a truck – a Scania truck – was supposed to look like.

Eventually, even Scania had to surrender to the shrinking sales volume of the once dominant design: while bonneted cabs – like steam engines – still enjoyed high popularity among the public, economic concerns among clients undermined their commercial viability. The Scania case, however, is illustrative of how the way in which technological features of an organization and/or its products become embedded in social and cultural understandings may coevolve with internal interpretations and decisions: although, on the one hand, external interpretations are partly the result of organizational decisions (such as persisting in the production of bonneted cab trucks when all the other producers are not), on the other hand, they may eventually come to reinforce – or constrain – internal interpretations of what is central and distinctive of the organization.

Proposition 4. *The greater the extent to which a technological attribute is socially acknowledged, the higher the likelihood that is will come to be considered as an identity referent.*

4. THE CONSEQUENCES OF TECHNOLOGY AS AN IDENTITY REFERENT

In the previous section, we have argued how technological features that are associated with foundational moments in the life of an organization, central to its business model, related to past accomplishments, and widely acknowledged by external audiences are more likely to become part of members' beliefs about central and distinctive features of their organization – or, in other words, to become identity referents. In this section, building on past research on organizational identities, we explore how, by being embedded in shared identity beliefs and reflected in institutional claims and strategies, these features are also less likely to be discarded in the face of external or internal pressures – hence they will become increasingly "enduring."

Research on organizational identity has shown how organizational features that are perceived as central and distinctive to an organization tend to influence how strategic decisions unfold (see Lerpold et al., 2007 for a review). According to Whetten (2006), organizational identities are most likely to be invoked in novel, consequential strategic choices, expected to have a profound effect on the organization. Ravasi and Schultz (2006) have shown how changes in the competitive environment may be perceived as "identity threats" – and addressed as such – to the extent that they challenge the viability of central, enduring, and distinctive features of an organization. Under these circumstances, organizational leaders would try to maintain a consistency between the past and the current identity of the organizations, and its future evolution. Although not always conscious, this drive reflects a fundamental human need to maintain direction and cohesion in action (Ashforth & Mael, 1996). As new strategic issues arise, then, organizational members are likely to look for responses that are perceived as coherent with the identity of the organization. Identity-referent technological features may inspire, orient, or even constrain the search for solutions. At Scania, for instance, as concerns for general safety in the case of collision arose throughout Europe and truck manufacturers were expected to find solutions, designers proposed a reinterpretation of the traditional bonneted cab, which used the front "nose" to buffer the impact of the crash and reduce damages to other vehicles (Brunninge, 2007).

This is not to say that, in the presence of strongly held organizational identity referents, strategic change will be impossible, but that strategic decisions would need to pass a test of coherence with the extant self-referential mental models of organizational members and with established patterns of activities (Nag et al., 2007). In this respect, organizational identities that are based on stringent definitions and few, narrowly understood identity referents may restrain the capacity of organizational leaders to envision new identity-congruent patterns of activities in the face of changing external conditions. Conversely, the adaptability of an organization may be increased by the inclusion among identity referents of broader, process-based technical capabilities, rather than specific technological features. Despite the immense popularity and success of products such as the Post It and Scotch tape, for instance, 3M was always considered by its members an "innovation company," rather than an "adhesive company," allowing for continuous growth and exploration of new technologies and businesses (Canato, 2008).

An additional source of enduringness for identity beliefs comes from their possible inclusion in formal organizational claims. Under normal circumstances, attempts to deliver a favorable image of the organization to its various audiences are likely to draw – more or less consciously – on members' beliefs about what is essential and distinguishing about their organization. By doing so, members genuinely manifest their beliefs and aspirations about the organization (Hatch & Schultz, 1997, 2002), try to avoid dangerous incongruence between what they claim and what they believe their organization really is and does (van Riel, 1995), and possibly search for consensus based on convergence of values with external audiences (Scott & Lane, 2000).

To the extent that certain features – including technological features – are perceived as central and distinguishing, therefore, they are likely to surface in organizational communication. Think, for instance, of the traditional emphasis of Benetton on color (as summarized in the tagline "United Colours of Benetton," but also reflected in the images selected for advertising campaigns, etc.), reflecting the organization's unique dyeing technology, or the emphasis of Toyota on quality, reflecting its massive efforts in developing superior manufacturing techniques. To the extent that these claims come to shape external constituents' interpretations and expectations about the organization, members' collective sense of self may be reinforced by "mirroring" these external images (Hatch & Schultz, 2002), and members themselves may be reluctant to revise their identity referents for fear of confusing organizational audiences and losing their support.

Finally, research has provided robust evidence of a more general unwillingness of organizational members to drop features that are perceived as part of the identity of the organization, even in the presence of deliberate attempts of organizational leaders to change collective self-conceptualizations (e.g. Humphreys & Brown, 2002; Nag et al., 2007). The replacement of identity referents or the introduction of new features that are perceived as incoherent with the identity of the organization may threaten members' sense of self and continuity, therefore eliciting emotional resistance to the proposed changes (Whetten & Mackey, 2002). New features may also require an adaptation of current mental models, unleashing the opposition of confused members who are required to revise their understanding of what the organization is and what it stands for (Reger et al., 1994). Also, organizational changes that touch identity-relevant features may be resisted as it may result in an alteration of established working practices and social relations that are underpinned by the identity of the organization (Nag et al., 2007).

On the basis of these considerations, we argue that technological features that are internally perceived as central and distinctive characteristics for the organization would display a natural tendency to resist change even against commercial, technical, and economic considerations:

> **Proposition 5.** *The inclusion of a certain technological feature among identity referents will increase the likelihood that it will be retained over time even in the face of external or internal pressures for change.*

In summary, in this section, we have pointed at how past research on organizational identity has observed how identity-related features are likely to be preserved over time. In part this occurs because of a more or less explicit resistance of members to proposed organizational changes that question the set of referents over which their conceptualization of the organization is built. In part this occurs more subtly as, under normal circumstances, strategic decisions as well as organizational claims tend to reflect and build on current identity beliefs. In doing so, these decisions commit the organization to the preservation and reinforcement of these features, as strategic decisions will be backed up by investments and organizational communication will create expectations that will have to be met. In this respect, although the claim of endurance was initially proposed as a constitutive requirement for "true" identity features, these observations seem to indicate that endurance may as well be both an antecedent *and* a consequence of the inclusion of a feature in the identity of an organization.

5. DISCUSSION AND CONCLUSIONS

Organizational research on technology suggests that, in addition to the requirements that organizational technologies pose on organizational structures and processes – as first evidenced by Joan Woodward – social schemata and social structures themselves tend to affect how technologies are developed and used in organizations.

In this chapter, we have investigated some antecedents and consequences of the inclusion of certain technological features of an organization among organizational identity referents – that is among those features that are likely to be part of collective self-conceptualization of an organization. On the basis of the idea that identity referents are characterized by centrality, distinctiveness, and enduringness, we have identified potential antecedents in the foundational nature of a technological feature, its centrality in the model of interaction between the organization and its environment, its association with past achievements, and its social acknowledgment. We have also argued how the inclusion of a technological feature among identity referents is likely to feed back on the endurance of the feature, with reinforcing effects on their identity-related status.

The claim of endurance has been the subject of an intense debate, as some scholars challenged the notion that identity is comprised only of those features that are preserved over time, even when everything else changes (Corley et al., 2006). Advocates of a social construction perspective, such as Dennis Gioia and colleagues, have observed how organizational adaptation to a changing environment may require a periodic renegotiation of the fundamental understandings shared by its members (Gioia, Schultz, & Corley, 2000). Although formal claims may remain the same, then, the underlying meanings may evolve along with expectations and demands from the environment. Recently, in a contribution aimed at clarifying and strengthening the notion of organizational identity, David Whetten has addressed these concerns about the rigidity of a strict interpretation of the concept endurance by observing how even relatively "recent" features may come to be perceived as an identity referent insofar as they are associated to "irreversible commitments" – that is to decisions that clearly signal the intent of an organization to commit to a certain feature and to make it central to its policies and practices (Whetten, 2006).

In this chapter, we build on this discussion – and on the analysis carried out in the previous sections – to suggest a partially different view. We propose to consider endurance not as an input but as an outcome of the process that leads a certain organizational feature to be included among identity referents. In other words, we argue that a given feature is not considered an identity referent simply because it has been around for a long time but that it will be retained over time even amid other changes exactly because it is considered an identity referent – i.e. something that is central and distinguishing for the organization. In the specific case of technological features, we argue that the willingness to preserve a given technological feature is a choice that organizational members have to face at different points in time, as changes inside and outside the organization come to question current ways of designing products, of producing them, and so on. If we accept this notion, then endurance can be conceived as a consequence of a more or less explicit understanding of a given technological feature as central and distinctive to an organization. In turn, because of the implications described in the previous section (i.e. emotional and cognitive resistance, salience to strategic decisions, and centrality in projected images), the inclusion of a certain technological feature among identity referents will result in the retention of this feature even when other opportunities for technological change may arise. Organizational strategies will build on and strengthen these technological features and the business model that rests upon them. Their incorporation in organizational communication will reinforce internal commitment to and external acknowledgment of them as a distinguishing feature of the organization. This path will ultimately lead to the stabilization of technologies in organizations, as the identification of a specific set of technological knowledge as relevant cognitive dimensions of the organizations would make organizational leaders and members less willing to abandon established configurations and induce them to continue over the same technological trajectory.

Although organizations may be reluctant to dispose of identity referents, they may eventually do so under intense internal or external pressure. As the case of Scania illustrates, however, this may not occur easily. Other times, such as in the case of Piaggio and the steel frame of Vespa scooters, identity-related technologies survive contingent adverse conditions and are eventually preserved through short-term, or short-sighted, pressures. As the case of Polaroid described by Tripsas and Gavetti (2000) seems to indicate, however, it is not uncommon that the stubborn refusal to challenge central, foundational, distinguishing technological features of the organization eventually results in undermining the very conditions of its survival in the face of radical environmental changes.

We believe that our emerging framework may contribute to literature in the fields of both technology and organizational identity. On the one hand, we expand studies of technology in organizations by tracing a link between technological features and some of the cognitive structures, namely organizational identity beliefs and understanding, which drive individual as well as collective behavior in organizations. More specifically, we observe how, under certain conditions, technological features may become embedded in relatively shared and emotionally laden members' conceptualizations of what the organization is and stands for, which in turn will consolidate the incorporation of the feature in organizational processes and products. In doing so, our chapter expands our understanding of the cognitive processes that underpin the use, preservation, and replacement of technology in organizations. Future research on the conditions that influence the adoption and discard of new technology may try to test our propositions, for instance, by empirically exploring the connections between the diffusion of a given technology within a population of organizations and their categorical identities.

On the other hand, our chapter attempts to extend current theorizing on organizational identity, by addressing explicitly the factors that influence the likelihood that a given organizational feature becomes an identity referent and under which conditions this occurs. We have attempted to disentangle the interrelation between centrality, distinctiveness, and endurance, by suggesting how the three attributes of identity referents may be tied by longitudinal, mutually constitutive relationships. We are aware that we have only begun to tackle the issue of how certain features – and not others – become embedded in members' beliefs and understandings about the identity of their organization. By no means do we consider our potential antecedents as exhaustive of the possible range of factors that cause a certain feature to become an identity referent. We believe that there is still ample room for longitudinal, qualitative studies to investigate in more depth and richness the conditions under which organizational features acquire – or lose – enduringness. In particular, future research may want to shed more light on multiple feedback effects between certain attributes of technological features and the consequences of these features becoming identity referents – think for instance of the potential relationships between the centrality in projected images and on the social acknowledgment of a certain feature, or the salience to strategic decisions and the centrality to the business model – which are only foreshadowed in our model and, given space constraints, could not be developed here.

Finally, the processes our model describes seem to occur spontaneously, as certain interpretations – and not others – emerge and consolidate among members. However, research shows that certain actors may have interests in shaping emerging interpretations and do engage in it (e.g. Gioia & Thomas, 1996; Humphreys & Brown, 2002). Indeed, future research may be aimed at developing a more comprehensive understanding of how relatively "emergent" processes of identity construction, such as those we described in this paper, are affected by deliberate attempts at influencing shared beliefs – and how these two parallel dynamics influence identity constructions in organizations.

NOTE

1. We gratefully acknowledge David Whetten's helpful examples and constructive comments to this section.

REFERENCES

Albert, S., & Whetten, D. A. (1985). Organizational identity. In: L. L. Cummings & M. M. Staw (Eds), *Research in organizational behavior* (Vol. 7, pp. 263–295). Greenwich, CT: JAI.

Ashforth, B. E., & Johnson, S. A. (2001). Which hat to wear? The relative salience of multiple identities in organizational contexts. In: M. A. Hogg & D. J. Terry (Eds), *Social identity processes in organizational contexts* (pp. 31–48). Philadelphia: Psychology Press.

Ashforth, B. E., & Mael, F. (1996). Organizational identity and strategy as a context for the individual. *Advances in Strategic Management, 13*, 19–64.

Bang, J., & Palshøy, J. (2000). *Bang and Olufsen, vision and legend.* Denmark: The Danish Design Center.

Barley, S. (1986). Technology as an occasion for structuring. *Administrative Science Quarterly, 31*, 78–108.

Barley, S. (1990). The alignment of technology and structure through roles and networks. *Administrative Science Quarterly, 35*, 61–103.

Benjamin, B. A., & Podolny, J. M. (1999). Status, quality and social order in the California wine industry. *Administrative Science Quarterly, 44*, 563–589.

Bijker, W. E., Hughes, T. P., & Pinch, T. J. (1987). *The social construction of technological systems: New directions in the sociology and history of technology.* Cambridge, MA: MIT Press.

Boje, D. M. (1995). Stories of the storytelling organization: A postmodern analysis of Disney as 'Tamara-Land'. *Academy of Management Journal, 38*, 997–1035.

Brown, T. J., Dacin, P. A., Pratt, M. G., & Whetten, D. A. (2006). Identity, intended image, construed image and reputation: An interdisciplinary framework and suggested terminology. *Journal of the Academy of Marketing Science, 34*, 99–106.

Brunninge, O. (2007). Scania's bonneted trucks. In: L. Lerpold, D. Ravasi, G. Soenen & J. van Rekom (Eds), *Organizational identity in practice* (pp. 19–34). London: Routledge.

Camuffo, A., Romano, P., & Vinelli, A. (2001). Back to the future. Benetton transforms its global network. *MIT Sloan Management Review*, *43*(1), 46–52.

Canato, A. (2008). *Exploring the interactions between organisational identity and organisational routines*. Unpublished doctoral dissertation, Bocconi University, Milano.

Collins, J., & Porras, J. I. (1996). *Built to last*. New York: Harper Business.

Corley, K. G., & Gioia, D. A. (2004). Identity ambiguity and change in the wake of a corporate spin-off. *Administrative Science Quarterly*, *49*, 173–208.

Corley, K. G., Harquail, C. V., Pratt, M., Glynn, M. A., Fiol, M., & Hatch, M. J. (2006). Guiding organizational identity through aged adolescence. *Journal of Management Inquiry*, *15*, 85–99.

Dean, J. W., Yoon, S. J., & Susman, G. I. (1992). Advanced manufacturing technology and organizational structure: Empowerment or subordination? *Organization Science*, *3*, 203–229.

De Sanctis, G., & Scott Poole, M. (1994). Capturing the complexity in advanced technology use: Adaptive structuration theory. *Organization Science*, *5*, 121–147.

Dosi, G. (1982). Technological paradigms and technological trajectories. *Research Policy*, *11*, 147–162.

Dutton, J., & Dukerich, J. (1991). Keeping an eye on the mirror: Image and identity in organizational adaptation. *Academy of Management Journal*, *34*, 517–554.

D'Adderio, L. (2003). Configuring software, reconfiguring memories: The influence of integrated systems on the reproduction of knowledge and routines. *Industrial and Corporate Change*, *12*, 321–350.

Elsbach, K. D., & Kramer, R. M. (1996). Members' responses to organizational identity threats: Encountering and countering the business week rankings. *Administrative Science Quarterly*, *41*, 442–476.

Ferdows, K., Lewis, M. A., & Machuca, J. A. D. (2004). Rapid-fire fulfilment. *Harvard Business Review*, *82*(11), 104–117.

Fiol, M. C. (1991). Managing culture as a competitive resource: An identity-based view of sustainable competitive advantage. *Journal of Management*, *17*, 191–211.

Fiol, M. C. (2002). Capitalizing on paradox: The role of language in transforming organizational identities. *Organization Science*, *13*, 653–666.

Fombrun, C. J., Gardberg, N. A., & Barnett, M. L. (2000). Opportunity platforms and safety nets, corporate citizenship and reputational risk. *Business and Society Review*, *105*, 85–106.

Garud, R., & Rappa, M. A. (1994). A socio-cognitive model of technology evolution: The case of cochlear implants. *Organization Science*, *5*, 344–362.

Gioia, D. A. (1998). From individual to organizational identity. In: D. A. Whetten & P. C. Godfrey (Eds), *Identity in organizations: Building theory through conversations* (pp. 17–31). Thousand Oaks, CA: Sage.

Gioia, D. A., & Chittipeddi, K. (1991). Sensemaking and sensegiving in strategic change initiation. *Strategic Management Journal*, *12*, 433–448.

Gioia, D. A., Schultz, M., & Corley, K. (2000). Organizational identity, image and adaptive instability. *Academy of Management Review*, *25*, 63–82.

Gioia, D. A., & Thomas, J. B. (1996). Identity, image and issue interpretation: Sensemaking during strategic change in academia. *Administrative Science Quarterly*, *41*, 370–403.

Gioia, D. A., Thomas, J. B., Clark, S. M., & Chittipeddi, K. (1994). Symbolism and strategic change in academia: The dynamics of sensemaking and influence. *Organization Science*, *5*, 363–383.

Glynn, M. A. (2000). When cymbals become symbols: Conflict over organizational identity within a symphony orchestra. *Organization Science*, *11*, 285–299.

Golden-Biddle, K., & Rao, H. (1997). Breaches in the boardroom: Organizational identity and conflicts of commitment in a nonprofit organization. *Organization Science*, *8*, 593–609.

Griffith, T. L. (1999). Technology features as triggers for sensemaking. *Academy of Management Review*, *24*, 472–488.

Hatch, M. J., & Schultz, M. (1997). Relations between organizational culture, identity and image. *European Journal of Marketing*, *31*, 356–365.

Hatch, M. J., & Schultz, M. (2002). The dynamics of organizational identity. *Human Relations*, *55*, 989–1018.

Helfat, C. E., & Lieberman, M. B. (2002). The birth of capabilities: Market entry and the importance of pre-history. *Industrial and Corporate Change*, *11*, 725–760.

Humphreys, M., & Brown, A. D. (2002). Narratives of organizational identity and identification: A case study of hegemony and resistance. *Organization Studies*, *23*, 421–447.

Kaplan, S., Murray, F., & Henderson, R. (2003). Discontinuities and senior management: Assessing the role of recognition in pharmaceutical firm response to biotechnology. *Industrial and Corporate Change*, *12*, 203–233.

Kaplan, S., & Tripsas, M. (2008). Thinking about technology: Applying a cognitive lens to technical change. *Research Policy*, *37*, 790–805.

Leonard-Barton, D. (1988). Implementation as mutual adaptation of technology and organization. *Research Policy*, *17*, 251–267.

Leonard-Barton, D. (1992). Core capabilities and core rigidities: A paradox in managing new product development. *Strategic Management Journal*, *13*, 111–126.

Lerpold, L., Ravasi, D., Van Rekom, J., & Soenen, G. (2007). *Organizational identity in practice*. London: Routledge.

Lounsbury, M., & Glynn, M. A. (2001). Cultural entrepreneurship: Stories, legitimacy and the acquisition of resources. *Strategic Management Journal*, *22*, 545–564.

Mazzanti, D., & Sessa, O. (2003). *Vespa. Italian style for the world.* Firenze: Giunti Editore.

Meyer, J., & Rowan, B. (1977). Institutionalized organizations: Formal structure as myth and ceremony. *American Journal of Sociology*, *83*, 333–363.

Nag, R., Corley, K. G., & Gioia, D. A. (2007). The intersection of organizational identity, knowledge and practice. *Academy of Management Journal*, *50*, 821–847.

Orlikowski, W. J. (1992). The duality of technology: Rethinking the concept of technology in organizations. *Organization Science*, *3*, 398–427.

Orlikowski, W. J. (2000). Using technology and constituting structures. A practice lens for studying technology in organizations. *Organization Science*, *11*, 404–428.

Orlikowski, W. J. (2007). Sociomaterial practices: Exploring technology at work. *Organization Studies*, *28*, 1435–1448.

Orlikowski, W. J., Yates, J., Okamura, K., & Fujimoto, M. (1995). Shaping electronic communication: The meta-structure of technology in the context of use. *Organization Science*, *6*, 423–444.

Patel, P., & Pavitt, K. (2000). How technological competencies help define the core (not the boundaries) of the firm. In: G. Dosi, R. R. Nelson & S. G. Winter (Eds), *The nature and the dynamics of organizational capabilities* (pp. 313–333). Oxford: Oxford University Press.

Peteraf, M., & Shanley, M. (1997). Getting to know you: A theory of strategic group identity. *Strategic Management Journal, 18*, 165–187.

Porter, M. E. (1996). What is strategy? *Harvard Business Review, 74*(6), 61–78.

Pratt, M. G., & Rafaeli, A. (1997). Organizational dress as a symbol of multilayered social identities. *Academy of Management Journal, 40*, 862–898.

Rao, H. (1994). The social construction of reputation: Certification contests, legitimation, and the survival of organizations in the American automobile industry: 1895–1912. *Strategic Management Journal, 15*, 29–44.

Rao, H., Monin, P., & Durand, R. (2003). Institutional change in Toque Ville: Nouvelle cuisine as an identity movement in French gastronomy. *American Journal of Sociology, 108*, 795–843.

Ravasi, D., & Rindova, V. (2008). Symbolic value creation. In: D. Barry & H. Hansen (Eds), *New approaches in management and organization* (pp. 270–284). London: Sage.

Ravasi, D., & Schultz, M. (2006). Responding to organizational identity threats: Exploring the role of organizational culture. *Academy of Management Journal, 49*, 433–458.

Ravasi, D., & Schultz, M. (2007). Organizational culture and identity at Bang and Olufsen. In: L. Lerpold, D. Ravasi, J. Van Rekom & G. Soenen (Eds), *Organizational identity in practice* (pp. 103–119). London: Routledge.

Reger, R. K., Gustafson, L. T., DeMarie, S. M., & Mullane, J. V. (1994). Reframing the organization: Why implementing total quality is easier said than done. *Academy of Management Review, 19*, 565–584.

Scott, S. G., & Lane, V. R. (2000). A stakeholder approach to organizational identity. *Academy of Management Review, 25*, 43–62.

Stevenson, H. H., Martinez, J. I., & Jarillo, J. C. (1989). *Benetton S.p.A.* Cambridge, MA: Harvard Business School Publications.

Tripsas, M. (2009). Technology, identity, and inertia through the lens of "The Digital Photography Company". *Organization Science, 20*(2), 441–460.

Tripsas, M., & Gavetti, G. (2000). Capabilities, cognition, and inertia: Evidence from digital imagining. *Strategic Management Journal, 21*, 1147–1161.

Van Riel, C. B. M. (1995). *Principles of corporate communication*. London: Prentice Hall.

Weick, K. (1990). Technology as equivoque. In: P. Goodman & L. Sproull (Eds), *Technology and organizations* (pp. 1–43). San Francisco, CA: Jossey-Bass.

Weick, K. (1995). *Sense-making in organizations*. Thousand Oaks, CA: Sage.

Whetten, D. A. (2003). *A social actor conception of organizational identity*. Unpublished manuscript.

Whetten, D. A. (2006). Albert and Whetten revisited. Strengthening the concept of organizational identity. *Journal of Management Inquiry, 15*, 219–234.

Whetten, D. A., & Mackey, A. (2002). A social actor conception of organizational identity and its implications for the study of organizational reputation. *Business and Society, 41*, 393–414.

Woodward, J. (1965). *Industrial organization*. Oxford, UK: Oxford University Press.

LETTING USERS INTO OUR WORLD: SOME ORGANIZATIONAL IMPLICATIONS OF USER-GENERATED CONTENT

Shahzad Ansari and Kamal Munir

ABSTRACT

It has been well established that organizations often need to restructure themselves to meet new technological challenges. We review the organizational impact of a recent technological development, sometimes referred to as Web 2.0 that enables users to leverage the Internet and generate "user-generated content" by acting as a supplier, co-producer, or even innovator of products and services. We draw on the social studies of technology, including actor-network theory to develop a conceptual understanding of how this phenomenon is challenging deeply entrenched mental models among managers and management theorists as well as problematizing the way organizational boundaries are conventionally drawn.

INTRODUCTION

Ever since Joan Woodward published her seminal work in the field of organization and management studies on how technological innovations

---

Technology and Organization: Essays in Honour of Joan Woodward
Research in the Sociology of Organizations, Volume 29, 79–105

ISSN: 0733-558X/doi:10.1108/S0733-558X(2010)0000029012

impact organizational structures, governance arrangements, and process choices (Woodward, 1965), it has been established that organizations often need to restructure themselves to meet new technological challenges. Woodward's stimulating comparative study using technology as an independent variable that explained the relationship between structure and performance, challenged classical management theories advocating universal rules of management (one best way of organizing a business) and set a generation of researchers to think and act differently (Thomas, 1993). Her influential work challenged the belief among classical management scholars in the existence of universal principles for the creation of effective organizations. Her work lead to the contingency approach, focusing instead on how effective organizational structure depends on context or external conditions. In a way, Woodward's work contributed to establishing the view that organizations are something we can "draw" a border around – everything inside is part of the organization and everything outside is part of the "environment."

While building on Woodward's seminal contribution that brought technology to the fore as a primary force impacting how organizations are managed, in this chapter, we develop a perspective that shows how a recent technological development is challenging the conventional dichotomy between an organization and its environment. Specifically, we review the impact of a technology, sometimes referred to as Web 2.0, on an organization's boundaries and its activities. Web 2.0 is a phrase used to describe how the Internet is now less about firms producing content for users to consume, as in Web 1.0, than it is about firms facilitating the presence of end-users as active, collaborative co-creators of content (termed as user-generated content), and affording tools and connectivity that allows an "architecture of participation" (Rheingold, 2003; *The Economist*, 2008; Wilson, 2006) based on a "we is better than me" logic (Libert & Spectors, 2007). As an open-source software expert noted: "Given enough eyeballs, all bugs are shallow" (Raymond, 1999).

Web 2.0 allows everyday users to leverage the Internet and act as a supplier, co-producer, or even innovator of products and services. An example is I-report, an initiative of the news channel CNN to take advantage of the power of "citizen journalism," where far flung people, closest to breaking news provide photos, videos, and first-hand accounts of that news that CNN then broadcasts. In the popular literature, user-generated content is given much significance (e.g., Leadbetter, 2007; McConnon, 2006), with several buzzwords such as "prosumers" (Toffler, 2006), "crowdsourcing"[1] (Hempel, 2006), and "democratization of the web" (Leadbetter, 2007), emerging to indicate the increasingly participative role of users in innovative activities. However, organizational scholars surprisingly have rarely studied this phenomenon.

Dominant models in strategic management (Porter, 1980; Barney, 1991) as well as various organizational theories (DiMaggio & Powell, 1983; Hannan & Freeman, 1977; Williamson, 1975) have typically given relatively less attention to the role of users and generally lack a "consumer orientation to the mix" (Brief & Bazerman, 2003, p. 187). Firms are mostly understood to assess and satisfy the users' needs, who remain at the periphery. In traditional industries, users are important because they buy products. In networked industries, they are important because of their sheer numbers (e.g., Katz & Shapiro, 1985). Even when users are seen as a source of ideas (e.g., Faulker & Runde, 2009; Franke & Shah, 2003; Jeppesen & Molin, 2003; von Hippel, 2001; von Krogh & von Hippel, 2003), the distinction between firms and consumers remains sharp and clear.

Recent technological developments – the increasing pervasiveness of the Internet (especially the new Web 2.0 version), interactive and converging digital media, peer-to-peer networks, along with evolving online business models (Silverstone & Sørensen, 2005) – have brought us to a point where such a conceptual distinction between producers and users is no longer feasible. To be sure, scholars have problematized conventional organizational boundaries and the neat distinction between producers and users. Describing it as the logic of "distributed capitalism," Zuboff and Maxmin (2002), for instance, have argued to shift the emphasis to distribution, rather than concentration, of assets – people, information, authority, and technologies – across the traditional divide, which separated producers and users (Garud & Karnøe, 2003). Under such a model, users are deemed to have far more power than they were attributed under the adversarial transaction economics of mass production. However, the continuation of a conceptual division between users and producers, and their respective roles, is preventing many managers from re-thinking their business models or from adjusting their roles in the new situations that confront them.

We discuss how user-generated content spurred by a technological development, Web 2.0, is challenging deeply entrenched mental models, among managers and management theorists as well as problematizing conventional organizational boundaries. We start out by reviewing the portrayal of users in the management literature, highlighting theories that allow for a richer conceptualization of how users matter. We then discuss the growing phenomenon of user-generated content and the meteoric rise of several firms and communities that are based around this notion. Finally, we develop a conceptual understanding of mass *participation* as against mass production and mass consumption and discuss theoretical and managerial implications of this phenomenon.

We draw on a framework from the social studies of technology, namely the actor-network theory (ANT) (e.g., Latour, 1987; Callon, 1991), where networks are social structures of people and things that are given meaning *relationally*. In ANT, both actors – producers, consumers, and institutional actors – and things – products and technologies (embodying social structures) – together termed as "actants" share the scene in the reconstruction of the network of interactions leading to the stabilization of a socio-technical system. None of the actants are accorded any agential priority (Callon & Latour, 1992), the emphasis being on the connections, interactions, and distributed agency among actants in a network. A key aspect of these interactions is "translation," a multifaceted interaction in which actors construct common meanings, define identities, and co-opt each other in the pursuit of individual and collective objectives. We draw on ANT because it links the social and the technical and does not privilege any actor or technology in understanding the changing role of users in product and service innovations.

HOW USERS ARE UNDERSTOOD IN MANAGEMENT RESEARCH

Users have figured in management research for a long time now. Innovation was one of the first research streams within the larger field of management that explored the role that users play in providing manufacturers with critical feedback (e.g., Burns & Stalker, 1961; Smith, 1776; Utterback, 1971). Burns and Stalker (1961), in particular, emphasized their role in their study of the design of a radar system during the Second World War, pointing out the benefits of establishing close relationships between manufacturers and users. However, as far as broader management research is concerned, in particular, strategy research with the development of the positioning and resource-based view (RBV) schools, the role of users has receded into the background.

In the 1950s and 1960s, the emphasis on an industry's structure was growing (Bain, 1956; Mason, 1939). The focus was on barriers to entry – such as economies of scale, product differentiation, and cost advantages – that would allow incumbent firms to earn above average profits. While sellers' activities were discussed, including promotional and pricing policies, research, and development and inter-firm competition or cooperation, buyers or users were mostly present to explain demand, with the focus being on the number and size of buyers and sellers, the degree of product differentiation, the extent of vertical integration, and the level of barriers to entry (Bain, 1956, p. 3; Scherer, 1980).

Interestingly, later work by Woodward (1965) and Burns and Stalker (1961) that formed the basis of contingency theory also tended to marginalize users despite focusing on technology. This, of course, should not be taken as a criticism – it was in line with the effects of various technologies observed by these eminent scholars at the time. In particular, Woodward's (1965) empirical research illustrated that the principles of the classical management theories are not always the right ones to follow, since different technologies impose different demands on organizations. Most of these technologies were producer-sponsored rather than user-centred with a view of gaining efficiencies in production and manufacturing. Thus, although this was an important step forward to understand how technologies mediate organizational structure, users were again not the focus of this analysis.

Another important study on the changing nature of technologies was by Zuboff (1984) who documented both the pitfalls and the promise of technology in business life. She noted that although automation could make humans the servants of the "smart machine," "informating" could potentially change the workplace by distributing management-controlled information and power among the workers and making them co-equals in the enterprise. Although the study drew attention to how technologies tended to redistribute power and reduce managerial authority, which depended in part upon control over the organization's knowledge base, the focus of analysis was still the organization – managers and employees – rather than users.

Although Burns and Stalker had talked about the need to work closely with the user during product development, Porter's (1980) positioning view, which gave a much-needed coherence to the area of strategic management, took a slightly different although no less important look at buyers. In highlighting the importance of "buyer-power," Porter focused on their number, knowledge, the choices available to them, and other such factors, all of which were seen as determinants of their bargaining power. Their existence, however, was very much distinct from that of the focal firm, with the power of users comprising only one of the five forces that determined whether a company would be able to achieve competitive advantage or not.

In a way, the RBV took us further away from users by focusing on the firm rather than the industry and reinforcing the firm-environment divide[2] (e.g., Barney, 1991; Teece, Pisano, & Shuen, 1997). This is unfortunate because in 1959, the role of customers as a key actor in creating value was explicitly recognized in Edith Penrose's study of the Hercules Powder Company, where the diversification of the firm was based on ideas generated by its customers and resulted in the assimilation of previously unexploited resources and skills (Penrose, 1959). However, as noted by several scholars, much of the RBV literature that has evolved since then has typically tended to neglect customers (Bowman & Ambrosini, 2000; Priem & Butler, 2001; Zander & Zander, 2005).

Within RBV, customers come across as an unobservable mass and almost irrelevant to value creation in inter-organizational networks. As Makadok (2001) notes, customer value is only one determinant among many, and it might not even be a necessary determinant of firm value. Citing the example of an Internet firm that produced a lot of customer value but little firm value, he states: "for the purpose of explaining profitability (firm value), customer utility or use value is relevant only insofar as it affects value captured by the firm, but it has no independent relevance of its own."

It is really in research on innovation that we come across accounts of users. For instance, Leonard-Barton (1995) and Leonard-Barton and Sinha (1993) argue that strong customer relationships usually lead to closer linkages between the knowledge that underpins product usage and the scientific and technical knowledge of designing and manufacturing the product. Design and use influence each other, and once a technology is implemented, designers can continue to modify the design through feedback from users. However, despite acknowledging the importance of users in technological design and implementation, these perspectives continued to see innovation as conducted from "the inside," with users at best playing a supporting role in innovation processes. The more recent and influential work on "disruptive" innovations by Christensen and colleagues (e.g., Christensen, 1997, 2006; Christensen & Bower, 1996) argues that organizations that focus on serving the customers of their core business may end up being held captive to their needs and lose out to rivals in their quest to find new customers and develop new markets. Although there is a distinction between the types of customers, core, high-end, and low-end, the focus is still on organizations and how they are impacted by disruptive technologies and business model innovations, rather than on users and their innovative capabilities.

An important body of work and perhaps the most user-centric in its approach concerns lead users and user communities and how firms benefit from incorporating user ideas in innovation processes. We discuss this work in more detail.

User Involvement and Co-Creation of Value – The Role of Lead Users

One of the leading proponents of this body of work, von Hippel (1976, 1986, 2005) powerfully illustrated that manufacturers need to directly engage users on possible solutions to understand and meet their needs. von Hippel (1978) developed an approach to innovation, which he described as "customer-active paradigm" (CAP) as opposed to a "manufacturer-active paradigm" (MAP). As later argued by other researchers, innovation was a joint process between manufacturers and users, and thus, CAP was more appropriate to the industrial innovation process (Biemans, 1991; Foxall, 1986). One particular way of involving users in the product development and innovation process is by focusing on "lead users" argues von Hippel (1986). Lead users are users who face needs that mainstream users and the market at large will face later, and they also expect to benefit significantly from solving these needs early (Morrison, Roberts, & Midgley, 2004; von Hippel, 1986, 2005). Involving lead users for new product development entails collecting information about both needs and solutions not only from users at the leading edges of the target market but also from users in other markets that face similar problems in a more extreme form. Manufacturers can thus use lead users to develop breakthrough products that tend to have higher performance and market potential than other innovations and in the process co-create value with their customer communities (Franke, von Hippel, & Schreier, 2006; Jeppesen & Frederiksen, 2006; Magnusson, 2003; Prahalad & Ramaswamy, 2003). Indeed, users have been described as "accidental entrepreneurs" who may engage in collective creative activity within the social context provided by user communities and develop an innovative idea, with preliminary adoption often occurring before that idea is formally developed (Shah & Tripsas, 2007). At times, users may also innovate in ways that are not anticipated by manufacturers. In a recent piece, Faulker and Runde (2009) describe how user innovations provided "scripts" for manufacturer-led changes in the form of products. They describe how a user innovation transformed the aging gramophone turntable from being simply a playback device into a musical instrument as "turntablists" used the product to create new sounds and music by physically manipulating vinyl records under a turntable stylus. This innovation then shaped the subsequent design of digital players to allow users to perform various techniques associated with "turntablism." Similarly, Ansari and Phillips (2009) describe how consumers appropriated a little-known functionality (SMS) in mobile phones to develop the practice of "texting" that later became widely diffused and institutionalized around the world and generated significant changes in the domain of mobile communications.

Some researchers have gone beyond the focus on the role of users as idea generators to focus on the role of users as active participants during product development. As Gulati and Kletter (2005) note, satisfied customers create value through co-developing and receiving solutions. From being mere passive audiences, customers are now increasingly being seen as active participants in the value network or "extended enterprise" (Prahalad & Ramaswamy, 2000, 2004). Indeed, companies are increasingly finding ways to mobilize customer communities to gain a competitive edge. This is because knowledge and new ideas from customer participation in the innovation process is regarded as essential in enabling innovation. Users may have unique need-related knowledge acquired through their own use as well as privileged access to both the needs and solutions of a community, especially in nascent markets, with few available estimates of market needs (Shah & Tripsas, 2007) as against stable environments with mature and relatively static needs. Users may also be in a unique position to understand the entire usage system, especially in industries characterized by interfirm modularity, where different components of a systemic product are made by different firms having knowledge of their own module (Baldwin & Clark, 2003). Finally, users may come up with higher levels of novelty due to collective creativity (Hargadon & Bechky, 2006).

It is important to note here that in marketing research (a stream of literature that we do not discuss in this chapter), customers have long been the focus of attention in innovation processes. However, customers continue to be regarded as a "target" of manufacturers and a "means to organizational ends" rather than as collaborators and co-producers of products and services (e.g., Vargo & Lusch, 2004).

Finally, the body of research that has emphasized the role of users more than others is the interpretive stream, for example, the social construction of technology (SCOT) literature (e.g., Bijker & Law, 1997) and ANT (Callon, 1986; Latour, 1987) that emphasizes the importance of understanding users and their needs in the co-development of technologies and products. In this research, scholars have argued against deterministic or linear notions of technological innovations and shown that innovation and technological development are socially embedded processes. Diverse groups with different interests in the design of technologies attempt to embody technologies with their own particular interests and shape their evolution and development. We elaborate further how researchers have theorized the role of users in this line of work.

The Role of Users in Interpretive Studies

The interpretive bend in organization studies recognizes that meaning of products or technologies arises in practice. As sociologists have long argued, the focus on production misses the fact that consumers have to become convinced about the value and legitimacy of products (Zelizer, 1983). The life insurance industry, for example, had to overcome the obvious moral ambiguity of people buying insurance that put a price on their deaths.

Studies in technology have shown that users can often ignore certain properties of the technology, work around them, or invent new uses (De Sanctis & Poole, 1994; Orlikowski, 2000; Rosenberg, 1982; Suchman, 1996) through post-adoption shaping of technology. Although producers act purposefully to promote their technologies or artifacts, their actions are often mediated by users, who "interpret" them in different ways (Bijker, 1995; Du Gay, Hall, Janes, Mackay, & Negus, 1997; Kline & Pinch, 1996; Oudshoorn & Pinch, 2003). Thus, there may be significant gaps between the "world inscribed in the object and the world described by its displacement" (Akrich, 1992). Scholars in this stream of work have argued that by drawing on their own particular sets of shared meanings and beliefs (structures), users develop regimes of worth in evaluating the products and services that may have little ontological affinity with what producers intended.

For example, the initial adoption of landline telephony was meant for safety and business-related reasons. Telephone companies failed to realize the "telephone's affordance for intimacy," (Frissen, 1995), as it quickly became a tool for chatting (Fischer, 1992). Also, the same artifact can mean different things to different social groups of users. In the early days of the bicycle, for young men, riding the risky "high wheeler"[3] meant the "macho machine," as opposed to the meaning given to it by elderly men and women who interpreted it as the "unsafe machine" (Bijker, 1995).

Within the interpretive stream, cultural and media studies have also acknowledged the importance of studying users arguing that human relations and identities are increasingly defined in relation to consumption rather than production (Appadurai, 1986; Lury, 1996; McKracken, 1988; Oudshoorn & Pinch, 2003). For instance, Bourdieu (1984) suggested that consumption has become increasingly important in the political economy of late modernity. Similarly, Baudrillard (1988) criticized the view that the needs of consumers are dictated, controlled, and manipulated by producers. He argued that consumption is not a passive and adaptive process but that consumption and production are mutually dependent with consumers being active agents in shaping consumption, social relations, and identities. This body of work has re-conceptualized the traditional distinction between production and consumption by reintroducing Karl Marx's claim that the process of production is not complete until users have defined the uses, meanings and significance of the technology with design and use being "two sides of the same coin" (Lie & Sørensen, 1996, p. 10). "Consumption is production" and use-value and exchange-value[4] form a dialectical unity (Marx, 1973[1858], p. 126). Marx realized that firms can never be totally indifferent to use-values, because inputs need to be managed in a manner that produces legitimate and profitable outputs.

To summarize, the role of users has largely been neglected in the management literature, and although innovation, SCOT, and lead-user literatures have put relatively more emphasis on the importance of understanding and incorporating user needs and ideas in design and innovation processes, they confine themselves to drawing on insights generated by the users or observing how they enact different products. Users have rarely been allowed to permeate the invisible but almost "sacrosanct" boundary around organizations. We argue that although existing conceptualizations are valuable in understanding users as both targets and sources of innovation, they can be usefully extended to capture contemporary developments such as the rapid growth of user-generated content in the wake of Web 2.0.

CHALLENGES FROM USER-GENERATED CONTENT – THE DEMOCRATIZATION OF INNOVATIONS

Over the past few years, there has been a rapid growth of several user-driven applications, such as blogs, podcasts, wikis, social networking websites, search engines, auction websites, games, and peer-to-peer services. Together, they are referred to as Web 2.0-based technologies or *social computing*, as they exploit the Internet's connectivity to foster online collaboration, participation, and networking of relevant people and content, where people share opinions, innovative ideas, insights, experiences, and perspectives.

In such arrangements, described by Leadbetter (2007) as innovation *by* the masses, not just *for* the masses, users do not simply want more "choice," something firms have long assumed in traditional business models and marketing campaigns, but more "say." Users are not just a supplier of content and services but also support the production, distribution, selection, and filtering of the relevant content and services. In other words, users are an integral part and co-producer of all the elements of a service delivered: of content (blogs), of taste/emotion (Amazon), of social contacts (MySpace), of relevance (Google page-rank), of feedback and reputation management (eBay), of storage/server capacity (P2 P), or of connectivity (wifi sharing).

These developments pose considerable challenges for managers who often appear reluctant to share control and rewards with users. In their existing mental models, new ideas and innovations are seen to emerge in orderly fashion from organizations or organization-sponsored market research that they can control and mandate and then convert into useful products and services for the users at large. Even if users contribute to these ideas, it is organizations that are seen to have the resources and expertise to translate these ideas into useful offerings.

For instance, online media companies have long viewed users as targets of their carefully expert manufactured content, as opposed to being co-producers. The increasing participation of users in creating content is posing a challenge for them. Besides media companies, even those firms that were born on the Internet, such as the search engine Yahoo!, are struggling to come to terms with the new reality posed by user empowerment, as they stand to lose user traffic on their firm-sponsored websites and platforms. Similarly, other large and well-entrenched web-based corporations such as Google, MySpace, Monster.com, and eBay currently have distribution models that may be considered inconsistent with self-adaptiveness, openness, and pervasiveness of the Web 2.0 (Pascu, Osimo, Ulbrich, Turlea, & Burgelman, 2007). Many have tended to neglect tapping into their user-base to eliminate spam and poor search results and have failed to differentiate their offerings in a meaningful way or push the frontiers of collective intelligence.

Later, we provide a few examples of new organizations and platforms based on user-generated content that are posing strategic and organizational challenges for many managers. These include web logs (blogs), Wikipedia (reference), YouTube (video sharing), Friction.tv (news sharing and debating), and Second Life (virtual reality).

Web logs are an important development in the network of social media, where a proliferation of content through blogs (short for Web logs) – online journals or diaries hosted on a website and often distributed to other sites or readers – poses a threat to established offline and online media companies. Not unlike chronicles or diaries, blogs, sometimes described as "naked conversations" (Scoble & Israel, 2006), provide commentary or news on a particular subject such as politics, sports, or music, or simply form an online diary written and published regularly by a blogger. A typical blog combines text, images, and links to other blogs, web pages, and other media related to its topic, where readers can leave comments in an interactive format. Blogs have threatened online newspapers since many bloggers are experts in their areas and greater authorities on a given subject than some newspaper reporters. For this reason, many newspapers have co-opted bloggers into their sites.

YouTube (recently purchased by Google) is an online video streaming service that allows anyone to view and share videos that have been uploaded by its members (with an audience of over 100 million). It is now ranked as the fourth most popular website in the world – behind only Yahoo! MSN, and Google itself. YouTube is a way to get your videos to others through uploading and sharing to connect with people with similar interests. As a result, instead of videos featuring celebrities and stars, the most unlikely videos that depict ordinary people and their lives can become big hits among user communities (Richards, 2007).

Friction.tv is an online platform for user-generated news and opinion that allows users to air their views, respond to the opinions of others, debate issues of local interest, or discuss points of global importance. It claims to provide a "stimulating alternative to the sanitised, agenda driven mediocrity of the conventional mass media" (Blakely, 2007).

Second Life is an online virtual community with nearly five million registered residents created by Linden Labs in what is being described as a "metaverse." Its users known as residents create "avatars," or customized online characters who represent their "in-worlds" selves and who build their own activities, objects, scripted gestures, and complex textures such as skin and hair in their "metaverse." Although in some ways similar, Second Life is not specifically a "game," however, because there is no score, and no traditional game narrative or characterizations (such as earn these points by performing this task). Among its millions of users, almost one participant in ten is co-creating with companies such as testing prototypes or contributing to design new products and services (Bughin, Chui, & Johnson, 2008).

Finally, *open-source movements*, based on collective effort, social interactions, and group influence (Chesbrough, 2006; Chesbrough & Rosenbloom, 2002) are in the vanguard of user-generated content. These movements are based on what has been described as the "private-collective model of innovation" (von Krogh & von Hippel, 2003) that allow social groups to accomplish the critical task of coordinating the actions of multiple individuals to achieve important outcomes (Kreiger & Muller, 2003; O'Mahony & Ferraro, 2007), where "customers also create the value you sell them" (Rheingold, 2003).

Examples include the Linux software – the fastest growing desktop operating software (Mauri, 2004) and Wikipedia. *Wikipedia* since its inception in 2001 has displaced all traditional encyclopedias.[5] Wiki has an abundance of articles accumulated in less than 6 years on far more subjects (6,100,000 articles) than Encyclopaedia Britannica (120,000 entries) and according to a report published in *Nature*, its entries on scientific subjects were generally just as accurate (Giles, 2005). Its website is now the 17th most popular site on the Internet, with users constantly improving and expanding the encyclopaedia by making thousands of changes an hour (Schiff, 2006). This phenomenon of tapping into the contributions of multiple distributed users and harnessing the power of mass collaboration has been described as "Wikinomics" (Tapscott & Williams, 2006).

These new entities pose a huge challenge to established organizations and the professionals and managers who design, control, and lead them. They embody a new ethic of collaborative and shared effort that blurs the boundary between producers and users as conceptualized in traditional management literature. Given the need to re-conceptualize the interface between users and producers, in the next section we draw insights from the social studies of technology research stream.

Towards a Richer Conceptualization of Users: Insights from Actor-Network Theory

We propose that the foundation for conceptualizing contemporary developments around user-generated content already exists within ANT (e.g., Callon, 1986; Latour, 1987). ANT posits that producers, users, and technologies constitute a "seamless web," and all these entities owe their existence to each other's presence in the actor-network. The term actor-network itself indicates that the actors and network are mutually dependent. Thus, its analysis seeks to be impartial with respect to the actors involved in the process, the vocabulary used to describe their viewpoints and their designation as either social or technical/natural (Munir & Jones, 2004). An important implication is that material entities, whether natural, like microorganisms, or technical, like keyboards, are (in principle) treated as actors in their own right on an equal footing with human entities such as scientists, technologists, or users. An actor-network for mobile telephony would include mobile operators, manufacturers, software engineers, interested customers, component suppliers, as well as the devices, switches, masts, and other relevant technologies. These actors are not seen as determining the outcome of technology evolution, however, but as providing affordances that open opportunities that may or may not be taken up.

ANT scholars argue that it is in a network of associations that value is created and appropriated. For example, in field of photography, "the Kodak Moment" identifies certain activities as worthy of being recorded. However, it is the network of actors (camera and film manufacturers, component manufacturers, competitors, widely, and cheaply available photofinishing services and end consumers) that allows one to capture a "Kodak Moment" (Munir & Jones, 2004). Such a network does not form automatically, but needs to be created and sustained by the active enrolment of other actors. Actors are enrolled by persuading them, and giving incentives to them, to become stakeholders. Without a chain of network members committing various types of resources to the provision of various components to deliver on a claim or a promising idea, new claims have little probability of being converted into facts (Latour, 1987).

Thus, in photography, the Kodak Moment was sustained because of a chain of associations in which it is embedded and which constitutes the context where film is cheap and widely available, cameras are simple to use and do not break down frequently, quick photofinishing services are widely available and affordable, and finally, preserving memories as pictures and displaying them is a valued activity. The agents providing these services, or enabling this chain of consumption, as well as the users sustaining popular photography had to be persuaded in a process of enrolment and that their participation was essential to the success and sustainability of the concept of Kodak Moment. In other words, actor-network theorists would argue that snapshot photography becomes a fact only because people are willing to treat it as such and act accordingly.

By suggesting that particular concepts and designs acquire their dominance not only because of the support of heterogeneous actors, including users but also as a result of association with artifacts, actor-network theorists have taken a significant step beyond the insights offered by technology management theorists. For instance, they offer a novel conceptualization of the role of users. As Callon (2007, p. 148) notes, rather than someone invited to live experiences, to feel at home, and to be entertained, "the consumer is considered as an active, interactive being, in the grip of emotions and drives, capable of taking part in experiences of which she is the heroine," where "subjectivity is constructed and proposed through the very act of consumption" – a form of "active and interactive individual attached to product-services that singularize her and that she singularizes."

Finally, ANT also helps us develop a theoretical understanding of an age-old dilemma that innovating organizations have faced, that is, even if the technology is a "breakthrough," it does not necessarily lead to profits (e.g., Teece, 2006). Although actor-network theorists do not address the issue directly, their concept of "obligatory points of passage" (Latour, 1987) may be used to understand how firms are able to successfully build a sustainable competitive advantage on their products and services. Thus, having enrolled a powerful network, including existing institutions, actors then seek to institutionalize their own products, technologies, and services by making them central to future industry development. Thus, firms can strategize to sustain key roles in an actor-network and not be sidestepped or bypassed by competitors, suppliers, or even consumers. For instance, IBM despite its vast resources, brand name, and innovative capabilities failed to create "obligatory passage points" (OPP) in the actor-network it operated in and as a result lost out to its suppliers, in particular Microsoft and Intel, when it came to generating profits from personal computers.

In short, ANT provides a useful vocabulary for understanding the producer–user nexus and to extend the conceptual range of the analysis. Its role may be particularly important in the context of the "democratisation" of innovations in the context of Web 2.0, where users have come to play an increasingly active and participatory role in the creation of value around technologies, products, and services. We describe some of the very recent developments in this domain.

DISCUSSION: USERS AS PARTICIPANTS IN VALUE CREATION NETWORKS

The phenomenon of users as producers, distributors, and consumers is blurring the distinctive boundaries between users and firms and threatening the top down models of delivering products, ideas, and services. Scholars need to rethink the traditional sacrosanct user–buyer distinctions among market participants. Conceptualizing this phenomenon in terms of actor-networks presents new possibilities in organizing people, processes, relationships, and knowledge (Saveri, Rheingold, Pang, & Vian, 2004) and have the potential to significantly alter the industrial, social, and cultural landscape, allowing for more complex forms of participation and cooperation (Brown & Duguid, 2000).

From Open Sourcing to Active Enrolment

In an annual survey of senior executives in the media and entertainment industry, the firm Accenture examined the strategies of companies across the landscape of advertising, film, music, publishing, radio, the Internet, videogames, and television. About 57% of the respondents identified the rapid growth of user-generated content – which includes amateur digital videos, podcasts,[6] mobile phone photography, wikis,[7] and social-media blogs – as one of the top three challenges they face today. The digital media head for Accenture's Media and Entertainment practice noted: "Traditional, established content providers will have to adapt and develop new business and monetisation models in order to keep revenue streams flowing. The key to success will be identifying new forms of content that can complement their traditional strengths."

From an actor-network perspective, such firms need to actively enrol users (at different levels) in networks, which also contain the products, other users and the firm. This conceptualization goes beyond the concept of "open sourcing," where organizations invite individuals to contribute to building a particular product. This is all the more important in media. When something radically disruptive happens and traditional media cannot cover it immediately, the collective efforts of a large number of people can create and distribute information in a very efficient manner. For instance, with photographs taken on mobile phones and content posted by users, one can get up-to-date information from social networking sites or YouTube almost immediately – a capability most firms are unable to match. Given the significance of this phenomenon, an important question that arises is how can organizations embrace the shift vis-à-vis the enhanced role of users while continuing to play a central role in an actor-network. What actions are likely to ensure that they are able to appropriate some of the new value that is being created from increasing user participation?

Value Appropriation through Building Obligatory Passage Points

The role of the user as a co-producer of value is changing the structural composition across several industries, especially media, and directly influencing their competitiveness. Not surprisingly, many organizations are not silent spectators to these developments and are coming up with innovative ways to engage with user communities and companies that are centred on user-driven content (*McKinsey Quarterly*, 2007a, 2007b). Two main approaches are being pursued in this regard:

First approach is through acquisition strategies, where many resourceful organizations are simply acquiring companies that are based on user-driven content and the Web 2.0. For instance, several blogs, wikis, and social networking sites such as MySpace.com and YouTube have been acquired for large sums by established players. Examples abound, such as News Corporation buying MySpace, eBay buying Skype, Yahoo! buying Flickr, Google buying Writely, and so on.

Second, firms are leveraging these applications for commercial and professional purposes (Bughin, 2007). For instance, blogs, wikis, and podcasts are increasingly used in the corporate world to collaborate and network both inside and outside the company, whereas several organizations leverage YouTube and Second Life for their advertisement and promotional campaigns. Many established old-economy companies have also joined in. Coca-Cola launched a website for uploading user-generated content; Wal-Mart launched a campaign for teenagers to create their sites linked to its corporate website; and MTV started a TV channel called Flux for user-generated content (Pascu et al., 2007).

In this way, firms are gradually competing to position themselves as OPP. The classic example of OPP is Microsoft, which has positioned its operating system between users and their alternatives. Each time a user accesses an application on Windows he/she pays a toll to Microsoft. And the larger the number of applications on its operating system platform, the harder it becomes to dislodge it. Microsoft's model is worth emulating for Web 2.0 firms or those who wish to embrace it. They need to position themselves in "structural holes" (Burt, 1992) linking users to other users and alternatives.

Firms' efforts and partial success in co-opting user communities and sustaining conventional organizational boundaries may suggest that the development around Web 2.0 is perhaps a brief "shining moment" before user-defined assets become corporatized and enter mainstream business. Although this is certainly plausible, it is worth noting the remarkable resistance of several user communities where members continue to provide one another support, advice, and feedback. Indeed, user communities have played a significant role in establishing and legitimizing services that range from open source software (e.g., Linux) to weight reduction programs (e.g., Weight Watchers) and substance abuse programs (e.g., Alcoholics Anonymous) and not all these communities succumb to the pressures of corporatization.

CONCLUSION

Firms have historically organized themselves around a sharp distinction between users and producers. Many see themselves as intellectual fortresses, with a territorial stance toward organizational boundaries as they seek to maintain control over the products and services their users adopt. This is not surprizing as allowing this boundary to dissolve would problematize for instance, the make-or-buy decisions that managers make as they seek to maximize value and earn rents from the resources and capabilities they own or access. Even dominant management paradigms such as the RBV and underpinning paradigms such as transaction cost economics exist around the notion of explicit boundaries around the firm with a clear distinction between an organization and the users it targets with its products and services. Much less attention has been paid to organizational forms that lack such distinct boundaries, for example, organizing in communities.

The rise of Information and Communication Technologies (ICTs) and media convergence has challenged these deeply entrenched beliefs by creating a sort of "digitized common." Almost four decades ago, Woodward's influential work contributed to bringing technologies to the fore in organizational and management studies and triggered a rich body of research into how technologies impact businesses and the way they are organized. At the same time, it also contributed to establishing a perspective where organizations are seen as distinct from their environments, including technologies and users. We have argued that recent technological developments pose a challenge to the conventional dichotomy between an organization and its environment. These technologies enhance relevant connections in an actor-network and increase the possibilities for interpersonal and interactive communication and connections among relevant people, artifacts, technologies, and dispersed pockets of content. User communities acting as innovators, producers, distributors, and consumers are leveraging these technologies and challenging traditional conceptualizations. This has spawned the development of new models of innovation, production, distribution, and consumption that are based on community, collaboration, and self-organization, rather than on hierarchy and control, highlighting the fact that these processes can be open and shared.

In this conceptualization, firms need to incorporate an understanding of users as participants in creative processes, where they co-create goods and services, rather than simply consume the end product while firms reap the dividends of tapping into the collective creativity of masses. With the ubiquity of the Internet and low-cost connectivity, innovation need not flow top down a pipeline, from experts to passive consumers. Instead it can be a social, cumulative, and collaborative activity with ideas flowing back up the pipeline from consumers who have the ability to share and develop ideas, without having to rely on formal organizations to do it for them. Firms thus need to rethink their top down business models and incorporate social and technological collaboration into their enterprising fibre with a shift from production–consumption dichotomies to interactive participation.

These developments increasingly point to the need for analysing "actor-networks" rather than inter-organizational networks. Actor-networks can be conceptualized as seamless webs, where particular configurations of heterogeneous networks, consisting of firms, users, technologies, and discourses together generate value by shaping interests, preferences, and inter-subjective contexts. Firms and their managers in these actor-networks need to break free of their existing cognitive frames and mindsets that privilege top-down models and an expert-based control system and enrol networks or societal communities in their business models and market-making strategies. A firm and its managers cannot successfully create value without the support of an extensive actor network that it is part of and that includes multiple nodes – social and technical – including user communities and technologies. In such a conceptualization, the context is not seen as a container and users viewed as "targets" outside a firm, or technology simply inserted into social relations. Rather (potential) users are seen as part of the organization and technology viewed as intertwined with the social in the changing nature of systems of relations being continually produced as actor-networks.

For instance, an important implication of this development causes us to re-examine the way we think about intellectual property and its role in technological and economic progress with an increasing need to "make room for consumers under copyright law" and acknowledge the participatory role of consumers under copyright theory. The perception of consumer-as-participant adds a new dimension to standard copyright analysis, which is particularly significant in the environment of user-generated content, where in many instances firms face significant challenges from actions such as the posting of copyrighted material – movies, music, and so on, or proprietary secrets over the Internet. If individuals are innovating and sharing those ideas voluntarily, should this be restricted or encouraged as part of the intellectual "commons" (Ostrom et al., 2002)?

An actor network increases in size and strength as more actors become enrolled. Thus, to be able to accomplish its tasks, innovate and create value, a firm needs to support and mobilize such an actor-network, enrol a sufficient number of actors into its fold and align its various social and technical nodes in a working configuration. In such a conceptualization, where agency is widely distributed and dispersed across organizations and communities, firms must neither be completely closed proprietary systems nor completely open systems with the user community in charge and where their unique offerings turn into "public goods." Rather, firms need to achieve a balance with hybrid organizational arrangements, where they develop more open and interactive approaches to innovation and leverage the individual contributions from users and their communities.

Researchers have only recently begun to theorize about these developments. Garud, Jain, and Tuertscher (2008) in a paper on technological design examine two cases relevant in this context, Wikipedia and Linux software – both based on user-generated content. The authors introduce the notion of "incomplete designs," where producers create technologies that allow for active user engagement and participation in the ongoing definition and characteristics of the technology. The final product emerges from user engagement with the "unfinished" technology. Although an emphasis on completeness may result in the creation of designs that foreclose future options, incompleteness of designs acts a trigger for action as users try and elaborate what has been left incomplete or unattended. This has important implications for what firms can do in terms of designing their products and services so that they continue to matter in the actor-network emerging around user-generated content.

FUTURE DIRECTIONS AND LIMITATIONS

Given that Web 2.0 and user-generated content are very recent developments, emergent practices related to these deserve more scrutiny. It could similarly be interesting to contrast the developments of Web 1.0 with Web 2.0 and the emergent "cloud computing." During the Internet bubble, based largely on what is referred to as Web 1.0, being the first in a particular market segment and soaring stock prices were thought to be critical to success (Pascu et al., 2007). However, a simple first-mover advantage does not necessarily provide a key competitive advantage in the domain of user-generated content. For instance, MySpace was a pioneer in social networking but stands to be overtaken by its rival Facebook. It can be argued that constituents who are part of this actor-network need to pay more attention to traditional business concepts, such as revenues and profits that provide a more stable economic base compared to market or stock-price valuations.

Similarly, it would be interesting to observe how the involvement of users is debated, constructed, and exploited in this domain. For example, how is the discourse being shaped in the field(s), or users being constructed within organizations? Are users actually being empowered? It would be fascinating to observe how groups of users (whether on user-support networks, or as nodes of a network) mobilize to determine the direction of a particular organization. Finally, it is also important to note that unorganized users as a collectivity may not always fare better than individuals, professionals, or experts especially in situations requiring highly developed skills and expertise. If people get biased in the same direction, collective wisdom (Surowiecki, 2004) can then turn into collective folly or what Charles Mackay in 1861, described as the "madness of the crowds" (Mackay, 1986). It would thus be worthwhile to examine the impact of tapping into user participation in different environments such as nondigitized spheres. We hope that this chapter inspires further research in the promising areas of user-generated content.

NOTES

1. As against outsourcing – sourcing ideas and resources outside the company – and open-sourcing – allowing targeted outsiders to directly contribute in a firm's innovation processes – crowdsourcing refers to tapping into the collective knowledge base of the masses with a view to generating new ideas, shortening research and development time, cutting development costs, and creating a direct, emotional connection with customers (*The Economist*, 2007).
2. Work in neo-institutional economics (e.g., North, 1990) has arguably challenged the classic organization/environment demarcation and is often presented as an alternative to the RBV. However, although the unit of analysis is the transaction rather than the organization, the literature maintains a clear distinction between what is inside the firm and what is outside the firm including users.
3. One could easily be thrown off the "high wheeler."
4. The use value refers to the intrinsic characteristics of a product that enable it to satisfy a human need and is realized only in the process of consumption, whereas exchange value represents what (quantity of) other commodities it will exchange for, if traded.
5. Even traditional companies are embracing user-generated content. For instance, LEGO invited its customers to its online gallery to interactively suggest new models for its toy-brick business and then gave financial rewards to those whose ideas were selected and marketed.
6. Audio or video recording and a multimedia form of a blog or other content, often distributed through an aggregator such as Apple Computer's iTunes.
7. Systems for collaborative publishing that allow many authors to contribute to an online document or discussion.

ACKNOWLEDGMENTS

We thank Graham Sewell and Nelson Phillips for their valuable suggestions to improve this chapter. We are also grateful to the participants, in particular, Lars Frederiksen, Catelijne Koopmans, and Sara Kaplan for providing valuable insights on this essay during an OTREG meeting at Imperial College Business School, London, UK in 2007.

REFERENCES

Akrich, M. (1992). The description of technical objects. In: W. E. Bijker & J. Law (Eds), *Shaping technology/building society: Studies in sociotechnical change* (pp. 205–224). Cambridge, MA: The MIT Press.

Ansari, S., & Phillips, N. (2009). *Text me! New consumer practices and change in organizational fields*. Working Paper presented at OTREG conference in 2007.

Appadurai, A. (1986). *Introduction: Commodities and the politics of value. The social life of things: Commodities in cultural perspective* (pp. 3–63). Cambridge: Cambridge University Press.

Bain, J. S. (1956). *Barriers to new competition*. Cambridge: Harvard University Press.

Baldwin, C., & Clark, K. (2003). Managing in an age of modularity. In: R. Garud, A. Kumaraswamy & R. Langlois (Eds), *Managing in the modular age: Architecture, networks, and organizations* (pp. 149–161). Malden, MA: Blackwell.

Barney, J. B. (1991). Firm resources and sustained competitive advantage. *Journal of Management*, *17*(1), 99–120.

Baudrillard, J. (1988). *Consumer society, in selected writings*. London: Polity Press.

Biemans, W. G. (1991). User and third-party involvement in developing medical equipment innovations. *Technovation*, *11*(3), 163–182.

Bijker, W. E. (1995). *Of bicycles, bakelites and bulbs. Towards a theory of sociotechnical change*. Cambridge, MA: MIT Press.

Bijker, W. E., & Law, J. (1997). *Shaping technology/building society*. MA: MIT Press.

Blakely, R. (2007). Friction.TV outpaces YouTube. *The Timesonline*, June 5.

Bourdieu, P. (1984). *Distinction: A social critique of the judgment of taste*. London: Routledge.

Bowman, C., & Ambrosini, V. (2000). Value creation versus value capture: Towards a coherent definition of value in strategy. *British Journal of Management*, *11*(1), 1–15.

Brief, A. P., & Bazerman, M. H. (2003). Bringing in consumers. Editor's comments. *Academy of Management Review*, *28*(2), 187–189.

Brown, J. S., & Duguid, P. (2000). *The social life of information*. Boston, MA: Harvard Business School Press.

Bughin, J. R. (2007). How companies can make the most of user-generated content. *McKinsey Quarterly*, August, pp. 1–3.

Bughin, J. R., Chui, M., & Johnson, B. (2008). The next step in open innovation. *McKinsey Quarterly*, June, pp. 1–8.

Burns, T., & Stalker, G. M. (1961). *The management of innovation*. London: Tavistock.

Burt, R. S. (1992). *Structural holes: The social structure of competition*. Cambridge, MA: Harvard University Press.

Callon, M. (1986). Some elements of a sociology of translation: Domestication of the scallops and the fishermen of St. Brieuc Bay. In: J. Law (Ed.), *Power, action and belief: A new sociology of knowledge?* (pp. 196–233). London: Routledge and Kegan Paul.

Callon, M. (1991). Techno-economic networks and irreversibility. In: J. Law (Ed.), *A sociology of monsters: Essays on power, technology and domination* (pp. 132–161). London and New York: Routledge.

Callon, M. (2007). An essay on the growing contribution of economic markets to the proliferation of the social. *Theory, Culture and Society*, *24*, 139–163.

Callon, M., & Latour, B. (1992). Don't throw the baby out with the bath school! A reply to Collins and yearly. In: A. Pickering (Ed.), *Science as practice and culture* (pp. 343–368). London: University of Chicago Press.

Chesbrough, H. (2006). *Open business models: How to thrive in the new innovation landscape*. Boston, MA: Harvard Business School Press.

Chesbrough, H., & Rosenbloom, R. (2002). The role of the business model in capturing value from innovation: Evidence from xerox corporation's technology Spinoff companies. *Industrial and Corporate Change*, *11*(3), 529–555.

Christensen, C. M. (1997). *The innovator's dilemma: When new technologies cause great firms to fail*. Boston, MA: Harvard Business School Press.

Christensen, C. M. (2006). The ongoing process of building a theory of disruption. *Journal of Product Innovation Management*, *23*, 39–55.

Christensen, C. M., & Bower, J. L. (1996). Customer power, strategic investment, and the failure of leading firms. *Strategic Management Journal*, *17*(3), 197–218.

De Sanctis, G. M., & Poole, S. (1994). Capturing the complexity in advanced technology use: Adaptive structuration theory. *Organization Science*, *5*(2), 121–147.

DiMaggio, P. J., & Powell, W. (1983). The iron cage revisited: Institutional isomorphism and collective rationality in organizational fields. *American Sociological Review*, *48*, 147–160.

Du Gay, P., Hall, S., Janes, L., Mackay, H., & Negus, K. (1997). *Doing cultural studies. The story of the Sony Walkman*. London: Sage Publications Limited.

Faulker, P., & Runde, J. (2009). On the identity of technical objects and user innovations in function. *Academy of Management Review*, *34*(3), 442–462.

Fischer, C. (1992). *America calling: A social history of the telephone to 1940*. Berkeley, CA: University of California Press.

Foxall, G. (1986). A conceptual extension of the customer-active paradigm. *Technovation*, *4*(1), 17–27.

Franke, N., & Shah, S. (2003). How communities support innovative activities: An exploration of assistance and sharing among end-users. *Research Policy*, *32*, 157–178.

Franke, N., von Hippel, E., & Schreier, M. (2006). Finding commercially attractive user innovations: A test of lead-user theory. *Journal of Product Innovation Management*, *23*(4), 301–315.

Frissen, V. (1995). Gender is calling: Some reflections on past, present and future uses of the telephone. In: K. Grint & R. Gill (Eds), *The gender-technology relation* (pp. 79–94). London UK: Taylor and Francis.

Garud, R., Jain, S., & Tuertscher, P. (2008). Incomplete by design and designing for incompleteness. In: R. Boland, M. Jelinek, & G. Romme (Eds), *Special issue on Organization studies as a science of design in Organization Studies*, *29*(3), 351–371.

Garud, R., & Karnøe, P. (2003). Bricolage versus breakthrough: Distributed and embedded agency in technology entrepreneurship. *Research Policy*, *32*(2), 277–300.

Giles, J. (2005). Internet encyclopaedias go head to head. *Nature*, *438*(7070), 900–901.

Gulati, R., & Kletter, D. (2005). Shrinking core, expanding periphery: The relational architecture of high-performing organizations. *California Management Review*, *47*(3), 77–104.

Hannan, M. T., & Freeman, J. (1977). The population ecology of organizations. *American Journal of Sociology*, *82*, 929–964.

Hargadon, A., & Bechky, B. (2006). When collections of creatives become creative collectives: A field study of problem solving at work. *Organization Science*, *17*(4), 484–500.

Hempel, J. (2006). Crowdsourcing. *Business Week*, September 25, Issue 4002.

Jeppesen, L. B., & Frederiksen, L. (2006). Why do user contribute to firm-hosted user communities? The case of computer controlled music instruments. *Organization Science*, *17*, 45–63.

Jeppesen, L. B., & Molin, M. J. (2003). Consumers as co-developers: Learning and innovation outside the firm. *Technology Analysis and Strategic Management*, *15*(3), 363–384.

Katz, M., & Shapiro, C. (1985). Network externalities, competition and compatibility. *American Economic Review*, *75*(3), 424–440.

Kline, R., & Pinch, T. J. (1996). Taking the black box off its wheels: The social construction of the automobile in rural America. *Technology and Culture*, *37*, 776–795.

Kreiger, B. L., & Muller, P. S. (2003). Making internet communities work: Reflections on an unusual business model. *Advances in Information Systems*, *34*, 50–59.

Latour, B. (1987). *Science in action: How to follow scientists and engineers through society*. Cambridge, MA: Harvard University Press.

Leadbetter, C. (2007). We Think: Why mass creativity is the next big thing. Draft version of book. Available at http://www.wethinkthebook.net/cms/site/docs/charles%20full%20draft.pdf

Leonard-Barton, D. (1995). *Wellsprings of knowledge: Building and sustaining the sources of innovation*. Boston, MA: Harvard Business School Press.

Leonard-Barton, D., & Sinha, D. K. (1993). Developer-user interaction and user satisfaction in internal technology transfer. *Academy of Management Journal*, *36*(5), 1125–1139.

Libert, B., & Spectors, J. (2007). *We are smarter than me: How to unleash the power of crowds in your business*. New Jersey: Wharton School Publishing.

Lie, M., & Sørensen, K. (1996). *Making technology our own? Domesticating technology into everyday life*. Oslo, Norway: Scandinavian University Press.

Lury, C. (1996). *Consumer culture*. London, UK: Polity press.

MacKay, C. (1986). *Extraordinary popular delusions and the madness of crowds*. Ithaca, NY: Cornell University Press.

Magnusson, P. R. (2003). *Customer-oriented product development: Experiments involving users in service innovation*. Stockholm: Stockholm School of Economics, EFI, The Economic Research Institute.

Makadok, R. (2001). A pointed commentary on Priem and Butler. *Academy of Management Review (dialogue)*, *26*(4), 498–499.

Marx, K. (1973[1858]). *Grundrisse*. Harmondsworth and New York: Penguin.

Mason, E. S. (1939). Price and production policies of large-scale enterprises. *American Economic Review*, *29*(March), 61–74.

Mauri, R. A. (2004). Unstoppable Linux. *Vital Speeches of the Day*, *70*(11), 340–344.

McConnon, A. (2006). Collecting the wisdom of crowds. *Business Week*, September 25, Issue 4002.

McKinsey Quarterly. (2007a). How businesses are using Web 2.0. A Mckinsey Global Survey. *McKinsey Quarterly*, March.

McKinsey Quarterly. (2007b). How companies can make the most of user-generated content. A Mckinsey Global Survey. *McKinsey Quarterly*, August.

McKracken, G. (1988). *Culture and consumption: New approaches to the symbolic character of consumer goods and activities*. Bloomington: Indiana University Press.

Morrison, P. D., Roberts, J. H., & Midgley, D. F. (2004). The nature of lead users and measurement of leading edge status. *Research Policy*, *33*, 351–362.

Munir, K. A., & Jones, M. (2004). Discontinuity and after: The social dynamics of technology evolution and dominance. *Organization Studies*, *25*(4), 561–581.

North, D. (1990). *Institutions, institutional change and economic performance*. Cambridge: University Press.

Orlikowski, W. J. (2000). Using technology and constituting structures: A practice lens for studying technology in organizations. *Organization Science*, *11*(4), 404–428.

Ostrom, E., Dietz, T., Dolsak, N., Stern, P., Stonich, S., & Weber, E. (2002). *The drama of the commons*. Washington, DC: National Academy Press.

Oudshoorn, N., & Pinch, T. (Eds). (2003). *How users matter. The co-construction of users and technology*. Cambridge, MA: The MIT Press.

O'Mahony, S., & Ferraro, F. (2007). The emergence of governance in an open source community. *Academy of Management Journal*, *50*(5), 1079–1106.

Pascu, C., Osimo, D., Ulbrich, M., Turlea, G., & Burgelman, J. C. (2007). The potential disruptive impact of Internet 2 based technologies. *First Monday*, *12*(3). Available at http://firstmonday.org/issues/issue12_3/pascu/index.htm

Penrose, E. T. (1959). *The theory of the growth of the firm*. New York: Wiley.

Porter, M. E. (1980). *Competitive strategy*. New York: Free Press.

Prahalad, C. K., & Ramaswamy, V. (2000). Co-opting customer competence. *Harvard Business Review*, *78*, 79–87.

Prahalad, C. K., & Ramaswamy, V. (2003). *The future of competition: Co-creating unique value with customers*. Boston, MA: Harvard Business School Press.

Prahalad, C. K., & Ramaswamy, V. (2004). *The future of competition, co-creating unique value with customers*. Boston, MA: Harvard Business School Press.

Priem, R. L., & Butler, J. E. (2001). Is the resource-based 'view' a useful perspective for strategic management research? *Academy of Management Review*, *26*(1), 22–40.

Raymond, E. (1999). *The cathedral and the bazaar. Musings and open source by an accidental revolutionary*. Sebastopol, CA: O'Reilly.

Rheingold, H. (2003). *Smart mobs. The next social revolution*. Cambridge, MA: Perseus Publishing.

Richards, J. (2007). YouTube to pay contributors. *The Timesonline*. May 8.

Rosenberg, N. (1982). *Inside the black box: technology and economics*. New York: Cambridge University press.

Saveri, A., Rheingold, H., Pang, K., & Vian, K. (2004). *Toward a new literacy of cooperation in business: Managing dilemmas in the 21st century* (Available at http://www.iftf.org/docs/SR851A_New_Literacy_Cooperation.pdf#search=%22'cooperation%20in%20business'%22). Menlo Park, NJ: Institute for the Future, Technology Horizons Program.

Scherer, F. (1980). *Industrial market structure and economic performance* (2nd ed.). Chicago: Rand McNally.

Schiff, S. (2006). Can Wikipedia conquer expertise? *New Yorker*. July 31.

Scoble, R., & Israel, S. (2006), Naked conversations: How blogs are changing the way businesses talk with customers, Wiley@wiley.com

Shah, S., & Tripsas, M. (2007). The accidental entrepreneur: The emergent and collective process of user entrepreneurship. *Strategic Entrepreneurship Journal*, *1*, 123–140.

Silverstone, R., & Sørensen, K. (2005). Towards the communication society. In: R. Silverstone (Ed.), *Media, technology and everyday life in Europe: From information to communication* (pp. 213–222). London: Ashgate.

Smith, A. (1776). *An Inquiry into the nature and causes of the wealth of nations*. London: Penguin Books.

Suchman, L. A. (1996). Supporting articulation work. In: R. Kling (Ed.), *Computerization and controversy* (2nd ed., pp. 407–423). San Diego, CA: Academic Press.

Surowiecki, J. (2004). *The wisdom of crowds*. New York, NY: Random House Inc.

Tapscott, D., & Williams, A. D. (2006). *Wikinomics: How mass collaboration changes everything*. New York, NY: Portfolio, Penguin Group Inc.

Teece, D. (2006). Profiting from innovation. *Research Policy*, *35*(8), 1107–1109.

Teece, D. J., Pisano, G., & Shuen, A. (1997). Dynamic capabilities and strategic management. *Strategic Management Journal*, *18*(7), 509–533.

The Economist. (2007). Working the crowd. *The Economist*, March 10, Vol. 382, Issue 8519.

The Economist. (2008). The road to e-democracy. *The Economist*, February 16, Vol. 386, Issue. 8567, p. 15.

Thomas, A. (1993). *Controversies in management*. New York, NY: Routledge.

Toffler, A. (2006). *Revolutionary wealth: How it will be created and how it will change our lives*. New York, NY: Random House Inc.

Utterback, J. (1971). The process of technological innovation within the firm. *Academy of Management Journal*, *14*, 75–88.

Vargo, S. L., & Lusch, R. F. (2004). Evolving to a new dominant logic for marketing. *Journal of Marketing*, *68*(1), 1–17.

von Hippel, E. (1976). The dominant role of users in the scientific instrument innovation process. *Research Policy*, *5*(3), 212–239.

von Hippel, E. (1978). A customer-active paradigm for industrial product idea generation. *Research Policy*, *7*(3), 240–266.

von Hippel, E. (1986). Lead users: A source of novel product concepts. *Management Science*, *32*(7), 791–806.

von Hippel, E. (2001). Innovation by user communities: Learning from open source software. *MIT Sloan Management Review*, *42*(4), 82–86.

von Hippel, E. (2005). *Democratizing innovation*. Cambridge, MA: MIT Press.

von Krogh, G., & von Hippel, E. (2003). Open source software and the 'Private-Collective' innovation model: Issues for organization science. *Organization Science*, *14*(2), 209–223.

Williamson, O. (1975). *Markets and hierarchies, analysis and antitrust implications: A study in the economics of internal organization*. New York, NY: Free Press.

Wilson, J. (2006). 3G to Web 2.0? Can mobile telephony become architecture of participation? Convergence. *The International Journal of Research into New Media Technologies*, *12*(2), 229–242.

Woodward, J. (1965). *Industrial organization: Theory and practice*. New York, NY: Oxford University Press.

Zander, I., & Zander, U. (2005). The inside track: On the important (but neglected) role of customers in the resource based view of strategy and firm growth. *Journal of Management Studies*, *42*(8), 1519.

Zelizer, V. A. R. (1983). *Morals and markets: The development of life insurance in the United States*. New Brunswick, NJ: Transaction Books.

Zuboff, S. (1984). *In the age of the smart machine*. New York: Basic Books.

Zuboff, S., & Maxmin, J. (2002). *The support economy: Why corporations are failing individuals and the next episode of capitalism*. New York, NY: Viking Press.

ENTREPRENEURSHIP AND THE CONSTRUCTION OF VALUE IN BIOTECHNOLOGY

Sarah Kaplan and Fiona Murray

The entrepreneurship literature typically depicts Schumpeterian entrepreneurs – those in a quest to profit from new technologies – as individuals seeking out preexisting opportunities and building organizations to create and capture financial profit (Shane, 2000; Shane & Venkataraman, 2000; Venkataraman, 1997). Implicit in this view is the idea that a technology is something to discover rather than something to influence and that technology evolution is exogenous to the entrepreneurial process (as noted by Shah & Tripsas, 2007). An alternative perspective argues that technologies are at least partially changeable and that the role of effective Schumpeterian entrepreneurs is to mould them to a particular (exogenously given) institutional environment (Hargadon & Douglas, 2001). Either view of technical change (and of the role of entrepreneurship in it) is at odds with findings from studies of the evolution of new technologies, which describe both deeply uncertain institutional environments and contested efforts to shape what the technology becomes (for an overview, see Kaplan & Tripsas, 2008). Specifically, the burgeoning literature on institutional entrepreneurship (Fligstein, 2001; Garud, Hardy, & Maguire, 2007; Garud, Jain, & Kumaraswamy, 2002; Lounsbury & Glynn, 2001; Munir & Phillips, 2005) argues precisely that neither the technology nor the institutional environment is fixed and that multiple actors with multiple goals (not always, or not

Technology and Organization: Essays in Honour of Joan Woodward
Research in the Sociology of Organizations, Volume 29, 107–147

ISSN: 0733-558X/doi:10.1108/S0733-558X(2010)0000029013

even often, the profit motive) act to shape the institutional setup that would govern activities in a particular field. From this standpoint, a technology is mutable and shaped as the field is shaped (Garud & Karnøe, 2001).

Certainly, in the case of biotechnology, which we analyze in this chapter, what biotechnology meant at any one point in time was up for grabs. The technology was often thought to hold huge potential but was equivocal (Weick, 1990) – multiple interpretations of its potential were possible. The institutional environment was also complex and highly uncertain. In this context, a large number of Schumpeterian entrepreneurs created new organizations (such as Genentech, Amgen, Biogen, and others) to commercialize various biotechnologies. It was also the case that a wide array of institutional entrepreneurs (including city governments, federal agencies, social movement organizations, etc.) mobilized around issues of safety, efficacy, intellectual property, and economic development. Each of these actors saw the opportunities and risks of biotechnology in different ways and acted according to these understandings of the value (either positive or negative) they perceived the technology could have.

We think of these interpretations of value as economic logics that comprise the organizing principles of what is valued and valuable in the institutional setup of a field (David, 2003; Friedland & Alford, 1991). Central to the biotechnology case we study, and to the institutional perspective on entrepreneurship more generally, is the idea that the financial profits motivating the Schumpeterian entrepreneur are only one of many interpretations of the value of the technology that exist in the field. Other institutional entrepreneurs whose notions of value may be focused on ends other than making profits will also articulate their perspectives. What animates our enquiry is to understand the evolution of biotechnology in the marketplace and the role entrepreneurial action has in shaping this process. We find that, where there are multiple interpretations, contests between all sorts of entrepreneurs (Schumpeterian and other) about which economic logic will dominate are likely. These contests about value are highly consequential because they have implications for the shape of the field and of the evolution of technologies within it. Yet, the mechanisms for resolving these disputes about value and the entrepreneur's role in such a process are poorly understood.

Conventionalist theory – as most comprehensively articulated by Boltanski and Thévenot (2006) (and also exemplified in Beunza & Stark, 2004; Callon & Muniesa, 2005; Stark, 2000) – provides a useful lens for unpacking these dynamics. This theory suggests that an economic logic defines what is of value in a particular context. Their insight is that there is no single economic logic and therefore no single articulation of value – multiple economic logics are possible and may often coexist. Each economic logic is based in its own internally consistent set of tests for establishing value and, more importantly, the evidence that satisfies those tests. The combination of tests and evidence provide the justification or legitimization of the value for a good. A particular sphere of action – the marketplace or elsewhere – will be governed by an institutional setup that is based in a compromise across multiple possible economic logics and that is sustained by a particular constellation of justifications. One implication of this perspective is that entrepreneurs – Schumpeterian as well as institutional entrepreneurs – will engage in contests with one another to propose and stabilize the economic logic. They seek to define the tests of value and to provide evidence that satisfies these tests.

With regard to commercializing new technologies, entrepreneurs produce or draw on a wide range of evidence: Courts and government agencies making decisions defining appropriability, financial markets placing value on technologies well before products materialize, scientists producing technical evidence on viability, and firms making sense of the technology and its commercial applications. The entrepreneurial task is therefore to establish or undermine different tests of value, mobilize or suppress evidence to satisfy or refute these tests, and construct a compromise across the contested values associated with a technology. Throughout this process, we argue, entrepreneurs take action to create new logics or transform existing ones, leading to a new set of opportunities. The outcome of such entrepreneurial action strongly shapes the evolution of a technology and, therefore, the organizations that exploit it.

Through our historical analysis of the evolution of biotechnology, we show that highly varied understandings of the value embodied in biotechnology existed. Across three eras (1973–1986, 1988–2000, and 2003 to present), entrepreneurs constructed different economic logics for biotechnology, often in highly contested settings against multiple entrepreneurial adversaries. We also find that an economic logic was not easily stabilized; biotechnology's evolution was arrested by moments when the stabilized constellations fell apart (in 1987–1989 and again in 2001–2002) and new logics were constructed. We argue that such breakdowns may occur when evidence fails to meet critical tests or when different understandings of value are in conflict. These breakdowns create new opportunities for other entrepreneurs to construct alternative economic logics.

By exploring these processes of contestation, (temporary) stabilization and subsequent breakdowns, we contribute first to the entrepreneurship literature by expanding the definition of the entrepreneurial act. We find that the entrepreneur creating a new firm to commercialize a technology, while being a Schumpeterian opportunity seeker, is also acting as an institutional entrepreneur, constructing the economic logics and institutional setups as they build their organizations. Not only does this perspective redefine the role of Schumpeterian entrepreneurs, it also opens up the discussion of entrepreneurship to a whole set of different entrepreneurial actors who may not be creating firms but who are seeking to shape the economic logic and institutions that will govern the system of exchange. This full complement of entrepreneurs function like Becker's (1963) "moral entrepreneurs," each seeking to set the rules of exchange and provide evidence to support a particular institutional setup (see also Epstein, 2007).

Second, we contribute to the literature on technical change by showing that entrepreneurs are central actors in this process. Their challenge is to exploit, negotiate, and resolve the uncertainties created during the emergence of a new technology. They must develop an economic logic and constitute the logic in an effective organization. In doing so, they act to change the institutional setup in a process that shapes and is shaped by the evolving technology. By taking this view, we present a broader definition of the institutional arrangements that are central to technical change, placing legal institutions promulgating and defining patent law alongside government agencies establishing safety regulations together with financial market institutions validating the financial value of a start-up. By examining the entire institutional setup, we can more precisely explain patterns of technical change. We show that such change is often not smooth, but instead can be arrested or change direction when compromises about the economic logic break down. As such, the forces shaping technology evolution are best understood as not purely technical, but also, and unavoidably, economic.

Third, while we have known since the pioneering work of Joan Woodward (1958) that different technologies require different organizational configurations, our analysis suggests that the entrepreneurial act of defining the value of a technology and creating new organizations to constitute this value actually shapes the direction that technologies evolve. Thus, it is not simply a matter of matching an organization to a technology but rather of seeing how the creation of new organizations to commercialize technologies interacts with the definition of the technology itself in the marketplace.

ECONOMIC LOGICS AND THE EVOLUTION OF TECHNOLOGY

By taking conventionalist view of the evolution of biotechnology, we suggest that the process by which entrepreneurs determined what made biotechnology valuable and figured out how to organize around such an economic logic was contested. The shape that biotechnology has ultimately taken emerged from the resolution of these contests. Convention theory – as elaborated in Boltanski and Thévenot's (2006) *On Justification*[1] – argues that our economy is shaped by participants affecting the rules of economic action. Whereas most economists would argue that the assignment of value underpins any system of exchange, conventionalists suggest that this value is not only given by the principles of optimization but instead can be derived from many possible spheres such as civic duty, attainment of fame, proof of technologic performance, and demonstration of creativity. More specifically, Boltanski and Thévenot (2006, p. 43) claim that the establishment of a particular logic "comes about as a part of a coordinated process that relies on two supports: a common identification of market goods, whose exchange defines the course of action, and a common evaluation of these objects in terms of prices that make it possible to adjust various actions." Simply put, economic logics embody principles of economic coordination or conventions that guide interpretation of the technology and its value.

We use the notion of a logic as it is defined by Friedland and Alford (1991, pp. 248–249) (and discussed in DiMaggio, 1997, p. 277); a set of "material practices and symbolic constructions" that are the "organizing principles" of the institutional setup. An *economic* logic concerns the organizing principles that define what is of value. It underpins a "system of exchange" (Biagioli, 2000, 552fn) that can be understood as being similar to Latour and Woolgar's (1979) cycles of credit that transform valued outputs into resources for further production. The guiding focus of the conventionalist perspective is in explaining how economic action is socially constructed and in analyzing how what is valuable is determined (Stark, 2000). It relies on the idea that multiple values can coexist, each being coherent within its own economic logic, and each of which entails its own metrics and standards of evidence for proving the value of any object or idea (Callon & Muniesa, 2005). Each logic has its own tests for value, and actions are taken with the idea that they will or at least could be subject to tests of "justification." There are various loci where the tests can play out, such as the courts, markets, labs, or government agencies. The process is one of mutual substantiation in which a particular test is determined to be a deciding factor and certain evidence is deemed to be a justification. The test and the evidence are coproduced.

Although the institutional perspective has highlighted the importance of logics and their institutional setup in the evolution of new industries (Lounsbury, Ventresca, & Hirsch, 2003), the key insight of the conventionalists is that what is valuable will differ in different spheres, not only the market but also social, religious, civic, and others. And, more importantly, that even within a given sphere, there can be a contest over which particular economic logic will prevail. For example, scientists engaging in research in the academic sphere may value intellectual contribution and recognition and follow the economic logic of Open Science (David, 2003; Latour & Woolgar, 1979; Merton, 1968). However, scientists in industry may value relevance to practical problems. Likewise, technologies can be subject to different economic logics in different spheres. In the market sphere, the value of a new technology will be associated with financial profit. But, in the civic sphere, the value may be in job creation or economic development. Or, in the social sphere, the value may be negative, coming in the form of fears of toxicity.

Just as Zelizer (1983, 2005) have shown that multiple logics – social and market – can affect the ways intimate goods and services are traded in the marketplace, the conventionalist view suggests that many potential economic logics can operate in a single sphere. This has been demonstrated by Lounsbury (2007) who, in his study of the mutual fund industry, identifies the contrasting trustee and the performance logics that defined the values of the Boston– and New York–based funds respectively. In publishing, Thornton and Ocasio (1999) describe the yielding of the editorial logic to a market-oriented logic as firms in the industry changed hands and brought in professional managers. And, specifically in biotechnology, both academic and commercial (or venture capital) economic logics have been shown to operate, often in highly conflictual ways, within the academic sphere (Murray, 2008; Powell & Owen-Smith, 2002; Vallas & Lee, 2008). In the context of the commercialization of a new technology, we argue that the conventionalist perspective makes room for the potential that different definitions of an economic logic associated with technology may be part of the compromise that structures the institutional setup surrounding it and allows a system of exchange to operate. The prevailing economic logic is therefore the set – or in Latour and Woolgar's (1979) language, the "lash-up" – of conventions that govern the action.

The conventionalist view sees the efforts to construct such "lash-ups" as a way of dealing with the Knightian uncertainty (Knight, 1921/1965) in the market. Indeed, "for the Conventions School, the process of justification (rationalization) is critical to actors assuaging their concerns about an unknowable future" (Biggart & Beamish, 2003, p. 456). Uncertainties can emanate from multiple parties or settings and threaten the stability of institutionalized conventions. There may be disruptions to the existing compromise about which logic should hold. Thus, the emergence of a new technology, for example, is a kind of *moment critique* (Boltanski & Thévenot, 1999, p. 359); a moment of crisis forcing reflexivity and a recognition that something has to change. Ambiguity is also created simply by the existence of multiple, overlapping logics. Interpretations of the value of a thing and of the thing itself are subject to debate, and actors' preferences are unknown, unclear, or multiple. Different actors may be in favor of different economic logics. When commercializing a new technology, Schumpeterian entrepreneurs may articulate and contest among themselves (and with their investors) different economic logics of what is valuable in a new technology. They may also find themselves in conflict with institutional entrepreneurs whose economic logic is dramatically different in conception. Competing parties will engage in efforts not only to bring justification of a certain definition of value but also to assure that their preferred economic logic be the one structuring the process of commercialization. Actors can challenge the validity of a test, avoid a test or introduce a test that is valid according to a different economic logic. However, the very uncertainties that usher in disputes also make negotiation and entrepreneurial action possible and even necessary (Sewell, 1992).

The entrepreneur may be seen as the actor who can break from the existing institutional setup in the market and create new economic practices (Biggart & Beamish, 2003). Thus, rather than being passive recipients of new technologies, logics, and institutions, it is likely that entrepreneurial actors will be active in developing the technology, creating an economic logic, and building a supporting institutional setup. In this sense, entrepreneurial actors of every type can engage in creative, strategic actions that can produce new sets of coordinated practices associated with a new economic logic that will shape subsequent activities in the field. Their role comes about because, as they develop and promote different economic logics, they work to generate evidence within existing institutions, act to change institutions, and try to change the tests associated with these institutions. They instantiate these ideas through the organizations they build to exploit the economic logic they are promoting. Through the success of their organizations, they provide evidence that their proposed economic logic is viable, just as other types of entrepreneurs seek evidence supporting alternative views.

The constellation of features characterizing conventionalist theory make it particularly well-suited to the analysis of the emergence of a new technology and the surrounding institutional setup. Because new technologies are inherently equivocal (Weick, 1990), it makes sense that multiple economic logics could apply. What evidence would constitute proof of the value of such a technology would itself be inherently subject to interpretation and potentially disputed. Because future outcomes of the development of the technology cannot be predicted, entrepreneurs are those skilled and knowledgeable actors (Fligstein, 2001; Giddens, 1984) generating evidence, sometimes in the form of creating start-up organizations, and changing institutions all in the service of establishing a particular economic logic surrounding the technology. They mobilize a wide range of evidence related to different economic logics, establish tests that match their evidence, and attempt to shape the interpretation of evidence provided by others. The outcomes of their efforts shape the direction that the technology, the organizations, the logic, and its underlying institutions take.

One can see a clear connection between the conventionalist perspective on technology we propose and ideas developed in the stream of research on the social construction of technology (SCOT) (Bijker, Hughes, & Pinch, 1987). They share a focus on the interpretive flexibility of technologies (and other goods) and on the mechanisms for closure and stabilization of an artifact. What conventionalist theory usefully adds is a focus on the establishment of tests and the mobilization of evidence as the underlying mechanisms for achieving some sort of compromise about the value of a technology. This highlights very naturally the role of advocacy and argumentation on the part of marketplace participants in shaping such outcomes. In doing so, the conventionalist conceptual toolkit directs us to explore the ways in which entrepreneurial actors go about constructing and stabilizing a particular economic logic to define whether, and under what conditions, stakeholders attach value to the new technology. In demystifying the tests and evidence that validate the tests, the conventionalist perspective also highlights the degree to which compromises are fragile (being perhaps only local and contingent) and therefore the possibility that such compromises may break down at critical moments. In the following section, we explore how these ideas that help explain the evolution of biotechnology.

CONSTRUCTING BIOTECHNOLOGY

We trace the development of biotechnology in human therapeutics[2] over a 30-year period from the first demonstration of recombinant DNA (rDNA) techniques in 1973 to the field characterized by a complex network of dedicated biotech firms, pharmaceutical firms, investors, and academics that, by around 2003, stabilized in number, organizational form, strategy, and financing (Biotechnology Industry Organization, 2008). The field of biotechnology has been extensively studied by organizational scholars, and its complex story has merited books and articles too numerous to count (for overviews, see Kenney, 1986; Kornberg, 1995; Pisano, 2006; Robbins-Roth, 2000). We therefore do not pretend to offer a full account of the field but rather seek to view 30 years of biotechnology through a particular lens, which we hope will shed light on some important dynamics shaping its evolution. Our analysis highlights entrepreneurial action across three eras. Each one characterized by the stabilization of a different economic logic. However, these trajectories were arrested by moments (1987–1989; 2001–2002) when the compromise over how to define the tests and the evidence of the economic logic broke down, only to be reconstructed in a different form later.

- Era 1: 1973–1986, when biotech came to be seen as a source of novel ("large molecule") human therapeutics developed by independent start-ups in competition with the "small molecule" drugs of pharmaceutical firms.
- Era 2: 1990–2000, when biotech became a set of firms providing a range of biology-based approaches supporting an alternative drug discovery platform to the traditional chemistry-based platforms used by pharmaceutical firms.
- Era 3: 2003 onwards, when biotech emerged as a method to combine biological techniques with other disciplines such as chemistry and computer science to develop various types of therapeutics for specific diseases by both independent biotech firms and pharmaceutical firms.

Most observers date the start of biotechnology in the marketplace to 1973, when the first rDNA techniques were demonstrated at Stanford University by Stanley Cohen, Herbert Boyer, and colleagues (Cohen, Chang, Boyer, & Helling, 1973). These results showed that DNA could be introduced into a bacterium and "switched on" to make a protein (Cohen et al., 1973). A plethora of methods for manipulating, isolating, and modifying DNA followed, and in their wake, the potential for an economic logic in the market place and a setting ripe for entrepreneurial action. Of course, biotechnology has a long "prehistory" in both academic research and practical applications that provided the foundations for these important experiments (Kenney, 1986). Evidence of thousands of years of basic expertise in biotechnology-related techniques is found in accounts of fermentation, beer production, and wine making (Legras, Merdinoglu, Cornuet, & Karst, 2007). However, it was in 1953, with the elucidation of the structure of DNA (Watson & Crick, 1953), that the scientific underpinnings for the development of new techniques were developed. This defined an academic agenda for the second half of the twentieth century of which Cohen and Boyer were only a part (Judson, 1979; Morange, 1998). Their discovery of rDNA techniques did, however, open up the possibility for commercial applications.

In the three decades following the Cohen and Boyer breakthrough, many Schumpeterian entrepreneurs launched start-ups to profit from biotechnology. From 1980 (the first initial public offering for a biotechnology firm) to 2003, over 470 firms were taken public and many more funded by venture capitalists and angel investors who invested over US$22 billion in early-stage biotechnology firms in the same period (Van Brunt, 2003; Lerner, 1992; Lerner & Merges, 1998). In examining their activities in the market, however, we found that they were far from pure opportunity seekers. Instead, they actively constructed and reconstructed justifications for the value of their firms by arguing for particular tests of value and mobilizing evidence to satisfy those tests. They instantiated economic logics for biotech in the organizations they built, and, in doing so, they raised millions from private investors and public markets.

The Schumpeterian entrepreneurs were not alone in their efforts to construct the value of biotechnology. Many actors, concerned with their own definitions of value, fought for different understandings of biotechnology and different definitions of the possibilities associated with it. Hence, biotechnology's economic logics were defined, contested, and stabilized (and sometimes destabilized) not only in the research labs, offices of venture capitalists, and biotech start-ups but also in the courts, Congressional hearings, government agencies, large pharmaceutical firms, and even in the streets (in political demonstrations).

Although the discovery of rDNA techniques made biotechnology's commercial application possible and generated enthusiasm among entrepreneurs, great uncertainty governed how, exactly, these applications would evolve and how the biotechnology opportunity would be constructed. Research on the history, economics, and sociology of technology has highlighted four domains in which the value of a technology can be established – technical, appropriability, market, and ethical, legal, and social dimensions. From a technical perspective, the uncertainties are about whether a technology would actually "work" (Dosi, 1982). Concerns about appropriability focus on establishing ownership and rights to future market rents and provide barriers to entry (Cockburn & Griliches, 1988; Levin, Klevorick, Nelson, & Winter, 1987; Teece, 1986). Uncertainties about the market focus on the degree to which investors and customers would pay for the technology (Gans & Stern, 2000; Roberts & Berry, 1985). Ethical and safety concerns also generate uncertainties (Kevles & Hood, 1992; Winner, 1977).

Our analysis of the evolution of biotechnology indicates that there were strong dependencies between those domains. It was not enough to show a technique worked, it was also crucial to demonstrate that the ideas could be owned, that customers or investors would be willing to pay, and that the social and human health risks were not too great. As a result, entrepreneurs of all sorts needed to "lash-up" evidence across these four domains to achieve compromises about the economic logic. In the sections that follow, we focus on how a constellation of evidence came to support the prevailing economic logic in each era, and, when that compromise failed, how it was reconstructed. These ideas are summarized in Table 1.

THE FIRST BIOTECH ERA (1973–1986)

Biotech as New Biological Drugs in Competition with Big Pharma

The Cohen and Boyer breakthrough made biotechnology techniques practicable for the first time, and many entrepreneurs founded firms in attempts to capture this potential. In the very early days, firms aimed at a wide range of applications in areas as diverse as agriculture, the environment, energy, industrial chemicals, and human health (Robbins-Roth, 2000). Cetus, founded in 1971, is considered by some as the first biotechnology firm as it focused on vaccines, therapeutic proteins, antibiotics, and even alcohol production from fermentation. Genentech was founded in 1976 with an initial focus on industrial chemicals and animal health in addition to human health. Amgen, founded in 1980, had a similarly diverse spread of applications including diagnostic kits, oil recovery, and animal health. Hybritech, founded shortly afterwards in 1978 with funds from Genentech's investors, focused on another promising new technology, monoclonal antibodies.[3] It was Genentech, however, founded by Boyer and venture capitalist Bob Swanson, which ultimately came to represent the economic logic of this era. The firm soon focused on applying rDNA techniques to develop therapeutic biological drugs – building blocks such as DNA or proteins made in genetically engineered cells – as an alternative to the big pharmaceutical firms whose drugs were small chemical entities designed and made using chemistry.

Table 1. Sources of Evidence in Each Biotechnology Era.

Eras	Technical Evidence	Appropriability/Legal Evidence	Regulatory Evidence – Safety, Ethics, etc.	Market Evidence
Era 1 1973–1986	Publications & patents FDA approval for different clinical phases & approval for recombinant Insulin (1982) FDA approval for large-scale manufacturing	Chakrabarty patent *Diamond v. Chakrabarty* final Supreme Court decision (1980) Granting of Cohen & Boyer Patent (1980)	NAS Committee on Biohazards of rDNA Asilomar Conference on rDNA safety NIH Regulations on rDNA Congressional Hearings	War on cancer – market for interferons Pharma market for new products through licensing deals, e.g., Genentech & Eli Lily, Genentech & Hoffman
De-construction 1987–1989	Failure of interferon in single-drug trials for cancer. Limited success in drug approval compared to investment in biotech R&D	Genentech vs. Hoffman patent suit Amgen Epogen patent dispute	California disputes over genetically modified strawberries. Rise of activist groups organizing against genetics	Slow down in big pharma partnerships
Era 2 1990–2000	Public funding for Human Genome Project and associated scientific promise Completed milestones from discovery service agreements with big pharma	Over 1,000 gene-sequence patents filed and granted	Limited regulatory requirements for platform approach Privacy of genetic information resolved through State and Federal regulation	Large-scale partnerships for biotech & big pharma to solve discovery crisis: HGS–Smith-Kline Beecham; Millennium–Bayer
De-construction 2001–2002	Limited technical success from biotech's discovery platforms Limited number of novel targets and drugs	USPTO utility guidelines for gene sequence patents – high hurdle for patentability. Clinton–Blair say genome placed in public domain	Patient groups debate ethics of high charges for gene testing	Overall stock market crash
Era 3 2003 onwards	Publications and patents on new targets & approaches Deal milestones FDA milestones	Patent portfolios of large & small molecules robust to patent disputes	No change	Unmet needs for disease Pharma alliances for joint development of single molecules or small programs

The founders were self-conscious in their desire to establish Genentech's approach as the prevailing economic logic in biotechnology. As Swanson (1996) described in an oral history:

> We decided to raise money in our initial public offering in 1980 ... We did it for a number of reasons. One is that we needed more money to complete our development. There was a lot of excitement about the technology, and we wanted to be the first company out to the public market because we felt that we were doing things right. We were basically managing the business conservatively; we were focused on getting to market; and we wanted to set the right tone–the idea being, if a bunch of other biotechnology companies were out there, and they disappointed investors or they weren't doing things right, then it would be more difficult for us. So we wanted to set the standard. We had been setting the standard on the science. We wanted to set the standard as a public company.

With a successful initial public offering (IPO), Genentech, its venture backers and investment bankers provided a blue print for a stable economic logic. Other firms followed, shedding their broad, multi-application orientation to focus on biological drugs ("large molecules") for human disease. From 1980 to 1986, over 60 biotech firms completed IPOs. Stelios Papadopoulos (the first dedicated biotech industry analyst) noted, "In the early to mid-80s, it became clear that the only meaningful game was pharmaceuticals" (quoted in Robbins-Roth, 2000, p. 25). However, this understanding of biotechnology, as a source of novel human therapeutics developed by independent start-ups in competition with pharmaceutical firms, could not have been reached if uncertainties across the technical, appropriability, regulatory, and market domains had not been contested and resolved.

The strongest evidence of technical viability came when experiments were published and patents were filed on rDNA and genetically modified organisms. In the first seven years after its founding and until the approval of its first drug, Genentech published more than 77 peer-reviewed publications in academic journals, jointly authored with scientists including both Cohen and Boyer and also a range of others at the University of California at San Francisco, Stanford, Johns Hopkins, and the City of Hope Medical School. Historical accounts of the period suggest that Cohen and Boyer had limited interest in and awareness of rDNA's commercial potential. However, an article in the *New York Times* (McElheny, 1974) influenced Stanford's Director of Technology Licensing to propose that the DNA cloning procedures be patented (Hughes, 2001; Ku, 1983). While Cohen was reluctant, the filing was made with only one week remaining before the U.S. limits on prior disclosure would have invalidated the patent.

The patent claimed both the process of making and the composition for biologically functional chimeras (mixes of cells from two different species), and its detailed disclosure descriptions provided additional evidence of technical viability. Two years earlier, Ananda Chakrabarty, a microbiologist at General Electric's Schenectady Laboratories, had also initiated the commercial move, filing for the first patent on a genetically modified organism – a modified form of *Pseudomonas* bacterium that was capable of breaking down crude oil (Patent no. 3,813,316, Chakrabarty, 1974; Patent no. 4,259,444, Chakrabarty, 1981). In an interview, Chakrabarty described his work: "I just shuffled the genes, changing the characteristics of a bacteria that already existed. The 'new' bacteria could guzzle the oil in case of oil-spills in seas or rivers, thus saving valuable marine life and preventing environmental degradation" (Chowdhury, 2002). In the late 1970s, critical approaches to genetic modification in plants were also patented (e.g., Patent no. 4,459,355, Cello & Olsen, 1984).

Although patents were evidence of technical viability, they also assigned ownership of the intellectual property. Not everyone agreed that such ownership of living organisms was appropriate. When Chakrabarty initially submitted his patent, the patent office declined to grant it. Chakrabarty brought suit against the Commissioner of Trademarks and Patents, Sidney A. Diamond, and in 1980, the Supreme Court deliberated over the Chakrabarty patent. Many different groups provided evidence to the court, each bringing not only his own evidence but his own views about which test should be considered by the court. For the Patent Office, the test was whether genetically modified life forms were patentable material under the U.S. Constitution and according to patent laws passed by Congress. In contrast, executives in various biotechnology start-ups, whose very existence depended on the ability to own biotechnology intellectual property, expressed the view that patentability should be granted in the interests of economic development. They were joined in their view by the Pharmaceutical Manufacturers Association (who filed a separate *Amicus* brief). They felt the patent should be justified in commercial terms and hoped to gain patent rights to boost their ability to earn rents on the technologies they developed. In their *Amicus* brief to the court, Genentech's executives summarized this perspective (Lyon & Lyon, 1979, p. 3):

> In Genentech's case the patent incentive did, and doubtless elsewhere it will, prove to be an important if not indispensable factor in attracting private support for life-giving research. And where the Patent System facilitates the interposition of small but fruitful companies like Genentech in pharmaceutical and other industries traditionally dominated by major concerns, it operates to best purpose, as an essentially

> pro-competitive mechanism. Having delivered very substantial benefits to the public in reliance on the patent incentive, Genentech is vitally interested in continued operation of the quid pro quo principle upon which the Patent System is based.

The debate about the Chakrabarty patent, and by implication about biotechnology more generally, was not only about who had the right to earn rents but also about whether such technologies should be developed at all, given concerns for safety. Activists such as Jeremy Rifkin, founder of the People's Business Commission, a Washington-based public interest group, saw the Supreme Court as another setting in which to bring evidence of safety concerns. In the only *Amicus* brief to the Supreme Court against the Chakrabarty patent grant, they argued that the test before the Supreme Court should relate to the possible hazards of biotech and described how genetic engineering might "irreversibly pollute the planetary gene pool in radical new ways" (quoted in Thackray, 1998, p. 68). The judgment describes how safety activists saw what tests and evidence should be used to decide on the appropriateness of patenting biotechnology-produced organisms, pointing to:

> grave risks that may be generated by research endeavors such as the respondent's. The briefs present a gruesome parade of horribles ... We are told that genetic research and related technological developments may spread pollution and disease, that it may result in a loss of genetic diversity, and that its practice may tend to depreciate the value of human life. These arguments are forcefully, even passionately, presented; they remind us that, at times, human ingenuity seems unable to control fully the forces it creates – that, as with Hamlet, it is sometimes better to bear those ills we have than fly to others that we know not of.

It was argued that the Supreme Court should weigh these potential hazards in considering whether the respondent's invention is patentable subject matter (US Supreme Court, 1980).

In allowing the Chakrabarty patent (and by precedent the Cohen and Boyer patent), the judges rejected the arguments that tests of safety or commerce should be used when determining patentability. They found that questions of regulation were for the legislative process – not the courts – and that "the grant or denial of patents on micro-organisms is not likely to put an end to genetic research or to its attendant risks." Instead, the Supreme Court determined the validity of the patent in accordance with the Constitution that anything "under the sun" should be patentable and with the Patent Act of 1952, specifically Title 35 of the U.S. Code, Section 101, describing the kinds of inventions that could be patented. Although they did not give credence to the economic arguments proposed by biotechnology firms, the successful outcome of the case provided evidence for the appropriability of invented biotech organisms, which validated the approach being pursued by Genentech. A press release for Genentech said that the Supreme Court's action had "assured this country's technology future" (Genentech, 1980).

The questions of safety began to recede in the wake of the *Diamond v. Chakrabarty* decision. However, throughout the very early years of biotechnology, actors who defined the value of biotechnology as related to the risk of human or environmental toxicity placed limits on research and commercialization. Universities, city governments, Federal regulatory agencies, activist groups, and researchers themselves worked to assure that safety concerns were factored into the approach taken to develop biotechnology.

One response to these pressures was an attempt by researchers at self-regulation. In 1974, a group of researchers – spearheaded by Paul Berg, a scientist at Stanford University who was himself conducting early experiments in rDNA – requested that the National Academy of Sciences (NAS) form a committee to study the safety of conducting research biotech (Lederberg, 1975). The NAS then convened the Committee on Recombinant DNA Molecules, which declared a moratorium on further research until scientists could establish guidelines for safety. The following year, more than 100 scientists, lawyers and journalists met under the auspices of the National Institutes of Health (NIH) (which took over from the NAS) at Asilomar State Beach for what has become known as the Asilomar Conference. Their goal was to set guidelines (rather than regulations) on research on rDNA that would allow scientific activity in biotechnology to continue while assuring that risks of mutant genes or toxicity were controlled (Carmen, 1985; Diringer, 1987). The debate dealt with both what tests for safety would be used and what the standards of evidence would be. The resulting compromise made research in biotechnology possible. The agreement was to match containment approaches to the level of risk associated with different classes of experiments, specifying types of facilities for minimal- to high-risk situations. It also banned certain kinds of highly dangerous experiments.

Subsequent to this conference, it became possible for various Federal agencies to set regulations for conducting biotechnology research. In 1976, the NIH released its own guidelines for NIH-sponsored genetic research (41 Federal Regulation 27902). Around this time, public hearings by the Committees on Labor and Public Welfare (94th Cong., 1st Sess. 1975), Commerce, Science, and Transportation (95th Cong., 1st Sess. 1977), and Interstate and Foreign Commerce (95th Cong., 1st Sess. 1977) further codified biotech regulation. These events established a new regulatory regime that allowed researchers in academia and firms to restart biotech research that had been previously halted. By 1980, the NIH had agreed to allow private-sector firms to register their experiments voluntarily and to receive NIH certification. Large-scale production of biological products (more than 10 liters) remained unregulated and unpopular among private-sector firms such as Cetus (McGarity & Bayer, 1983). When developed with Federal funds, it required prior approval, but privately funded projects were a gray area.

With this movement at the Federal level, local attempts to contain biotechnology research met with only partial success. For example, in Cambridge, Massachusetts – the home of the Massachusetts Institute of Technology and Harvard University as well as some of the early biotech start-ups – the city government initially placed its own moratorium on rDNA experiments (in response to a 1976 Harvard proposal to renovate its biology labs). The city created the Cambridge Experimentation Review Board that conducted over 75 hours of hearings during which a broad range of possible outcomes were considered. However, the Federal regulatory process, which was occurring contemporaneously, established a precedent for allowing research, and so the city ultimately decided to encode NIH guidelines into city law. This struggle for influence represented a significant turning point in the contest between regulators and for-profit constituents in influencing a leading institution – in this case, the Cambridge City government. The winners argued that the potential health benefits and the economic opportunities outweighed any risks (Wright, 1986).

The net effect of these debates among scientists and at the local and the Federal governmental levels in the late 1970s was to lay out a path for continuing research (at least in the United States) using the rDNA techniques initially proposed by Cohen and Boyer. Biological drugs for human health began to dominate biotechnology as agricultural applications had not yet achieved a stable regulatory environment. It was not until 1986 that a Coordinated Framework for Regulation of Biotechnology in plants was announced (National Research Council (U.S.). Committee on Genetically Modified Pest-Protected Plants, 2000; Office of Science and Technology Policy, 1986).

Assuring a regime for appropriability and safety paved the way for the further development of biotechnology for human therapeutics. Subsequent advances would be dependent on what kinds of research would be viable in the market and therefore receive funding. Entrepreneurial firms were often in the lead in creating market evidence. One example was the production of human insulin. Researchers at Genentech worked in 1978 with the City of

Hope National Medical Center to show it was possible to produce human insulin using rDNA technology. Robert Swanson, president of Genentech at the time, noted, "The development of human insulin demonstrates the viability of using recombinant DNA technology to produce products with practical application" (Genentech, 1978).[4] Most of the evidence of manufacturability was generated at the small 10-liter laboratory scale approved by the NIH, although in 1979, Genentech created a minor furore by making organisms for insulin production in batches of 100 liters. They took advantage of ambiguity in the rules to establish more dramatic evidence of rDNA's potential. The tests also allowed Genentech to show their partner – Eli Lilly – that they could meet important technical milestones in the deal that gave Eli Lilly the right to produce and distribute recombinant insulin as an alternative to Lilly's bovine insulin (Yansura, 2001).

Another example was the pursuit of Interferon, the first promising lead to emerge from the war on cancer announced by President Nixon in his 1971 State of the Union Address. Its promise was to replace small-molecule chemotherapies being pursued by large pharmaceutical firms. The possible application of biotech to cancer provided entrepreneurs with compelling evidence to bolster claims of market opportunity. As a result, many of the biotechnology start-ups of the day, including Genentech, Amgen, Biogen, and Cetus, pursued this opportunity. Indeed, much of the excitement around Genentech's IPO was due to its interferon alpha project. The appeal to the war on cancer also helped counter continuing concerns about safety hazards. The possibility that biotech firms might develop capabilities to manufacture interferons and therefore cure cancer seems to have been a turning point that, according to at least one media analyst and observer, "swept away much of the public and governmental uneasiness over the possible dangers associated with the research" (O'Malley, 1980).

The success (in the case of insulin) and the potential promise (in the case of interferon) of early biotechnology drugs were recognized by some of the large pharmaceutical firms (Kaplan, Murray, & Henderson, 2003). Eli Lilly had been the predominant player in insulin and therefore saw both the threat and the opportunity in Genentech's work. Having bought the worldwide rights to Genetech's recombinant human insulin, the firm made significant investments in building rDNA production capabilities. In 1980, Hoffmann-La Roche bought rights to market Genentech's interferon, and Schering Plough did the same for Biogen's interferon. These deals substantiated the market value of biotechnology among corporate buyers.

However, another critical market test was achieving Federal Drug Administration (FDA) approval to distribute biotechnology drugs. Initially, no guidelines for FDA tests existed and the agency sought to incorporate the NIH guidelines into the design of clinical trials (43FR 35210, August 8, 1978). However with the complexity and criticism of these guidelines and their rapidly changing standards, the FDA moved to a position, supported by industry, that the 1902 Biologics Control Act could guide the tests and standards for appropriate technical evidence (McGarity & Bayer, 1983). As a result, the FDA was able to begin approving recombinant drugs. In 1982, the first successful approval of a recombinant drug was Genentech's human insulin, and approvals for human growth hormone (1985) and alpha interferon (1986) followed, with eventual blockbuster erythropoietin (approved for Amgen) coming a few years later in 1989.

By 1986, an apparently stable compromise about biotechnology's economic logic had emerged. Tests had been established and evidence weighed. High-profile IPOs, licensing deals and drug approvals suggested there was a market for biotechnology. The IP regime had been clarified and safety concerns mitigated. Breakthroughs in the lab and in manufacturability indicated that large-molecule drugs were technically viable. All signs pointed to a burgeoning industry that would yield medically efficacious products to save lives and deliver high investor returns.

Breakdown of the Logic of the First Biotech Era (1987–1989)

If the story ended here, it would provide a rich, if simple, account of an economic logic constructed around a technology rich in entrepreneurial opportunities and institutional uncertainties. Yet, this initial "Genentech" model of biotechnology failed as a commercial project. While over $1.4 billion in funding had been raised in the public markets through IPOs (Lerner & Merges, 1998), investors began to weary of the fading promise of biotech. By 1986, the FDA had approved only six biotechnology drugs (the three mentioned above and another form of alpha interferon, a monoclonal antibody for graft rejection and lastly Recombivax – the hepatitis B vaccine). The industry was failing tests of commercial viability. Stocks "lapsed into a near comatose languor as investors tired of waiting for all the visionary promises to be fulfilled" (Stevens, 1986). The financial markets closed to biotech firms funding only 13 IPOs between 1987 and 1990 compared to 22 in 1986 alone.

How did the compromise, crafted so carefully, fall apart? Howard Greene, former chairman of San Diego-based biotech firm Hybritech (and a prominent venture investor), described the challenge in 1987: "All it took to form a company five or six years ago was finding a Nobel laureate from one of a dozen illustrious universities who was going to spiritually associate with the company. It was assumed that was all it took to succeed. Now people have found out that, like any business, it takes management" (Kraul, 1987). However, more than simply a managerial failure on the part of biotech's early Schumpeterian entrepreneurs, the problem lay in the instability of the evidence across all domains: technical, appropriability, safety, and the market.

Technical evidence suggested that one of the centrepiece drugs in biotechnology, interferon, was not as effective a cancer cure as many had hoped (Panem, 1984). Numerous industry observers and scholars noted the disappointing results. An article in the *British Medical Journal* suggested that the euphoria surrounding interferon as a "miracle cure for cancer was short lived and faded when it seemed that interferon's performance in large scale cancer trials had been disappointing" (Pieters, 1998, p. 1231). Interferon often produced various unwanted side effects in patients (Powledge, 1984). Later research showed that interferon could be incorporated into multi-drug therapeutic regimes for cancer treatment and (in different variants) for hepatitis B and C, multiple sclerosis, and numerous other indications. However, the particular test chosen by these early biotech firms and scientists – single-drug trials – highlighted evidence bolstering safety concerns while failing to provided technical evidence of efficacy.

This was not limited to rDNA products. There was considerable disappointment with monoclonal antibodies (MABs) as well, with firms confronting the rejection by the human immune system of MABs made using mouse genes. Regulatory approval procedures became so formidable that industry analysts called for a national panel to facilitate the process. According to Steve Burrill, a high-profile industry analyst, "The hurdles are placing a burden on biotech companies to the point they could make that world non-economic" (quoted in Kraul, 1987). The FDA countered that while the earliest biotech drugs were recombinant versions of widely understood drugs such as insulin, the recent new drug applications were more complex scientifically, particularly the MABs undergoing clinical trials, and the agency had limited expertise in the area (Gibbons, 1991).

Legal evidence of the appropriability of biological drugs also weakened with Genentech's 1986 announcement that the Hormone Research Foundation and its licensee, Hoffman-La Roche, were suing the firm for patent infringement in recombinant human growth hormone. Amgen entered a series of legal battles with Johnson & Johnson over its Epogen (erythropoietin) patents. This underscored the uncertainty that remained around appropriability and raised legal questions about the viability of the industry. Biotech firms also had to fight renewed challenges by safety-oriented consumer groups, in particular, the Washington-based Foundation on Economic Trends founded by Jeremy Rivkin and by local communities. For example, in California, Advanced Genetic Sciences spent four years clearing legal hurdles and finding a community willing to host its outdoor test of frost-fighting bacteria. Even when a location was approved, opponents tried to prevent the test by destroying thousands of the experimental strawberry plants that served as the material for the bacteria tests during night-time raids (Diringer, 1987). As a result, market evidence continued to weaken – investors were concerned that there was insufficient interest among pharmaceutical firms in licensing biotech's products (Kraul, 1987).

CONSTRUCTING A NEW LOGIC FOR THE SECOND BIOTECH ERA (1990–2001)

Biotech as a Platform for Drug Discovery and Other Applications

In the period 1973–1990, as the biotechnology-as-large-molecule-for-human-therapy trajectory was being pursued, scientists, firms, and universities added numerous tools and techniques to biotechnology's toolkit including polymerase chain reaction to amplify DNA, DNA sequencing technologies to decode DNA, and gene chips to map the patterns of DNA, in particular tissues and other samples. After the breakdown of the economic logic for biotechnology in the late 1980s, profit-seeking Schumpeterian entrepreneurs shifted from thinking of these tools and techniques as mere enablers of biotechnology to positioning them as biotechnology itself. Rather than drugs, biotechnology would be a platform for the discovery of drugs of any kind – both large and small molecule. This approach, while connected to the prior biotechnology activities, required new scientific expertise. This "rational" (grounded in biology) drug discovery stood in stark contrast to the trial-and-error (grounded in repeated chemistry experiments) approach traditionally used by large pharmaceutical firms (Henderson, Orsenigo, & Pisano, 1999).

A few biotech firms – Human Genome Sciences (HGS) and Millennium – came to exemplify the new economic logic in the marketplace. HGS was founded in 1992 by Bill Haseltine, a former scientist at Harvard, and by Craig Venter, formerly a scientist at the NIH. Rather than focus on particular biological drugs, the company based their business on combining a diverse set of biotechnologies. This discovery platform, they argued, could be used to examine precisely the mechanisms of disease taking place in the human body and provide critical information scientists could use to design drugs to block the disease-causing mechanisms. At the core of their platform was the sequencing and collection of large amounts of genetic information, particularly for very small DNA fragments called expressed sequence tags (ESTs) whose patentability would be the source of considerably controversy. When HGS successfully completed its IPO in 1993, it provided a blueprint other start-ups could follow. With a similar logic, a high-profile group of academic scientists (including Eric Lander who was leading part of the Human Genome Project) founded Millennium Pharmaceuticals. While Millennium's specific biotechnologies focused on targeted gene sequencing and the identification of gene function, like HGS, the firm was also an important model that other entrepreneurs followed, especially after completing an extremely successful IPO in 1996. Rather than focusing on single drugs, the new logic allowed firms to combine a collection of diverse biotechnologies to build a drug discovery "platform" – a novel combination of tools and the information essential for the new rational approach to drug discovery. By 1997, these firms captured over 30 percent of the market capitalization in biotechnology (Cohen, 1997).

The first challenge for these start-ups was to generate technical evidence to bolster their claims. They needed to prove that biotech-based drug discovery platforms were more effective than traditional trial-and-error discovery methods that had dominated the pharmaceutical sector. The test was not as clear as going to the FDA and arguing about the design of a clinical trial, as Genentech and others had done in the 1980s. Initially, they focused on scientific publications of results through the academic system of peer review as a source of technical evidence. In the seven years after its founding in 1991, HGS published almost 100 peer-reviewed articles, including some in prestigious journals such as *Nature* and *Science*, coauthored with academic researchers at Johns Hopkins, Harvard, and the University of Michigan. Millennium published over 150 in its first seven years (1993–1999) again collaborating closely with academics, mainly at Harvard and the Harvard Medical School. Like their predecessors, this generation of biotech firm founders established high-profile scientific advisory boards made up of well-regarded academics (Ding, Murray, & Stuart, 2006; Stuart & Ding, 2006). However, these relationships were more likely to focus on testing out specific platform technologies and exploring newly identified drug targets than on the joint development of manufacturing expertise or specific therapeutic drugs that had characterized Genentech and the other early firms.

If genetic analysis and discovery tools were to become central to biotech's newly constructed economic logic of drug discovery, evidence of appropriability would be essential. Patents on biological molecules themselves such as recombinant insulin were not enough. The new platform companies were not constructed to discover these new molecules. Instead, they provided critical knowledge that served as an input into the discovery process. The question was what evidence would convince investors that they could appropriate value? Established patent law covered some aspects of the new discovery platforms because they were new techniques to "probe" the genome – equipment, reagents, processes, and so on. However, many entrepreneurs wanted to sell the information they discovered. Most of this was information about gene sequences and a complex legal debate followed over the validity of patenting the "code of life." Reminiscent of the debates in the 1970s over rDNA patents, lawyers, entrepreneurs, and ethicists argued for different tests of patentability and provided different evidence to bolster their claims. Craig Venter initiated this debate while still a scientist at the NIH, when, together with NIH Director Bernadine Healy, he filed patent applications on DNA fragments discovered as part of the Human Genome Project.

The core controversy of the 1991 filing was the possibility of patenting small pieces of DNA – DNA fragments of a gene whose function was not yet determined, having no link to a specific disease and only speculative utility. The NIH patents contained hundreds of gene fragments but disclosed only a narrow understanding of their utility; no one was sure of the ways in which these fragments could be useful, and therefore, the patents typically speculated about their use in various experiments rather than in their therapeutic application (Holman & Munzer, 2000). Although scientists had provided evidence in favor of patenting in the earlier *Diamond v. Chakrabarty* case (in their *Amicus* briefs), this time, scientists had a wide variety of reasons to argue against it.

Academic geneticists, who had often spent their entire careers (at the NIH and elsewhere) exploring a single gene and its role in disease, wanted the tests of value to be based on the impact of patents on scientific life, suggesting that DNA patents would allow corporations to control a priceless resource (Nash, 2000). They also framed the argument in terms of fairness and the appropriate use of patents as a reward. Their argument was exemplified by a patent filed by HGS on a gene called *CCR5*. At the time of filing, the firm had no idea of its role in disease. By the time of patent grant, Robert Gallo, a leading researcher in the field, and his team had discovered that *CCR5* was critical for HIV and the HGS share price jumped 21 percent. HGS could directly benefit from the discoveries of others. In response, Gallo was quoted in *Science*: "As a society, we have to ask if it's fair to give the main commercial prize to the company that simply sequences a gene rather than to those who do the hard work of figuring out its biological function" (Marshall, 2000b, p. 1375).

Other scientists including James Watson, who was leading the Human Genome Project, and his UK counterpart, John Sulston, argued that this type of patenting would stifle the international collaboration that characterised the Human Genome Project and lead to a patent war among research institutions. Watson argued that the idea of patenting small gene fragments was "sheer lunacy" (cited in Kevles & Berkowitz, 2001, p. 237; Roberts, 1991, p. 184). Their fear was realized in June 1992 when the British government's Medical Research Council filed its own patent applications for 1,000 partial human gene sequences (Veggeberg, 1992). Unlike the *Diamond v. Chakrabarty* case, the gene patenting debate did not play out in front of the Supreme Court as it was not framed around a single patent. Instead, the scientific press (mainly the editorial pages of *Science* and *Nature*), as well as the mass media, gave widespread coverage.

This was followed by various Congressional hearings. Public interest groups, including ethicists and activists such as Jeremy Rifkin, again objected to gene patents but argued for a moral test rather than a utilitarian one: genes should be seen as a sacred code – the blueprint of life (Kevles & Berkowitz, 2001). While a gene patent did not equate to the ownership of a person, the very notion of property rights on a human gene violated human dignity. Other vocal opponents included representatives of disease foundations whose funding went toward solving complex and life-threatening diseases. They argued that gene patents would increase the price of genetic tests to diagnose life-threatening diseases (Merz, 1999). Moreover, they argued, patients with breast cancer, Canavan disease, and PXE disease whose genes formed the basis for gene patents should, they contended, have a right to the research results. These patients spoke out vocally at Congressional hearings (Merz, 1999; Anonymous, 1996).

Biotechnology and pharmaceutical firms were divided in their view of the value of gene sequence patents. In Congressional hearings, press statements and at the NAS, the newer start-ups, such as HGS, pointed to the extensive investments in new biological drugs enabled by strong patent rights on human genes of therapeutic importance. The Association of Biotechnology Companies endorsed EST patents (Eisenberg, 1992). However, the more established biotechnology firms, those that survived from the first biotechnology era, worried that strong patent claims on gene fragments would crowd the patent landscape for their research and make it more difficult for them to make money on biological drugs. Their position was represented by the Industrial Biotechnology Association that argued that while a company might be willing to pay a single licensing fee to access to a full gene for drug development, they were reluctant to sign multiple licenses on a plethora of gene fragments that happened to map to a gene that they had discovered through long and costly R&D (Henry, Cho, Weaver, & Merz, 2002).

Nevertheless, by 1997, the USPTO had issued over 400 human gene sequence patents providing evidence for appropriability of gene sequences and some DNA fragments (Jensen and Murray, 2005). Under continued pressure, the USPTO continued to seek guidance on this issue, inviting comment on its newly proposed utility guidelines for gene patenting. Corporations again expressed concern that if gene fragment patents constituted sufficient prior art, patents on complete genes would be precluded, thus undermining their claims on certain appropriability (U.S. Patent and Trademark Office, 1999). This time the USPTO changed its position and, in 2001, published new utility guidelines that required inventors to identify a specific gene target, the biological reaction involving a specific protein and a real world use linked to a disease (Duke Law & Technology Review, 2001).

The challenge for establishing the value of this new economic logic would not be the same as in the earlier biotechnology era. For one, it was not necessary to generate new regulatory evidence. Conceived as providing new ways of discovering drugs, these firms did not create any new safety concerns, nor did they have to worry about working to create new FDA approval standards. Existing tests for the safety and efficacy remained salient. Instead, entrepreneurs quickly had to contend with new questions about information privacy, and the possibility of genetic discrimination. In the late 1980s, the government sought to include studies of ethical, legal, and social issues (ELSI) in all areas of genetics and genetic information. Entrepreneurs such as Millennium cofounder Steve Holtzman played an active role in shaping discussions of the appropriate tests and evidence for the use of clinical genetic information in research (Office of Technology Assessment (U.S. Congress), 1991), in the criminal justice system (National Research Council 1992; Office of Technology Assessment (U.S. Congress), 1990) and in diagnostic genetic testing (Holtzman, 1989).

In 1991, the Government Operations subcommittee on government information held two hearings on legislation proposed to protect the privacy of genetic information. According to Congressman Robert E. Wise (D-West Virginia), chairman of the subcommittee, "One of the most serious and most immediate concerns is that genetic information may be used to create a new genetic underclass ... People may be unable to obtain jobs and insurance, or participate in other routine activities, because of the stigma of having an undesirable gene" (quoted in Breeder, 1991). The privacy of genetic information was also considered by the California legislature, which passed a bill prohibiting genetic discrimination by employers or insurers (California Government Code: §§12926, 12926.1 (2001), 1998), a requirement that extended not only to genetic testing but also to the use of family histories (Nedelcu et al., 2004). The emergence of these concerns pointed out that, even as some evidence might be stabilized, new vectors of concern could be opened (in this case privacy) and had to be confronted.

The question remained whether pharmaceutical firms, the target customer for these new platform-based biotechnology firms, would pay a substantial price for drug discovery services. It was increasingly recognized that large pharmaceutical firms were experiencing a problem with R&D productivity. The number of new drug approvals was stable while spending on drug development continued to rise (DiMasi, 2001). Patent expirations on blockbuster products would leave the pharma companies searching for new product opportunities that might be filled by new biotech discovery techniques (Teitelman & Coletti, 1989). This left pharmaceutical companies with underused sales capacity and declining profits.

To translate this crisis into demand for their services, new biotechnology start-ups had to find established pharmaceutical companies willing to pay for their drug discovery tools. Just as Genentech's deal with Eli Lilly provided critical market evidence for biotech firms in the first biotechnology era, in this era, it was a $125 million HGS deal with SmithKline Beecham to provide access to HGS's database of genetic codes that validated this new model. HGS CEO Bill Haseltine took credit for creating the market evidence needed (quoted in Edwards & Hamilton, 1998):

> This is the deal that changed everything. It was the shot, the deal that has transformed the life sciences. Now, you see a shift away from an industry based on chemistry to an industry based on genes ... What we did – me personally – I was the first one to realize the practical application of this new gene discovery.

The deal established the value of information about genes for drug discovery. Haseltine argued that "The value is now from the ability to work with genes" (quoted in Edwards & Hamilton, 1998). This was followed with similar deals such as Millennium's 1998 agreement with Bayer to provide access to over 200 new drug targets over a five-year period. In 1997, Monsanto paid Millennium over $200 million for access to its suite of genomic technologies. Through the joint venture, Millennium would apply their expertise to help Monsanto to apply genomics to agribusiness.

These deals, following on the heels of successful IPOs by HGS (1993) and Millennium (1996), secured vital market evidence for the economic logic of platform-based discovery. Entrepreneurs also used the achievement of milestones in alliance relationships to provide evidence that their technology was validated by thorough scientifically trained experts with full access to the scientific details. Firms publicized successes in hitting milestones. For example, in April 1996, HGS announced that it had achieved the first milestone in its collaboration with Pioneer Hi Bred and received a milestone payment. The press released noted that "This first milestone was the successful installation and testing of HGS proprietary bioinformatics software at Pioneer. This will allow Pioneer to analyze the corn cDNA sequence information being compiled by HGS as a part of the collaboration" (Human Genome Sciences, 1996). Like Swanson before, Haseltine and Millennium CEO Mark Levin were self-conscious in their desire to set a standard and gain legitimacy for their particular economic logic. Industry observers, such as the press, recognized the role of these entrepreneurs in the success and failure of commercial biotech, describing how [HGS's] "media-savvy chairman, William Haseltine, has become a poster boy for the entire genomics industry" (Red Herring, 2001). Alan Walton, a venture capitalist with Oxford Bioscience Partners in Boston and a founding investor with HGS, was also clear about the role HGS and others played in shaping the logic of the entire sector: "If HGS's first drugs should fail, the public, and certainly Wall Street, will say, 'See, all this excitement about genomics has led nowhere' " (quoted in Stipp, 2001).

BREAKDOWN AND RECONSTRUCTION OF THE BIOTECHNOLOGY ECONOMIC LOGIC IN THE 2000S

Biotech Firms Discover Drugs for Specific Diseases in Partnership with Big Pharma

The constellation of evidence lashed up by various types of entrepreneurs in the 1990s did indeed begin to collapse as the high-tech bubble burst in 2001–2002. Public funds for investing in all technological sectors, including biotechnology, diminished dramatically. With no foreseeable market payouts, venture capital investing also dried up. At the same time, an announcement by Britain's Prime Minister Tony Blair and U.S. President Bill Clinton on the appropriability of the human genome invalidated a critical piece of evidence supporting the economic logic of biotechnology in the 1990s. The two leaders declared that the sequence of the human genome "should be made freely available to scientists everywhere" (quoted in Berenson & Wade, 2000). Many biotech firms including HGS and Incyte lost more than 20 percent of their value in one day (Marshall, 2000a). Soon after, the USPTO finalized a fairly restrictive set of guidelines for gene patents. They required that a human DNA patent must be specific and must identify a gene target, specify the biological reaction involving a specific protein, and have a real world use linked to a disease (Duke Law & Technology Review, 2001).

These two events undermined much of the evidence for appropriability of gene sequences. On the regulatory side, patient advocates who had earlier spoken out against ownership of genes became more vocal. In his presidential address to the American College of Medical Genetics, Dr. Edward McCabe described the challenges of gene patenting and for-profit use of genetics and genomics more broadly. He cited a pending lawsuit brought by the parents of children with Canavan disease against Miami Children's Hospital. Having provided samples for the development of a diagnostic test, the families claimed the lack of access and high test price to be inappropriate. The Pseudozanthoma Elasticum (PXE) Foundation for children with this disease took the more dramatic measure of seeking patent rights on a test developed using their samples. The value of genomics and the complex of technologies, data and samples upon which it was constructed, was again subject to debate and discussion that as the title of McCabe's address aptly described, mixed "compassion, access, science and advocacy" (McCabe, 2001).

These events made a broad platform approach infeasible and forced firms to focus on specific disease targets. Some firms such as HGS developed a portfolio of protein and MAB drug candidates that are under clinical development for use in large markets including immunology, infectious disease, and oncology. Part of their approach was to promote their own internal candidates. On the other hand, they also made acquisitions including buying Principia Pharmaceuticals – a company whose technology for protein stability allowed HGS to develop more stable versions of existing protein drugs. Others, such as Millennium, took the significant cash reserves amassed in the technology bubble and acquired companies for their drug project portfolios. The firm acquired COR Therapeutics for over $2 billion to gain access to the revenues from their approved cardiovascular drug. They also made acquisitions in oncology. Others such as Incyte chose to continue selling genomic information but also narrowed the applications of their discovery platforms to focus on one or a few diseases. In Incyte's case, the program they selected was a small-molecule program in inflammation initiated through the acquisition of Maxia.

Because of questions about appropriability (patents would provide protection for drug molecules but not genes sequences), doing licensing or other deals in the early phases of research was no longer practicable. As a result, biotechnology firms had to acquire more expertise in the downstream analysis and testing of drugs – proteins, MABs, and small molecules – (a capability they had previously relied on their large pharmaceutical firm partners to provide). While this did not replace their academic licensing, sponsored research, and partnership activities, it did refocus their activities towards the clinic. This enabled deals to be struck in later phases where biotechnology start-ups and pharmaceutical firms could collaborate on moving drugs into clinical trials. These drugs could then move through now well-established procedures for toxicity studies, animal tests, and later clinical evidence from tests on humans.

After the downturn in 2000, the next few years were full of turmoil as firms once again sought to redefine a sustainable logic for biotech through widespread acquisitions, strategic changes, and mergers. Through the middle of 2003, the IPO market remained almost closed with only 10 percent of the industry's funding coming from public markets. Many IPOs were shelved including those of Medarex, Scios, and Xoma. Overall equity into biotech dropped dramatically from almost $12 billion in the first quarter of 2000 to only $2.2 billion in the first quarter of 2001.

In the later part of 2003, the IPO window reopened. No specific event precipitated this resolution. What was distinctive, and reflective of the redefinition of value that took place well beyond the existing cash rich biotech firms, was that 33 of the 38 companies that went public from September 2003 to the end of 2004 had products in clinical development compared to only 28 percent of the IPOs in the 1999–2000 "bubble" (Van Brunt, 2005). This rewarded the logic of the genomics-based technology platform. By highlighting the market for unmet medical needs and focusing on drugs (of all types) to solve those needs, it seemed that biotech's economic logic was resolved again. It was clearly elaborated but flexible enough to accommodate a wide range of underlying science to discover and validate new drugs.

The model that emerged in the 2000s is one in which biotech firms, whose core technologies came either from academia or from established firms, raised substantial early-stage investment from venture capitalists. As they developed their biotechnologies in pursuit of novel drugs (proteins, MABs, small molecules and today even RNAi, gene therapy, antisense, etc.), they sought partnerships with big pharma to share in the costs, risks, and benefits of drug development. Conversely, big pharma relied on biotech firms to explore risky new drug discovery approaches and targets and to find the most interesting technologies emerging from universities. "Biotechnology" has therefore come to mean a certain way of organizing drug research and development. Biotech is less about specific, narrowly defined biotechnologies per se, and more about an organizational form and its associated economic logic. The stability of this compromise over time will depend on the degree to which the links between this set of tests and evidence are durable, uncontested, and maintained over time.

DISCUSSION AND CONCLUSION

In our analysis of the evolution of biotechnology, we take a conventionalist lens to focus on the value associated with biotechnology in the marketplace over a 30-year period; how it was defined, changed, and stabilized. We show that what biotechnology was understood to be and how it was seen to create value changed dramatically over the course of the first 30 years of the industry. While initially hailed as an exciting biological technique that could be used in wide ranging applications, it was quickly defined as a means to discover and produce large-molecule protein drugs. Only after 30 years did entrepreneurs, executives, investors, academics, and even social activists come to regard biotechnology as a widely encompassing set of technologies used for more effectively discovering and developing a plethora of therapeutic drugs – large molecule and small. With this stable definition of value came a clearly delineated industrial field, constituted through a complex network of interactions between dedicated biotech firms, large pharmaceutical firms, venture capital, capital markets, universities, and lawyers.

Biotechnology's path was not inevitable; many untrodden paths might have been taken. Had uncertainties been resolved in different ways, by different actors, with different evidence of what could be of value, the trajectory biotechnology took would have been different. We contend that it is through entrepreneurial efforts by multiple actors that the particular path was constructed. Entrepreneurs mobilized a wide range of evidence, established tests that matched their evidence and attempted to influence the interpretation of evidence provided by others. The outcomes of their efforts shaped the direction that biotechnology took – as a technology and as a field within the marketplace instantiated in specific organizations and institutions. The economic logic for biotechnology in the marketplace was the one that sustained a particular set of justifications for at least a period and ultimately came to stabilize a particular organizational form. This perspective has broad implications for our understanding of technical change and value construction and of the role of entrepreneurial actors in these processes.

The study of technical change has evolved over the years from one that portrayed technology as an exogenous shock to one that has acknowledged the social forces at play. Research has shown that the evolution of a technology is not simply the inevitable result of "normal problem solving" (Dosi, 1982, p. 152) but rather socially and organizationally constructed (Bijker, Hughes, & Pinch, 1987). Furthermore, recent models suggest that this social construction involves the interpretive processes of multiple actors in scientific, governmental, commercial, and other spheres of action (Garud & Rappa, 1994; Kaplan & Tripsas, 2008; Lounsbury et al., 2003). These models suggest that different actors bring different interests, different perspectives, and different experiences to the table as they interpret a technology, make choices, and act. Because actors may conflict, they engage in contests to get their own interpretation to predominate (Kaplan, 2008). By using conventionalist theory as a lens for exploring this process, we show that the struggle over interpretations is not just about the technology itself but also about what value(s) should be attached to it. Constructing a technology thus is also about constructing the economic logic that underpins it.

This perspective also suggests that various institutions are both actors and arenas in these struggles (Kaplan & Tripsas, 2008; Kaplan & Radin, 2010). They can be sources of uncertainty (as when regulators are unclear about standards or activist groups challenge existing rules) and also decision-makers who resolve uncertainties and in doing so provide evidence for one particular economic logic over others (as when the Supreme Court validates a patent). Rather than privileging one type of institution, such as regulators (Schneiberg & Soule, 2005) or social activists (Lounsbury & Ventresca, 2002; Weber, Thomas, & Rao, 2009), we raise the possibility that multiple institutions play a role in technical change. In particular, we include the previously overlooked role of legal institutions in shaping technical change. Typically considered an immutable element of the institutional setup (Teece, 1986), the contestation of patent rights in the courts and in government agencies highlights the flexibility of the legal framework and its potential to be constructed as technology is constructed (Murray & Stern, 2008). This highlights the ways in which the field and its institutional setup coevolves with the construction of the technology.

We find that, in the case of biotechnology, the entrepreneurial actor plays a critical role in this construction. From this, we can make three contributions to the understanding of entrepreneurs and entrepreneurship. First, Schumpeterian entrepreneurs do not simply identify opportunities that exist "out there," start up new companies, or seek venture capital (Shane, 2000). Nor do they merely mould their technology to the institutional setup (Hargadon & Douglas, 2001). Entrepreneurs construct the very landscape in which they operate. This is not just the social construction of technology but also the social construction of the economic, and therefore of the organizations and institutions that instantiate a particular economic logic. As a result, Schumpeterian entrepreneurs are also institutional entrepreneurs (Fligstein, 2001; Santos & Eisenhardt, 2009) who, through their actions, shape the whole set of conventions that will govern value and exchange in a particular sphere of action. They break from existing conventions with the goal of finding new ways to create and justify value.

Second, the central job for the entrepreneur, if one takes the conventionalist lens, is not only to build an organization but also to identify, establish, or challenge particular tests of value and mobilize or dispute evidence that would justify value according to these tests. They can use different means to generate evidence: obtaining funding, applying for or litigating a patent, launching a product, securing favorable regulations, or establishing deal terms with partners. The organization is, therefore, not only the product of their efforts but also part of the process for justifying an economic logic. Success in building an organization (as validated by obtaining patents, getting FDA drug approvals, achieving milestones in alliances, doing licensing deals, or conducting a successful IPO) becomes evidence of the validity of a particular approach. It also plays a central role in establishing the categories that investors use in the evaluation of firms (Zuckerman, 1999). As a result, what is of value becomes endogenized in the actual process of entrepreneurship (Garud & Karnøe, 2001). As definitions of value are resolved, the categories that shape financial markets also emerge endogenously, highlighting the critical role of entrepreneurs in enabling commensuration, investment and valuation (Espeland & Stevens, 1998; Zuckerman, 2004).

Third, Schumpeterian entrepreneurs are not the only entrepreneurial actors who attempt to shape the economic logic of a technology. Our analysis of the biotechnology story places many institutional entrepreneurs in sharp relief – scientists, city governments, regulatory agencies, lawyers, judges, and so on – who contributed to the establishment of justifications of particular economic logics. These other entrepreneurs operated alongside Schumpeterian entrepreneurs in influencing the evolution of a technological field. We should think of these entrepreneurial actors then, not just as the mythical heros of start-up ventures but also as the executives of established firms seeking to profit from a new technology, civil servants in governmental agencies seeking to prevent risks, judges interpreting patent law, and activists giving expression to their social conscience. Each of these actors employ different strategies of entrepreneurial action (Baum & McGahan, 2009).

From this portrayal, we conclude that constructing a technology is deeply intertwined with the construction of organizations and of the institutions that will govern their operation. Conventionalist theory provides the micro-level underpinnings to the macro-level phenomena in the field (Biggart & Beamish, 2003). It gives us a conceptual apparatus for exploring the micro-level processes by which new technologies emerge and find a market, how the practices in those markets get institutionalized (Fligstein & Dauter, 2007; Baum & McGahan, 2009). By suggesting that technologies are economic constructions shaped by the on-the-ground actions of entrepreneurial actors battling to get a particular economic logic to predominate, we highlight the emergent nature of coordination in markets (Latsis, 2006), and we show how institutions get created and changed in addition to how they eventually become congealed (Lounsbury & Crumley, 2007). Reciprocally, we show that an economic logic breaks down if it does not sustain a set of justifications. Stabilized economic logics may only be "provisional settlements" (Girard & Stark, 2002; Kaplan & Orlikowski, 2009) that are specific to a certain place and time. This analysis shows that the development of technologies and organizations, as well as the institutions in which they are embedded, are intimately intertwined and highlights the immense entrepreneurial effort required to construct the economic that shapes their emergence.

As this chapter is part of a volume devoted to the impact of Joan Woodward's work, we want to point out how our conventionalist understanding of technology commercialization and valuation has its roots in her concerns with the relationship between new technologies and organizations (Woodward, 1958). Woodward proposed a contingent view in which different technologies require different kinds of organizational configurations. Her work was an important advancement of a field previously based on the idea that these factors were not causally related and was foundational for contingency theory and theories about the management of technology. She left open for future scholars questions about how the match between new technologies and organizations might emerge. In our study of biotechnology, we show how entrepreneurial actors of all types construct this match as they search for economic logics that can be supported over time by particular justifications. We also show that these matches are not stable but subject to breakdowns if new sets of actors mobilize evidence to justify alternative economic logics. Thus, we argue that technologies, organizations, and economic logics coevolve as entrepreneurial actors engage in contests over what is economic about technology.

NOTES

1. This discussion of the economies of convention is also deeply influenced by David Stark's work including Stark (2000), Girard and Stark (2002), and Beunza and Stark (2004) as well as the opportunity to read the manuscript from his book before it was published by Princeton University Press (Stark, 2009).

2. Occurring in parallel was the application of recombinant DNA and other techniques in other fields such as agriculture. Because the industry and market dynamics were quite different in these other contexts, we chose to examine the trajectory of development in human therapeutics only. This allows us to constrain our discussion to a particular set of institutions and actors.

3. The commercialization of monoclonal antibodies follows a similar path to rDNA with many of the same uncertainties. An important part of the immune system, experiments undertaken at the Medical Research Council laboratories in Cambridge, England, in the mid-1970s by Kohler and Milstein (1975) were part of on-going research on the immune system that continued the academic agenda of immunology. Like rDNA, this research showed significant potential for commercial application. The first commercial step was taken in San Diego by Hybritech.

4. Note that these attempts to establish viability often came into conflict as Genentech also licensed out the associated patents and was found by courts in 2002 to have concealed this information. The Los Angeles Superior Court awarded the City of Hope National Medical Center over $500 million to compensate for losses associated with this collaboration (Hamilton, 2002).

ACKNOWLEDGMENTS

The authors would like to thank Dorothy Griffiths, Michael Lounsbury, Anita McGahan, Nelson Phillips, Graham Sewell, Mary Tripsas, the slump_management research group and participants in the Society for the

Social Studies of Science Annual Conference, and the Joan Woodward Memorial Conference at Imperial College for helpful comments on earlier drafts of this paper. All errors or omissions remain our own.

REFERENCES

Anonymous. (1996). US coalition counters breast gene patents. *Nature*, *381*, 265.

Baum, J. A. C., & McGahan, A. M. (2009). *The reorganization of legitimate violence: Private military companies in the post-cold war era*. Working Paper.

Becker, H. S. (1963). *Outsiders; studies in the sociology of deviance*. London: Free Press of Glencoe.

Berenson, A., & Wade, N. (2000). A call for sharing of research causes gene stocks to plunge. *New York Times*, March 15, pp. A1, C16.

Beunza, D., & Stark, D. (2004). Tools of the trade: The socio-technology of arbitrage in a Wall Street trading room. *Industrial and Corporate Change*, *13*, 369–400.

Biagioli, M. (2000). Replication or monopoly? The economies of invention and discovery in Galileo's observations of 1610. *Science in Context*, *13*, 547–590.

Biggart, N. W., & Beamish, T. D. (2003). The economic sociology of conventions: Habit, custom, practice, and routine in market order. *Annual Review of Sociology*, *29*, 443–464.

Bijker, W. E., Hughes, T. P., & Pinch, T. J. (1987). *The social construction of technological systems: New directions in the sociology and history of technology*. Cambridge, MA: MIT Press.

Biotechnology Industry Organization. (2008). Biotechnology industry facts. Available at http://www.bio.org/speeches/pubs/er/statistics.asp

Boltanski, L., & Thévenot, L. (1999). The sociology of critical capacity. *European Journal of Social Theory*, *2*, 359–377.

Boltanski, L., & Thévenot, L. (2006). *On justification: Economies of worth* (Published in 1991 in French as *De la justification: les economies de la grandeur*. Paris: Gallimard). Princeton, NJ: Princeton University Press.

Breeder, D. C. (1991). Congress studies issue of genetic privacy. *The Omaha World-Herald Sunrise*, pp. 5A, Col. 3.

Callon, M., & Muniesa, F. (2005). Economic markets as calculative collective devices. *Organization Studies*, *26*, 1229–1250.

Carmen, I. H. (1985). *Cloning and the constitution: An inquiry into governmental policymaking and genetic experimentation*. Madison: University of Wisconsin Press.

Cello, L. M., & Olsen, W. L. (1984). Method for transforming plant cells. US Patent Number 4459355-A. Int Paper Co.

Chakrabarty, A. M. (1974). Microorganisms having multiple compatible degradative energy-generation plasmids and preparations thereof. US Patent Number 3813316. General Electric Company.

Chakrabarty, A. M. (1981). Microorganisms having multiple compatible degradative energy-generating plasmids and preparation thereof. US Patent Number 4259444. General Electric Co.

Chowdhury, S. (2002). Engineering life. *The Hindu*, December 04, accessed at www.hinduonnet.com

Cockburn, I., & Griliches, Z. (1988). Industry effects and appropriability measures in the stock market's valuation of R&D and patents. *The American Economic Review*, *78*(2), 419–423.

Cohen, J. (1997). The genomics gamble. *Science*, *275*, 767–772.

Cohen, S., Chang, A., Boyer, H., & Helling, R. (1973). Construction of biologically functional bacterial plasmids in vitro. *Proceedings of the National Academy of Sciences of the United States*, *70*, 3240–3244.

David, P. A. (2003). The economic logic of "open science" and the balance between private property rights and the public domain in scientific data and information: A primer. In: *The role of the public domain in scientific and technical data and information*. Washington, DC: National Academies Press.

DiMaggio, P. J. (1997). Culture and cognition. *Annual Review of Sociology*, *23*, 263–287.

DiMasi, J. A. (2001). Risks in new drug development: Approval success rates for investigational drugs. *Clinical Pharmacology & Therapeutics*, *69*, 297–307.

Ding, W. W., Murray, F., & Stuart, T. E. (2006). Gender differences in patenting in the academic life sciences. *Science*, *313*, 665–667.

Diringer, E. (1987). Scientific optimism vs. a skeptical public. *The San Francisco Chronicle*, April 30.

Dosi, G. (1982). Technological paradigms and technological trajectories: A suggested interpretation of the determinants and directions of technical change. *Research Policy*, *11*, 147–162.

Duke Law & Technology Review. (2001). *The fate of gene patents under the new utility guidelines*. Vol. 008, February 28, 2001.

Van Brunt, J. (2003). The year of the bear. *Signals Magazine*, January 24, accessed at www.signalsmag.com

Edwards, M., & Hamilton, J. O'C. (1998). Ten deals that changed biotech. *Signals Magazine*, November 17.

Eisenberg, R. S. (1992). Genes, patents, and product development. *Science*, *257*, 903–908.

Epstein, S. (2007). *Inclusion: The politics of difference in medical research*. Chicago: University of Chicago Press.

Espeland, W. N., & Stevens, M. L. (1998). Commensuration as a social process. *Annual Review of Sociology*, *24*, 313–343.

Fligstein, N. (2001). Social skill and the theory of fields. *Sociological Theory*, *19*, 105–125.

Fligstein, N., & Dauter, L. (2007). The sociology of markets. *Annual Review of Sociology*, *33*, 105–128.

Friedland, R., & Alford, R. R. (1991). Bringing society back in: Symbols, practices, and institutional contradictions. In: W. W. Powell & P. DiMaggio (Eds), *The new institutionalism in organizational analysis* (pp. 232–266). Chicago: University of Chicago Press.

Gans, J. S., & Stern, S. (2000). Incumbency and R&D incentives: Licensing the gale of creative destruction. *Journal of Economics and Management Strategy*, *9*, 485–511.

Garud, R., Hardy, C., & Maguire, S. (2007). Institutional entrepreneurship as embedded agency: An introduction to the special issue. *Organization Studies*, *28*, 957–969.

Garud, R., Jain, S., & Kumaraswamy, A. (2002). Institutional entrepreneurship in the sponsorship of common technological standards: The case of Sun Microsystems and Java. *Academy of Management Journal*, *45*(1), 196–214.

Garud, R., & Karnøe, P. (2001). In: *Path dependence and creation* (pp. 1–38). Mahwah, NJ: Lawrence Erlbaum Associates.

Garud, R., & Rappa, M. A. (1994). A socio-cognitive model of technology evolution: The case of cochlear implants. *Organization Science*, *5*, 344–362.

Genentech. (1978). *First successful laboratory production of human insulin announced.* Company press release, September 6.

Genentech. (1980). *Supreme court decision will spur genetics industry*. Company press release, January 1.

Gibbons, A. (1991). Biotech pipeline-bottleneck ahead. *Science*, *254*, 369–370.

Giddens, A. (1984). *The constitution of society: Outline of the theory of structuration.* Berkeley: University of California Press.

Girard, M., & Stark, D. (2002). Distributing intelligence and organizing diversity in new-media projects. *Environment and Planning A*, *34*, 1927–1949.

Hamilton, D. P. (2002). *Genentech faces $500 million charge after large punitive-damage award. Wall Street Journal*, June 25, p. 4.

Hargadon, A. B., & Douglas, Y. (2001). When innovations meet institutions: Edison and the design of the electric light. *Administrative Science Quarterly*, *46*(3), 476–501.

Henderson, R. M., Orsenigo, L., & Pisano, G. (1999). The pharmaceutical industry and the revolution in molecular biology: Interactions among scientific, institutional and organizational change. In: D. C. Mowery & R. R. Nelson (Eds), *Sources of industrial leadership: Studies in seven industries* (pp. 267–311). Cambridge: Cambridge University Press.

Henry, M. R., Cho, M. K., Weaver, M. A., & Merz, J. F. (2002). Genetics: DNA patenting and licensing. *Science*, *297*, 1279.

Holman, M. A., & Munzer, S. R. (2000). Intellectual property rights in genes and gene fragments: A registration solution for expressed sequence tags. *Iowa Law Review*, *85*, 735–848.

Holtzman, N. A. (1989). *Proceed with caution: Predicting genetic risks in the recombinant DNA era*. Baltimore: Johns Hopkins University Press.

Hughes, S. S. (2001). Making dollars out of DNA – The first major patent in biotechnology and the commercialization of molecular biology, 1974–1980. *Isis*, *92*, 541–575.

Human Genome Sciences. (1996). *Human genome sciences achieves milestone in pioneer hi-bred collaboration*. Company press release, April 9.

Jensen, K., & Murray, F. (2005). Intellectual property landscape of the human genome. *Science*, *310*(5746), 239–240.

Judson, H. F. (1979). *The eighth day of creation: Makers of the revolution in biology*. New York: Simon and Schuster.

Kaplan, S. (2008). Framing contests: Making strategy under uncertainty. *Organization Science*, *19*(5), 729–752.

Kaplan, S., Murray, F., & Henderson, R. M. (2003). Discontinuities and senior management: Assessing the role of recognition in pharmaceutical firm response to biotechnology. *Industrial and Corporate Change*, *12*, 203–233.

Kaplan, S., & Orlikowski, W. (2009). *The temporality of strategy making*. Working Paper.

Kaplan, S., & Radin, J. (2010). *Bounding an emerging technology: Deconstructing the Drexler-Smalley Debate about Nanotech.* Rotman School of Management Working Paper.

Kaplan, S., & Tripsas, M. (2008). Thinking about technology: Applying a cognitive lens to technical change. *Research Policy*, *37*, 790–805.

Kenney, M. (1986). *Biotechnology: The university-industrial complex.* New Haven: Yale University Press.

Kevles, D., & Berkowitz, A. (2001). The gene patenting controversy. *Brooklyn Law Review*, *67*, 233–248.

Kevles, D. J., & Hood, L. E. (1992). *The code of codes: Scientific and social issues in the Human Genome Project*. Cambridge, MA: Harvard University Press.

Knight, F. H. (1921/1965). *Risk, uncertainty and profit* (first published in 1921 Hart, Schaffner & Marx). New York: Harper & Row.

Kohler, G., & Milstein, C. (1975). Continuous cultures of fused cells secreting antibody of predefined specificity. *Nature*, *256*, 495–497.

Kornberg, A. (1995). *The golden helix: Inside biotech ventures*. Sausalito, CA: University Science Books.

Kraul, C. (1987). Biotech companies seeking capital have roller coaster year. *The San Diego Union-Tribune*, January 26, p. 41.

Ku, K. (1983). Licensing DNA cloning technology. *Les Nouvelles*, *18*, 112–115.

Latour, B., & Woolgar, S. (1979). *Laboratory life: The construction of scientific facts*. Princeton, NJ: Princeton University Press.

Latsis, J. (2006). Convention and intersubjectivity: New developments in French economics. *Journal for the Theory of Social Behaviour*, *36*, 255–277.

Lederberg, J. (1975). DNA splicing: Will fear rob us of its benefits? *Prism*, *3*, 33–37.

Legras, J. L., Merdinoglu, D., Cornuet, J. M., & Karst, F. (2007). Bread, beer and wine: *Saccharomyces cerevisiae* diversity reflects human history. *Molecular Ecology*, *16*, 2091–2102.

Lerner, J. (1992). *ImmuLogic pharmaceutical corporation*. Harvard Business School Case Study no. 9-293-066 through 9-293-071.

Lerner, J., & Merges, R. P. (1998). The control of technology alliances: An empirical analysis of the biotechnology industry. *Journal of Industrial Economics*, *46*, 125–156.

Levin, R. C., Klevorick, A. K., Nelson, R. R., & Winter, S. G. (1987). Appropriating the returns from industrial research and development; comments and discussion. *Brookings Papers on Economic Activity*, *3*, 783–831.

Lounsbury, M. (2007). A tale of two cities: Competing logics and practice variation in the professionalizing of mutual funds. *Academy of Management Journal*, *50*, 289–307.

Lounsbury, M., & Crumley, E. T. (2007). New practice creation: An institutional perspective on innovation. *Organization Studies*, *28*, 993–1012.

Lounsbury, M., & Glynn, M. A. (2001). Cultural entrepreneurship: Stories, legitimacy, and the acquisitions of resources. *Strategic Management Journal*, *22*, 545–564.

Lounsbury, M., & Ventresca, M. J. (2002). Social structure and organizations revisited. *Research in the Sociology of Organizations*, *19*, 3–36.

Lounsbury, M., Ventresca, M. J., & Hirsch, P. M. (2003). Social movements, field frames and industry emergence: A cultural-political perspective on US recycling. *Socio-Economic Review*, *1*, 71–104.

Lyon & Lyon. (1979). Amicus brief in *diamond v. Chakrabarty 79–136* on Behalf of Genentech, Inc., Amicus Curiae Counsel to Amicus Curiae Genentech, Inc.

Marshall, E. (2000a). Clinton and Blair back rapid release of data. *Science*, *287*(March), 1903.

Marshall, E. (2000b). Gene patents: Patent on HIV receptor provokes an outcry. *Science*, *287*, 1375–1377.

McCabe, E. R. B. (2001). Clinical genetics: Compassion, access, science, and advocacy. *Genetics in Medicine*, *3*, 426–429.

McElheny, V. E. (1974). Gene transplants seen helping farmers and doctors. *New York Times*, May 20, 60:1.

McGarity, T. O., & Bayer, K. O. (1983). Federal-regulation of emerging genetic technologies. *Vanderbilt Law Review*, *36*, 461–540.

Merton, R. K. (1968). *Social theory and social structure*. New York, NY: Free Press.

Merz, J. F. (1999). Disease gene patents: Overcoming unethical constraints on clinical laboratory medicine. *Clinical Chemistry*, *45*, 324–330.

Morange, M. (1998). *A history of molecular biology*. Cambridge, MA: Harvard University Press.

Munir, K. A., & Phillips, N. (2005). The birth of the 'Kodak moment': Institutional entrepreneurship and the adoption of new technologies. *Organization Studies*, *26*, 1665–1687.

Murray, F. (2008). *The oncomouse that roared: Hybrid exchange strategies as a source of productive tension at the boundary of overlapping institutions*. MIT Sloan School of Management Working Paper. Cambridge, MA.

Murray, F., & Stern, S. (2008). *Learning to live with patents: Acquiescence & adaptation to the law by the life sciences community*. MIT Sloan School of Management Working Paper. Cambridge, MA.

Nash, J. M. (2000). Who owns the genome. *CNN*, April 10, available at www.cnn.com

National Research Council. (1992). *DNA technology in forensic science*. Washington, DC: National Academy Press.

National Research Council (U.S.). Committee on Genetically Modified Pest-Protected Plants. (2000). *Genetically modified pest-protected plants: Science and regulation*. Washington, DC: National Academy Press.

Nedelcu, R., Blazer, K. R., Schwerin, B. U., Gambol, P., Mantha, P., Uman, G. C., & Weitzel, J. N. (2004). Genetic discrimination: The clinician perspective. *Clinical Genetics*, *66*, 311–317.

Office of Science and Technology Policy. (1986). *Coordinated framework for regulation of biotechnology*. Washington, DC: U.S. Government Printing Office.

Office of Technology Assessment (U.S. Congress). (1990). *Genetic witness: Forensic uses of DNA tests*. Washington, DC: U.S. Government Printing Office.

Office of Technology Assessment (U.S. Congress). (1991). *Biotechnology in the global economy*. Washington, D.C.: U.S. Government Printing Office.

O'Malley, B. (1980). Money in the genes. *The Multinational Monitor 1*, *1*(7). Available at www.multinationalmonitor.org

Panem, S. (1984). *The interferon crusade*. Washington, DC: Brookings Institution.

Pieters, T. (1998). Marketing medicines through randomised controlled trials: The case of interferon. *British Medical Journal*, *317*, 1231–1233.

Pisano, G. P. (2006). *Science business: The promise, the reality, and the future of biotech*. Boston, MA: Harvard Business School Press.

Powell, W. W., & Owen-Smith, J. (2002). The new world of knowledge production in the life sciences. In: S. G. Brint (Ed.), *The future of the city of intellect: The changing American university* (pp. 107–132). Stanford, CA: Stanford University Press.

Powledge, T. M. (1984). Interferon on trial. *Biotechnology*, *2*, 214–228.

Red Herring. (2001). These fashionable genes are too expensive. *Red Herring*, September 14. Available at www.redherring.com/HOME/9441

Robbins-Roth, C. (2000). *From alchemy to IPO: The business of biotechnology*. Cambridge, MA: Perseus Pub.

Roberts, E. B., & Berry, C. A. (1985). Entering new businesses: Selecting strategies for success. *Sloan Management Review*, *3*.

Roberts, L. (1991). Genome patent fight erupts. *Science*, *254*, 184–186.

Santos, F. M., & Eisenhardt, K. M. (2009). Constructing markets and shaping boundaries: Entrepreneurial power in nascent fields. *Academy of Management Journal*, *52*(4), 643–671.

Schneiberg, M., & Soule, S. A. (2005). Institutionalization as a contested, multi-level process: Politics, social movements and rate regulation in American fire insurance. In: G. F. Davis, D. McAdam, W. Richard Scott & M. N. Zald (Eds), *Social movements and organization theory* (pp. 122–160). Cambridge, NY: Cambridge University Press.

Sewell, W. H. (1992). A theory of structure: Duality, agency, and transformation. *The American Journal of Sociology*, *98*, 1–29.

Shah, S. K., & Tripsas, M. (2007). The accidental entrepreneur: The emergent and collective process of user entrepreneurship. *Strategic Entrepreneurship Journal*, *1*, 123–140.

Shane, S. (2000). Prior knowledge and the discovery of entrepreneurial opportunities. *Organization Science*, *11*, 448–469.

Shane, S., & Venkataraman, S. (2000). The promise of entrepreneurship as a field of research. *Academy of Management Review*, *25*, 217–226.

Stark, D. (2000). For a sociology of worth. *Keynote address for the meetings of the European association of evolutionary political economy*. November 2–4, Berlin.

Stark, D. (2009). *The sense of dissonance: Accounts of worth in economic life*. Princeton, NJ: Princeton University Press.

Stevens, C. (1986). Biotechnology up close. *Financial World*, January 22, p. 52.

Stipp, D. (2001). He's brilliant. He's swaggering. And he may soon be genomics' first billionaire. *Fortune*, June 25, pp. 100–106.

Stuart, T. E., & Ding, W. W. (2006). When do scientists become entrepreneurs? The social structural antecedents of commercial activity in the academic life sciences. *American Journal of Sociology*, *112*, 97–144.

Swanson, R. (1996). Interview with Robert Swanson, Co-Founder, CEO, and Chairman of Genentech, Inc., 1976–1996. University of California Berkeley, Regional Oral History Office. The Program in the History of the Biological Sciences and Biotechnology.

Teece, D. J. (1986). Profiting from technological innovation: Implications for integration, collaboration, licensing and public policy. *Research Policy*, *15*, 285–305.

Teitelman, R., & Coletti, R. (1989). Financial world global report: Pharmaceuticals. *Financial World*, May 30, p. 54.

Thackray, A. (1998). *Private science: Biotechnology and the rise of the molecular sciences*. Philadelphia: University of Pennsylvania Press.

Thornton, P. H., & Ocasio, W. (1999). Institutional logics and the historical contingency of power in organizations: Executive succession in the higher education publishing industry, 1958–1990. *American Journal of Sociology*, *105*, 801–843.

U.S. Patent and Trademark Office. (1999). Revised utility examination guidelines. Request for Comments, 64, Federal Register 71440, December.

US Supreme Court. (1980). *Diamond v. Chakrabarty*. 447 U.S. 303, 309.

Vallas, S. P., & Lee, D. L. (2008). Contradiction, convergence and the knowledge economy: The confluence of academic and commercial biotechnology. *Socio-Economic Review*, *6*, 283–311.

Van Brunt, J. (2005). Investors fuel biotech's future. *Signals Magazine*, January 18. Available at www.signdsmag.com

Veggeberg, S. (1992). Controversy mounts over gene patenting policy-scientists in industry and academia foresee trouble as NIH persists in claiming ownership over partial sequences. *Scientist, 6*, 1ff.

Venkataraman, S. (1997). The distinctive domain of entrepreneurship research: An editor's perspective. In: J. Katz & R. Brockhaus (Eds), *Advances in entrepreneurship, firm emergence, and growth* (pp. 119–138). Greenwich, CT: JAI Press.

Watson, J. D., & Crick, F. H. C. (1953). Molecular structure of nucleic acids – A structure for deoxyribose nucleic acid. *Nature, 171*, 737–738.

Weber, K., Thomas, L. G., & Rao, H. (2009). From streets to suites: How the anti-biotech movement affected German pharmaceutical firms. *American Sociological Review, 74*(1), 106–127.

Weick, K. E. (1990). Technology as equivoque. In: P. Goodman & L. Sproull (Eds), *Technology and organizations* (pp. 1–44). San Francisco: Jossey-Bass.

Winner, L. (1977). *Autonomous technology: Technics-out-of-control as a theme in political thought*. Cambridge, MA: MIT Press.

Woodward, J. (1958). *Management and technology*. London, UK: H.M. Stationery Office.

Wright, S. (1986). Molecular-biology or molecular politics-the production of scientific consensus on the hazards of recombinant-DNA technology. *Social Studies of Science, 16*, 593–620.

Yansura, D. G. (2001). *Interview with Daniel G. Yansura, senior scientist at Genentech* (Program in the History of the Biological Sciences and Biotechnology. An Interview Conducted by Sally Smith Hughes, Ph.D. in 2001 and 2002). Berkeley: University of California.

Zelizer, V. (1983). *Morals and markets: The development of life insurance in the United States*. New Brunswick: Transaction Books.

Zelizer, V. (2005). *The purchase of intimacy*. Princeton, NJ: Princeton University Press.

Zuckerman, E. W. (1999). The categorical imperative: Securities analysts and the illegitimacy discount. *American Journal of Sociology, 104*, 1398–1438.

Zuckerman, E. W. (2004). Structural incoherence and stock market activity. *American Sociological Review, 69*, 405–432.

INSTITUTIONAL SOURCES OF TECHNOLOGICAL KNOWLEDGE: A COMMUNITY PERSPECTIVE ON NANOTECHNOLOGY EMERGENCE

Tyler Wry, Royston Greenwood,
P. Devereaux Jennings and Michael Lounsbury

ABSTRACT

Although the cottage industry of neoinstitutional research gained its momentum through a conceptual architecture that was centred on a bifurcation of technological/material forces and cultural dynamics, current research in this genre has begun to re-examine the utility of such distinctions. One of the downsides of such a conceptual distinction is that the institutional approach to technology is anachronistic, treating it as an exogenous force. Even though early work by Woodward and others usefully contributed to our understanding of organizations by highlighting how different technologies correlate with various organizational forms, recent scholarship has enhanced our more functional understanding of technology by highlighting processes of coevolution and structuration. In this chapter, we draw on such social constructionist developments in the study of technology to reanimate institutional analysis. More specifically, drawing on the case of the development of nanotube intellectual property,

Technology and Organization: Essays in Honour of Joan Woodward
Research in the Sociology of Organizations, Volume 29, 149–176

ISSN: 0733-558X/doi:10.1108/S0733-558X(2010)0000029014

we focus on how technological knowledge production is embedded in community cultures. Our arguments and evidence suggest that there are distinctive community cultures around intensive versus extensive knowledge-generating patents, highlighting how an approach that appreciates the interactive dynamics of technology and culture can yield important insights into the institutional dynamics of technology development.

Neoinstitutional theorists have aptly demonstrated how cognitive, normative, and regulative forces facilitate organizational isomorphism across a wide variety of contexts (e.g., see Powell & DiMaggio, 1991). However, the development of much of this body of work relied on a sharp distinction between technological/material factors and more cultural/institutional processes (Scott, 2001). This conceptual break is particularly vivid in neoinstitutional research on diffusion that emphasizes a two-stage process, whereby early adopters are driven by technical considerations and later adopters imitate each other in a way that is decoupled from rational calculation (e.g., Tolbert & Zucker, 1983; Zhou, 1993; Westphal, Gulati, & Shortell, 1997). Even though many scholars have complained that this a-rational depiction of late adopters has limited the scope of institutional arguments (e.g., Hirsch & Lounsbury, 1997), this contagion model of diffusion has remained dominant in institutional theorizing (Strang & Macy, 2001). Reflecting on early neoinstitutional developments, Scott (2008) commented that:

> A focus on the explanation of non-rational features of organizations threatened to condemn institutional theorists to play the role of subordinate hand-maiden to rational analysts (in their numerous guises), who would themselves attend to the adult concerns of constructing accounts of efficient organizations, leaving to institutionalists the scraps, accounting for the error-term in their equations.

In this chapter, we aim to contribute to the development of a conceptualization of institutional dynamics that eschews a separation between technology and rationality on the one hand and institutional and cultural processes on the other (see also Garud & Kumaraswamy, 1996; Hargadon & Douglas, 2001; Lounsbury, 2007). To this end, we endeavor to cultivate a perspective that is attentive to the institutional forces that shape the development of different varieties of technological knowledge. Although organizational scholars initially conceptualized technology as an exogenous force that shapes organizational structure (e.g., Woodward, 1965; Thompson, 1967), more recent ethnographic accounts inside organizations illuminate the social processes through which technologies emerge and become socially organized (e.g., Barley, 1986; Orlikowski, 2000; Thomas, 1994). We believe that institutional theory can contribute usefully to this perspective by showing how technological developments are embedded in, and shaped by, broader institutional environments (e.g., Lounsbury, Ventresca, & Hirsch, 2003; Munir & Phillips, 2005).

We conceptualize the development of technological knowledge as fundamentally shaped by cultural dynamics in particular communities (Marquis, Glynn, & Davis, 2007). Geographic communities occupy a prominent place in research on knowledge creation and technology development. This work focuses on the role of industrial districts, or regional clusters, as key drivers in the development of knowledge-intensive industries (Adams, 2005; Harrison, 1992; Porter, 1998). This research, however, focuses mainly on regional economic factors to the exclusion of more culturally based institutional processes (but see Saxenian, 1994). Recent developments in institutional analysis have begun to show how practices vary among geographic communities (e.g., Lounsbury, 2007; Marquis & Lounsbury, 2007). We build on this work and argue that communities have different knowledge creation cultures that lead to systematic variation in the types of technological knowledge that they produce.

In particular, we focus on the creation of two forms of *knowledge-generating* technological knowledge: relatively "deep" knowledge that facilitates subsequent technological development within specific niches and more "robust" knowledge that enables technological developments across a wide array of niches. Although some have argued that the longstanding conceptual distinction between "basic" and "applied" scientific inquiry (e.g., Kuhn, 1962; Merton, 1973; Dasgupta & David, 1987, 1994) has broken down in recent years with the advent of biotechnology and other developments (see e.g., Powell & Snellman, 2004; Rhoten & Powell, 2007), we suggest that such a bifurcation still has utility – especially in theorizing how different kinds of universities facilitate different kinds of technological knowledge production. Empirically, we examine how variation in *knowledge-generating* technological knowledge (deep versus robust) is produced within the field of intellectual property (IP).

We posit that the creation of IP that fosters deep knowledge creation is produced in communities that have a cultural foundation rooted in fundamental knowledge development. Such communities are often dominated by elite research universities that are staffed with scientists who value basic inquiry and act as the gatekeepers of normal science. Although it is certainly an ideal-type, "normal" science focuses on confirming and incrementally elaborating knowledge, thus deepening understanding in specific knowledge domains (Kuhn, 1962). Alternatively, we assert that other communities have more of an applied culture that is built around second-tiered universities that valorize direct application and relevance. By focusing more pointedly on use in applications, the type of inquiry in this applied community tends to emphasize technological knowledge that is more elastic and trades off deep understanding for broader relevance across a more extensive range of domains (Laudon, 1986; Mansfield & Lee, 1996).

In addition, although we think some insights can be gained by examining the types of knowledge produced by different institutions in a fine grained way, we argue that important insights can be gleaned by exploring the phenomenon at a broader, community, level. To this end, we argue that a university's knowledge creation culture is amplified on a regional level with the presence of corporate research and development (R&D) and when the density of universities with similar status increases. As Owen-Smith and Powell (2004) showed, the productivity of the Boston region in biotechnology was importantly catalyzed by traditional universities and research hospitals that set the tone for innovation in the broader community through their knowledge creation activities.

Our empirical case concentrates on the creation of technological knowledge as manifested in patents in the techno-scientific field of nanotubes, which comprises one of the most well-defined and well-developed areas of nanotechnology (Hoffman et al., 2006). Research into nanotubes is generating excitement because of their unique electrical conducting properties that have fuelled efforts to develop and commercialize new kinds of transistors, probes, sensors, actuators, field emission arrays, and flat panel displays. Patenting began immediately after the initial discovery of carbon-based nanotubes by Iijima (1991). There was steady growth in nanotube IP through the 1990s followed by a marked spike following the passage of the US National Nanotechnology Initiative (NNI) in 2000. In sum, 880 nanotube patents were issued between 1992 and the end of 2004 when we ended our data collection.

Our chapter proceeds as follows. We begin by developing our theoretical perspective and hypotheses focussing on community-level variation in technological knowledge creation. We follow with a discussion of our methods, data, and results. Our analyzes concentrate on the creation of patents that provide a foundation for further technological knowledge developments through patenting within the same technological niche as the focal patents (deep knowledge development) as well as across various other technological niches (robust knowledge development). Given that there has been little research on the topic, the research we report on is preliminary and exploratory. Nonetheless, our findings are pronounced and suggestive of the utility of our conceptual distinctions. We conclude by discussing the implications of our findings as they relate to the institutional dynamics of knowledge and technology development.

THEORETICAL PERSPECTIVE

Communities have long been recognized as an important level of analysis that gives insight into the dynamics behind innovation and technology. One important stream of research focuses on regional agglomeration (or clustering) where a critical mass of organizations emerges around a particular industry, and the interactions among these organizations has a generative effect on local innovation (Porter, 1998; Storper, 1997). For instance, Saxenian (1994) argues that close linkages among colocated firms creates a virtuous cycle where networks spur regional innovation and innovation strengthens regional networks.

However, there is still much debate about the factors that allow for explosive, cluster-based, technological development within communities (Martin & Sunley, 2003). Bresnahan, Gambardella, and Saxenian (2001) have pointed out that many of the characteristics put forward as critical for regional success are drawn from established clusters post-hoc and that the factors that catalyze cluster emergence may differ from those that sustain its success. To wit, the conditions that led to the successful development of the US Capitol region were very different from those identified in many established clusters (Feldman, 2001). Others have questioned whether the interpretations put forward in early research on cluster emergence are accurate. Adams (2005), for one, has challenged many of the widely shared assumptions of how Silicon Valley developed, and Markysen (1996) rejected the idea of a single set of factors underlying regional success (see also Swann & Prevezer, 1996; Paniccia, 1998).

One feature common to *all* discussions of regional clusters is that they are premised upon the generation, diffusion, and commercialization of technological knowledge. Thus, the spatial distribution of knowledge creation capabilities is critical for understanding variation in the types of knowledge created in different regions. This is particularly important given the mounting evidence on the context-dependent nature of knowledge development (Garud & Rappa, 1994; Hargadon & Douglas, 2001; Powell &

Snellman, 2004). Building on this, we argue that the types of institutions within a region (i.e., universities, corporations), and the interactions among them, will play a key role in shaping the types of technological knowledge that a region generates.

Universities and Knowledge Creation Cultures

Although some view collaborations between firms and universities negatively, arguing that corporations are perverting the aims of university-based research (Krimsky, 2003; Press & Washburn, 2000), we maintain that universities are still key drivers of community knowledge creation cultures. Since gains in rapidly developing techno-scientific domains rely heavily on advances in academic research (Powell & Owen-Smith, 1998), managers in sectors such as biotechnology and pharmaceuticals report looking to universities as key sources of "inventions" (Mansfield, 1991; Rosenberg & Nelson, 1994); we expect that nanotechnology is no different. Though the majority of nanotechnology patents are taken out by corporations, most government research dollars flow through universities. In sum, over $1 billion per year in government funding is allocated to nanotechnology research in the United States (Berube, 2006; Hoffman et al., 2006). Moreover, although elite universities may receive higher rates of funding, nanotechnology research grants are distributed among a wide variety of universities located throughout the United States (NNI, 2007). As such, a large portion of nanotech research in a region – especially the high impact, foundational, variety – is likely carried out in its universities.

On the basis of these factors we expect that, although companies may influence the targets of regional research (Rosenberg & Nelson, 1994), universities play a key role shaping cultural norms about *how* this knowledge is created. This role has been exacerbated in some circumstances by the fact that universities are increasingly pursuing commercially oriented inquiry and taking out patents on their research (Powell & Owen-Smith, 1998). This has led to further increases in interaction between universities and firms (e.g., Vallas & Kleinman, 2008), including the growth of partnerships and other hybridized arrangements such as "open source" communities in software, biotechnology, and other technological spheres (Rhoten & Powell, 2007).

To explain variation in the kinds of knowledge-generating patents produced in a region, our argument starts with the established premise that different types of universities have different knowledge generation cultures. For instance, Feldman (2001, p. 868) argues that "not every research university has spawned technology-intensive economic development ... [because] ... universities have different academic cultures and offer various incentives and rewards for entrepreneurial activity." This notion of culture is often overlaid upon an emphasis on high-status universities such as Stanford and MIT, which pioneered the development of technology transfer offices and actively seek patents on the outcomes of academic research (Press & Washburn, 2000; Rosenberg & Nelson, 1994). However, despite the growing allure of commercially oriented science, elite universities still attract high levels of funding for basic scientific research (Press & Washburn, 2000) and are generally linked with the pursuit of "basic" science focused on generating deep understandings within specific domains (Kuhn, 1962; Laudon, 1986).

As a result, we posit that the technological knowledge generated in communities with a high number of elite universities will tend to be foundational for technologies in particular niches. For example, such communities may produce key process patents that enable the growth of specific technologies and complementary technological knowledge that also focuses on process development as opposed to product application. We posit that this will become manifested in subsequent patents that cite focal patents and are located in the same patent class as the focal patents. Thus,

H1. A higher number of elite research universities in a region will result in higher levels of deep knowledge-generating patents.

Further to this, we expect differences in the knowledge creation cultures of different universities. In particular, we expect differences between elite and second-tiered universities. Although patenting scientific research was pioneered by elite universities, the practice has diffused widely since the passing of the Bayh-Dole Act in 1980, which gave universities IP control of inventions resulting from federally funded research. As a result, patents are now registered by both elite and nonelite universities (Powell & Snellman, 2004).

However, focusing on the fact that university output is not uniform and that different forms of knowledge-generating technological knowledge can be created (e.g., deep versus robust), we argue that elite versus lower tiered universities may valorize and generate different forms of technological knowledge. Specifically, lower-status universities, such as those with land grant missions, may emphasize a more applied orientation geared toward more general product enabling technologies as opposed to focusing on developing more fundamental process technologies for specific domains (Mansfield & Lee, 1996). In addition, such universities receive less funding from granting institutions and may be more dependent on and more eager to produce knowledge that serves industry. As a result, we expect that these institutions will tend to create technological knowledge that may be utilized across a wider array of technological niches and industry needs. We posit that this will become manifested in subsequent patents that cite focal patents but are located in different patent classes from the focal patents. As such,

> **H2.** A higher number of second-tier research universities in a region will result in higher levels of robust knowledge-generating patents.

Community Isomorphism

Although the influence of geographic communities was featured prominently in early institutional work (e.g., Selznick, 1949; Zald, 1970), it has largely been ignored in the development of contemporary neo-institutionalism. Only recently has attention shifted back to the influence of communities as rich contexts that shape an organization's institutional environment. For example, Marquis et al. (2007) have expanded upon the way that organizations within regions develop strong norms that produce a form of "community isomorphism" (see also Galaskiewicz & Burt, 1991; Lounsbury, 2007). They refer to community isomorphism to explain how and why different communities develop norms around specific acceptable behaviors and converge on similar sets of practices. Empirically, this phenomenon has been illustrated in a wide range of contexts. For example, Deephouse (1996) showed that there was convergence in the asset profiles of Minneapolis banks, and that divergent banks were subject to legitimacy challenges. Lounsbury (2007) also showed how distinct institutional logics affected the products offered by mutual fund providers in Boston and New York. Community-level forces have also been shown to affect discretionary practices such as charitable giving (Galaskiewicz, 1997; Guthrie, 2003). Building on this work, we argue that technological knowledge creation is shaped by a region's broader, community-level, culture of technological knowledge creation. Although we have suggested that universities are key contributors to regional cultures, interaction patterns between universities and industry also play a fundamental role.

Some evidence suggests that knowledge generation in the United States is fundamentally shaped by local research cultures that emerge at the interface of universities and industry actors. According to Rosenberg and Nelson (1994), the research orientation of many universities (particularly those formed on the basis of land-grants) has been isomorphic with region-specific needs and problems. For example, the University of Akron gained renown for its expertise in polymer chemistry that resulted from its history serving the needs of its local rubber industry. Similarly, the University of Minnesota Mines Station owed its formation (and considerable funding) in large part to efforts to find commercial applications for low iron content ore deposits in the nearby Mesabi Range (Davis, 1964).

As with other rapidly evolving technological areas such as biotechnology (see Powell & Owen-Smith, 1998), the development of nanotechnologies are closely linked to advances in academic research and local networks of corporations and universities (Berube, 2006). As such, technological gains in these areas crucially depend on the exchange of resources and expertise among researchers at universities and corporations (Powell, Koput, & Smith-Doerr, 1996). Moreover, patterns of collaboration tend to develop on a regional-level, leading to community-specific trajectories of knowledge development. Indeed, the colocation of universities and corporations is highlighted in regional agglomeration arguments as a key driver of local technological development (Porter, 1998; Saxenian, 1994, 2001). Reflecting this, evidence shows that innovation in biotechnology relies extensively on collaborations that are facilitated by regional proximity (Powell et al., 1996). In many regions, these interactions have resulted in the creation of common knowledge creation communities (Powell, 1996).

In nanotechnology, the creation of such technological communities has been facilitated by the US NNI, which provides the overarching framework for research funding in nanotechnology. This framework includes provisions that make intersectoral collaboration a key funding consideration (Berube, 2006). Moreover, this type of collaboration has been formally institutionalized through "centres and networks (which) provide opportunities and support for multidisciplinary research among investigators from different research sectors, including academia, industry, and government" (NNI, 2007). These centres bind local research communities together in networks of close collaboration. In sum, there are 38 of these centres distributed fairly equally among elite universities such as Harvard and Stanford and second-tier universities such as Ohio State and the University of Oklahoma.

Since norms of appropriate action flow through networks, resulting in isomorphism among linked actors and organizations (Marquis et al., 2007; Uzzi, 1997), we believe that the role of universities in shaping community cultures of technological knowledge generation will be enhanced by the presence of high levels of industry R&D spending. Although we do not have detailed relational data, we believe that R&D expenditures provide a reasonable, albeit coarse, proxy for the propensity to engage in collaborations with universities in an effort to enhance the research part of R&D. To the extent that this is true, the effects of universities in promulgating a culture of intensive versus extensive knowledge generation should be exacerbated. Reflecting this, Powell and Owen-Smith (1998) and Powell, Koput, and Owen-Smith (2005) show that strong networks can constrain the types of research that is pursued in various arenas of technological development. Thus,

H3(a). A greater intensity of corporate research and development in a region combined with a higher number of elite research universities will result in higher levels of deep knowledge-generating patents.

H3(b). A greater intensity of corporate research and development in a region combined with a higher number of second-tier research universities will result in higher levels of robust knowledge-generating patents.

In addition to the normative pressures created by collaborative research networks within a community, we argue that regional knowledge creation cultures will be strongest in communities with higher concentrations of similar universities. Institutional theorists maintain that organizations with similar institutional standing will converge on similar practices based on pressures for competitive isomorphism (Scott, 2001). We expect that competitive isomorphic pressures will be strongest in regions dominated by similar universities because the strength and salience of norms will be more easily enforced. Moreover, the dominance of universities with similar research cultures will likely increase the concentration and influence of scientists who ascribe to a specific orientation of knowledge production within regional research networks. As such, we would expect that a region like St. Louis, which has three second-tier universities (St. Louis University, University of Missouri and Washington University), would have a stronger culture of applied knowledge creation than a region like Phoenix, which has a similar population but only one second-tier university (Arizona State). Thus, a region's population will also provide an important moderator of the ability of universities to establish a coherent regional culture of technological knowledge production.

H4(a). A higher concentration of elite research universities in a region will result in higher levels of deep knowledge-generating patents.

H4(b). A higher concentration of second-tier research universities in a region will result in higher levels of robust knowledge-generating patents.

DATA AND METHODS

To examine the types of knowledge generated by different communities, we focused on nanotubes patenting rates in combined statistical areas (CSAs) in the United States, from 1994 to 2004. Nanotube patenting began in earnest in the early 1990s after the publication of an article in *Science* that illustrated carbon nanotube synthesis (Iijima, 1991). Commercial applications are wide ranging and include areas as diverse as drugs, catalysts, polymers, industrial coatings, and electronics (Hoffman et al., 2006).

We coded all nanotube patents in the United States Patent Office (USPTO) database as gathered from Nanobank (Zucker & Darby, 2007). For each patent, we recorded its title, year of issue, assignees, type of assignee (e.g., corporation, university and government), geographic location of assignee, classification, and information on references made to the focal patent by other USPTO patents. To identify relevant patents, we searched Nanobank for the terms "nanotube," "carbon and nanotube" and related terms such as "buckeyball," and "fullerene" in the title, abstract, and claims section of patents. This yielded 880 patents issued between 1992 and 2004 in the last year of our analysis. Since the number of patents in 1992 was trivial ($n = 3$) and our independent variables are lagged one year, our analyzes run from 1994 to 2004.

Fig. 1 plots the number of nanotube patents granted by year. Patenting was fairly steady up until around 2000 when it began to accelerate with the

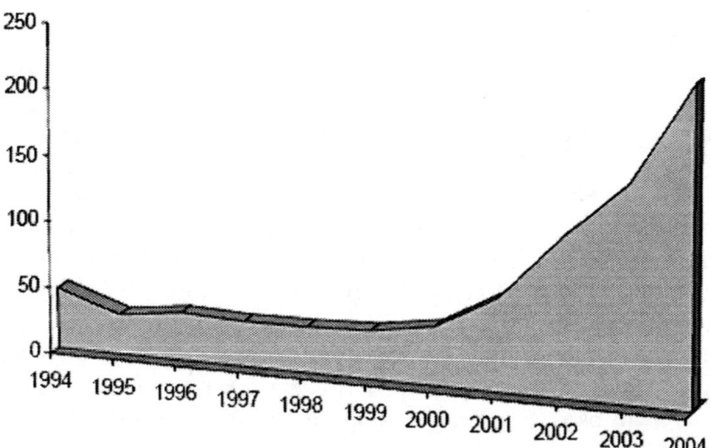

Fig. 1. Number of Carbon Nanotube Patents Granted by the USPTO, 1994–2004.

passing of the NNI that earmarked $500 million in 2001 to support nanotech ventures. The US government has continued to increase nanotech funding and invested approximately $1 billion dollars in 2007.

We captured the regional dynamics of nanotube knowledge creation by gathering data on the 50 regions in the United States that generated nanotube patents between 1992 and 2004. We gathered all our region-level variables based on CSAs. We chose CSAs over Metropolitan Statistical Areas (MSAs) to provide a more conservative test of our hypotheses. CSAs are the most inclusive measure of urban areas for which the US government gathers official statistics. This measure captures broader social and economic interactions as well as daily commuting patterns that are not identified by individual MSAs (OMB, 2006). Furthermore, a number of key universities are excluded from regions when defined according to MSAs. For example, Princeton University is contained within the New York City CSA, but not the New York City MSA. In sum, our dataset includes 550 region/year observations.

Dependent Variables

Our dependent variables are count variables that aim to capture two types of knowledge-generating patents that emanate from a region. *Deep knowledge* is based on patents that further knowledge development in their own domain. *Robust knowledge* is based on patents that spur knowledge creation in a range of technological areas that are distinct from the technological niches of the focal patents.

We constructed these variables by examining the number of citations made to a focal patent in the prior art section of other USPTO patents throughout the time period of our investigation (1992–2004). The USPTO classifies patents according to a scheme that reflects areas of commercial applicability (USPTO, 2005). As such, USPTO classifications reflect the state of technological knowledge in domains such as nanotubes. For example, patents with applications in superconductor technologies are categorized in the 505 class and those with applications for industrial coatings fall within the 427 class.

Deep knowledge–generating patents were captured by counting the number of patents that cite a focal patent and that share the focal patent's primary classification. We captured robust knowledge–generating patents by counting the number of patents that cite a focal patent and that do not share the focal patent's primary classification. We summed these citations to create weights for focal patents, essentially capturing the impact that patents had within and across technological niches (through USPTO class).

Thus, our dependent variables are patent counts by region year that are weighted to reflect their relative impact in helping to generate deep versus robust technological knowledge in subsequent patents.

Independent Variables

To identify the universities in each region that have capabilities in nanotube research, we consulted the US National Research Council study of research-doctoral programs in the United States (Goldberger et al., 1995). This study provides a detailed inventory of academic departments in the US broken down by research discipline. Literature suggests that the component disciplines of nanotechnology include physics, chemistry, math, biology, chemical engineering, electrical engineering, mechanical engineering, biological engineering, and materials science (Meyer, 2000; Schummer, 2004). To determine whether this discipline breakdown applied to nanotubes, we searched for "nanotube," "carbon and nanotube" and related terms in databases including CA (chemistry), Medline (biology), Inspec A and B (physics and electrical engineering), SD-MatSci (materials science), MathSciNet (math), and Ceaba (chemical engineering). Each search returned a considerable number of articles, thus supporting our sampling frame. From this, we identified each university where nanotube research might be expected within each of the 50 CSAs in our sample.

To differentiate between *elite* and *second-tier universities*, we used the Academic Ranking of World Universities (ARWU) compiled by researchers from Shanghai Jiao Tong University. These rankings are widely cited and have been used as a measure of university status in publications such as *The Economist* (see Wollridge, 2005). The rankings take into account alumni and staff who have won Nobel Prizes and Fields Medals, the size of an institution and articles published in *Nature* and *Science*, the Science Citation Index, and the Social Sciences Citation Index (Shanghai Jiao Tong University, 2004). On the basis of these criteria, the ARWU rankings measure the status of research universities as opposed to liberal arts colleges. We considered the top 25 research institutions in the United States to be elite universities.[1]

Control and Interaction Variables

To combat temporal effects, we included *year of analysis* as a control variable (e.g., see Sorenson & Fleming, 2004, p. 1629). This is a dummy variable with 2004 excluded as the baseline category. We also controlled for the *overall patent activity* in a region.

Additionally, we constructed variables to differentiate between basic science and engineering research capabilities in a region's universities. Evidence suggests that basic science and engineering research departments may produce different types of knowledge (Dasgupta & David, 1994). Science departments are typically oriented toward basic science, whereas engineering departments are thought to have a more applied focus. As such, we constructed control variables reflecting the number of *basic science* and *engineering research departments* in a region. Basic science departments included physics, chemistry, math, and biology. Engineering departments included chemical, electrical, mechanical, and biological engineering, as well as materials science. Our analysis showed a very high correlation between these variables (.910), suggesting that most research universities possessed both types of departments in similar quantities. Therefore, we combined the two into a composite measure of regional *research capabilities* to control for variation in the extent of nanotube research capabilities in a region's universities. We also constructed unreported models which included orthogonalized basic science and engineering variables; neither variable was significant in any model.

Hypotheses 3(a) and 3(b) argue for interactions between *corporate R&D* and *elite* and *second-tier universities*, respectively. The intensity of *corporate R&D* in a region was captured by gathering information on the research expenditures of all publicly traded firms with headquarters in a CSA. To gather this information, we started by identifying all three-digit NAICS codes that corresponded to industries where nanotubes have potential applications. According to Lux Research, nanotubes have applications for drugs, catalysts, polymers, industrial coatings, fabrics, chemical compounds, manufacturing, and electronics (Hoffman et al., 2006). As such, our list of NAICS codes includes areas such as 315 (apparel manufacturing), 325 (chemical manufacturing), 334 (computer and electronics manufacturing), and 927 (space research and technology). Appendix lists all the NAICS codes that we included in our sample. We used the Wharton Research Database Service (WRDS) to gather a list of all publicly traded firms classified according to the NAICS codes that we identified. This list was groomed to delete non-US firms and duplicate entries. Finally, we used WRDS to gather yearly R&D expenditures for each firm in each CSAs. We summed these expenditures to construct yearly measures of corporate R&D intensity.

Last, we include a measure of *regional population* to control for effects related to the size of a region. Population figures were gathered from US

Census Bureau estimates. Hypotheses 4(a) and 4(b) also argue that regional knowledge creation cultures will be stronger in communities with higher concentrations of *elite* and *second-tier universities,* respectively. To examine this, we divided the number of each type of university by a region's population.

All independent and control variables are lagged by one year. Also, as Table 1 shows, some of our variables are fairly highly correlated. To guard against collinearity in our regression models, we centred each independent and control variable around its mean and standardized it, as this helps to reduce inter-correlation (Cohen, Cohen, West, & Aiken, 2002).

METHOD OF ANALYSIS

Our dependent variables are two different counts of patent citations – from within and outside of its technological classification. As such, each can be conceptualized as arrival processes where the dependent variable is a non-negative count variable. The parameter of interest in this process is the arrival rate, defined as the instantaneous probability of arriving at state $(y+1)$ at time $(t+\Delta t)$, as given in the following:

$$\lambda_y(t) = \lim_{\Delta t \to 0} \frac{Pr[Y(t+\Delta t) - Y(t) = 1 \mid Y(t) = y]}{\Delta t} \quad (1)$$

where $Y(t)$ is the cumulative number of entries up to time t. The baseline model formulation assumes that $\lambda_y(t) = \lambda$ and that the conditional probability of Y_t arrivals in any time interval is governed by the probability law:

$$Pr\left(Y_t = y_t x_t\right) = \frac{\left[e - \lambda(x_t)\lambda(x_t)y_t\right]}{Y_t!} \quad (2)$$

Table 1. Correlation Matrix.

Variables		2	3	4	5	6
1	Population	.757	.421	.601	.539	.437
2	Corporate R&D	–	.511	.558	.721	.319
3	Cumulative patents		–	.595	.785	.462
4	Research competencies			–	.736	.716
5	Elite universities				–	.393
6	Second-tier universities					–

where the expected number of entries in each period $E(Y_t) = \lambda_t$ equals the variance. This is the procedure for a normal Poisson regression where λ_t is the deterministic function of the covariates. Post hoc goodness of fit analysis of our models, however, indicated over-dispersion, which is when the conditional variance of the entry process exceeds the conditional mean. In such cases, a stochastic component is needed in the entry rate to address this problem.

To address this problem, negative binomial regressions (nbregs) are conventionally used (see Cameron & Trivedi, 1986; Carroll & Hannan, 2000). We used the *nbreg* command in STATA 8.0, which generates estimates using maximum likelihood techniques, to conduct our analyzes. We used the *irr* option to generate *incident rate ratios* that capture the likelihood that patents from a region will generate deep or robust technological knowledge. Coefficients greater than 1.00 reflect higher a likelihood of incidence, whereas coefficients less than 1.00 indicate lower likelihoods. Specifying incident rate ratios does not affect the underlying process by which nbregs calculate coefficients or standard error estimates. We also controlled for the number of years that a region's patents had to accrue citations using Stata's *exposure* option. Our exposure variable was the product of a region's patents in a year and the number of years since issue. For example, if a region generated 5 patents in 2000 its exposure for that year would be *(5*(2005-2000))* or 25 patent-exposure years. Last, we used the *cluster* option to group observations by region. This option is used in situations, like ours, where observations are independent across groups but not necessarily within them. Specifying clusters provides robust variance estimates that affect standard error estimates but not coefficient estimates.

In addition to negative binomial regression, we also ran each of our models using ordinary least squares (OLS) regression. We did this to determine whether the correlations among our independent variables created problematic collinearity in our models. Post hoc variance inflation factor (VIF) estimation in OLS regression provides collinearity diagnostics that are not available with NB regression. VIF estimation chooses each independent variable and regresses it against a constant and the remaining explanatory variables. This procedure produces VIF values for each predictor variable that reflect the degree to which its variance has been inflated by collinearity. Although there is no specific threshold for unacceptable VIF levels, values below 10 are generally considered acceptable (Stine, 1995). The highest VIF in our models was slightly above 7.

RESULTS

Table 1 reports the correlations among our independent variables. Table 2 reports results from our negative binomial analyzes for both *deep* and *robust* knowledge creation. We constructed two regression models for each dependent variable. Model 1 includes all control and marginal variables. Model 2 specifies our full model including interaction terms.

Overall, we observe that population, research capabilities, and corporate R&D – highly touted factors in more traditional views of knowledge generation – have *no* significant marginal effects on the creation of deep or robust knowledge within a community. These results lend support to our argument that it is not corporate-based activities, but universities-based activities that are the key drivers of community knowledge creation cultures. In addition, the fact that the coefficient for corporate R&D shows a suppressing effect in three of our models (and is significantly negative in Model 2 for deep knowledge creation) suggests that critical nanotechnology developments rely on university-based research. We also note significant temporal effects in robust knowledge creation beginning in 1998. This is consistent with the volume of categories that nanotube patents began entering in the late 1990s (Lounsbury, Jennings, & Wry, 2007).

Additionally, we observe that the cumulative number of patents issued within a region significantly suppressed the likelihood that subsequent patents from a community would generate citations from patents within a focal patent's class. This is not surprising considering the fact that not all patents generate citations and that most are cited at only low levels. To the extent that a region specializes in particular areas of IP development, subsequent patents may only pick up on a few key pieces of a region's IP, whereas others are cited more sparsely. Furthermore, this finding suggests that the regional mechanisms that give rise to high patent levels may be different from those that generate high-impact IP in intensive or extensive domains.

UNIVERSITY KNOWLEDGE CREATION CULTURE

Hypothesis 1 argues that regions with a greater number of elite research universities will generate higher levels of deep knowledge. Our results support this argument. In both models 1 and 2 for *deep knowledge creation*, elite universities have the strongest positive coefficient of any variable. Indeed, as the number of elite universities increases, the likelihood that a

Table 2. Negative Binomial Analysis of Regional Knowledge Generation, 1994–2004.

Variables	Model			
	Deep knowledge creation		Robust knowledge creation	
	1	2	1	2
1994	.409*	.448*	.750	.670
	(.178)	(.190)	(.252)	(.219)
1995	.425	.498	1.626	1.681
	(.300)	(.341)	(.753)	(.768)
1996	.446	.486	1.089	.983
	(.226)	(.250)	(.400)	(.334)
1997	.471	.567	1.412	1.312
	(.297)	(.359)	(.553)	(.484)
1998	.595	.736	2.421**	2.120**
	(.263)	(.370)	(.839)	(.718)
1999	.818	.973	2.306**	2.143*
	(.360)	(.469)	(.907)	(.844)
2000	.906	.960	2.875*	2.645*
	(.410)	(.491)	(1.582)	(1.392)
2001	1.066	1.133	2.211**	2.651**
	(.462)	(.519)	(1.592)	(1.347)
2002	.991	1.017	2.526**	2.112**
	(.449)	(.475)	(1.045)	(.947)
2003	1.425	1.514	1.555*	1.563*
	(.517)	(.556)	(.462)	(.506)
Population	.914	1.197	.797	.856
	(.113)	(.265)	(.159)	(.127)
Corporate R&D	1.031	.618*	.984	.962
	(.137)	(.158)	(.061)	(.108)
Cumulative patents	.871***	.866***	.992	.992
	(.043)	(.045)	(.044)	(.041)
Research competencies	1.249	1.351	1.115	1.038
	(.316)	(.399)	(.230)	(.194)
Elite universities	2.523***	2.749***	.994	1.105
	(.948)	(.716)	(.265)	(.354)
Second-tier universities	.989	.727	1.123*	1.492**
	(.142)	(.207)	(.138)	(.298)
Elite universities × corporate R&D		1.560***		.906
		(.273)		(.098)
Second-tier universities × corporate R&D		1.04		1.100*
		(.051)		(.077)
Elite universities × inverse population		2.030***		.613***
		(.587)		(.130)

Table 2. *(Continued)*

Variables	Model			
	Deep knowledge creation		Robust knowledge creation	
	1	2	1	2
Second-tier universities × inverse population		.781* (.138)		1.604*** (.309)
Log pseudolikelihood	−333.42	−329.55	−496.06	−538.76
Wald R^2	106.88	852.65	65.69	82.17

Notes: Incidence rate ratios reported; standard errors in parentheses; one-tailed tests for hypothesized variables.
$^{*}p<.10$; $^{**}p<.05$; $^{***}p<.01$.

region's patents will generate narrow citations increases by over 2.5 times. As such, we find strong support for our hypothesis that elite universities tend to promulgate basic science cultures that manifest in the types of IP that they produce.

We also find support for Hypothesis 2. Our models for *robust knowledge creation* show that second-tier universities have a positive effect on the likelihood that a region's patents will generate citations outside of their focal class. Thus, our results suggest that second-tier universities have more applied research cultures that increase the likelihood of robust knowledge creation.

COMMUNITY ISOMORPHISM

Hypotheses 3(a) and 3(b) argue that university knowledge creation cultures will be amplified on a regional level through corporate-university research networks. We find strong support for the interaction between corporations and elite universities, but somewhat less support for the interaction with second-tier universities. It is well established that elite universities occupy central positions in local knowledge creation networks. Indeed, initial advances in commercial biotechnology were spurred by networks surrounding key scientists at elite universities in the San Francisco and Boston regions (Powell & Owen-Smith, 1998).

Our results suggest that similar dynamics apply in nanotechnology. The research culture of elite universities appears to be amplified community-wide when combined with high levels of corporate R&D, significantly affecting the character of the knowledge produced in a region. Indeed, as model 2 for deep knowledge creation shows, when a region encompasses elite universities and high levels of corporate R&D, the likelihood of its patents generating deep citations increases significantly beyond the effect of elite universities on their own. Conversely, model 2 for robust knowledge creation shows that regions with research cultures dominated by elite universities are considerably less likely to produce extensive knowledge.

Our results show a similar, but weaker, pattern with respect to second-tier universities and corporate research. Model 2 for robust knowledge creation shows that the interaction between these variables is positive and significant, but at lower levels than for elite universities.

As such, we find that second-tier universities significantly affect the knowledge creation culture of a community, but not to the same extent as elite universities.

Hypotheses 4(a) and 4(b) argue that universities will have a stronger effect on research cultures when similar types of universities are highly concentrated in a region. Results support both hypotheses. Looking at model 2 for deep knowledge creation, we observe that regions with higher concentrations of elite universities are significantly more likely to generate deep knowledge. Conversely, regions with a higher concentration of second-tier universities are considerably less likely to generate robust knowledge. Model 2 for robust knowledge creation shows similar results, but with the pattern reversed. Indeed, a high concentration of second-tier universities has the strongest positive effect on robust knowledge creation among all our hypothesized variables. In addition, the dominance of elite universities has a strong suppressing effect on this variable. Thus, we find strong support for our argument that university research norms have a stronger effect on knowledge creation cultures when a community is dominated by universities of a particular kind.

DISCUSSION AND IMPLICATIONS

Institutional theory has traditionally relied on a sharp distinction between technological/material factors and more cultural/institutional processes (Scott, 2001). Although this distinction is useful for showing how forces that motivate the adoption of some practices change over time (Tolbert & Zucker, 1983; Zhou 1993), it creates a blind spot in institutional theory where technology is disembedded from broader cultural/institutional processes. In this chapter, we build on work emphasizing that the creation of technology (and the scientific knowledge that enables this) is embedded in social contexts that fundamentally affects its development (Garud & Rappa, 1994; Hargadon & Douglas, 2001; Orlikowski, 2000). This perspective emphasizes processes that are opposite of those in early formulations that viewed technology as an exogenous force affecting organizations (e.g., Woodward, 1965). In particular, we show how an institutional view on spatial knowledge cultures can enrich understandings of technological development by illuminating dynamics that take place at a broader community level.

In this chapter, our focus is on the role of community dynamics in shaping the types of knowledge that different regions generate. We argue that the distinction between basic and applied science provides useful insight into how different universities approach the creation of technological knowledge. While taking out patents on university research is no longer the exclusive domain of elite institutions, we argue that differences in the research cultures of elite and second-tier universities manifests in the impact that patents from these institutions have on technological advances. Specifically, we argue that the "basic" research culture of elite universities contributes to the deep foundational knowledge creation that contributes to gains in specific technological niches. The more "applied" culture of second-tier universities contributes to the creation of robust knowledge that spurs development across a range of niches.

Building on recent work highlighting regional communities as important sources of institutional pressures (Lounsbury, 2007; Marquis et al., 2007), we argue that examining knowledge creation at this level illuminates important dynamics not readily apparent at individual organization or overall field levels. To this end, we posit that dense networks of similar universities and corporate researchers give rise to local norms of knowledge creation that affect the character of IP emanating from a region. Moreover, we see universities playing a central role shaping these community-level knowledge creation cultures.

Overall, our results provide considerable support for our arguments. We find strong support for the hypothesis that the culture of elite universities manifests in deep knowledge creation. We also find that regions with second-tier universities are significantly more likely to generate robust knowledge. Moreover, we find that community-level factors have a considerable effect on knowledge production that extends beyond the marginal contributions of a region's research institutions. It appears that regions possess distinct knowledge creation cultures that mirror the norms of local universities. Indeed, we found significant interactions with corporate R&D and elite universities for deep knowledge creation and with second-tier universities for robust knowledge creation. The interaction with elite universities was particularly strong, suggesting that developments in nanotechnology may be mirroring those in analogous areas, such as biotechnology, where dense local networks formed around key universities (Powell & Owen-Smith, 1998). We also found evidence suggesting that strong research cultures form in regions dominated by similar status universities. Although our findings provide support for these assertions, much more detailed research is necessary to examine the types of technological knowledge produced in communities and how universities contribute to the development of such knowledge producing cultures. Nonetheless, our findings have implications for institutional theory, the sociology of science and regional agglomeration arguments.

Implications

Our chapter provides further support for the development of communities as a meaningful level of analysis in institutional theory. Although a body of empirical work hints at the presence of community isomorphism (e.g., Deephouse, 1996; Galaskiewicz, 1997; Guthrie, 2003) a direct focus on this phenomenon is only beginning to emerge (Lounsbury, 2007; Marquis & Lounsbury, 2007; Marquis et al., 2007). We find support for the existence of community-level norms and illustrate tangible impacts that result from them. Indeed, it appears that regions have distinct knowledge creation cultures that fundamentally shape the types of IP that they generate. These dynamics are not apparent at micro-organizational or macro-field levels of analysis. As such, although future research should examine how community-level processes interact with broader field-level developments, our results show the utility of institutional theory to generate insights into meso-level processes. Moreover, this suggests that some of the disquiet among institutionalists concerning the lack of definitional consensus surrounding "institutions" and "fields" (e.g., Dacin, 1997; Scott, 2001) may be unnecessary since the plasticity of these terms contributes to the power of the theory. Our study shows that an institutional community perspective can generate novel insight with implications for other research domains. In particular, we find implications for literature on regional agglomeration and the sociology of science.

Regional agglomeration arguments emphasize that technological development is spurred by dense networks of technology firms, which creates a virtuous cycle whereby networks lead to increased innovation and innovation strengthens regional networks. Furthermore, the presence of elite universities in Boston and San Francisco is highlighted as a key factor behind the development of high-technology clusters around Silicon Valley and Route 128 (Saxenian, 1994, 2001). Still, this literature has assumed that the technological knowledge produced in different regions is unitary. Our arguments and evidence suggest that it is useful to probe further into the *content* of technological knowledge and how varying types may be systematically produced in different communities. As such, institutional dynamics illuminated at the community level offer valuable insight and nuance to economically based agglomeration arguments.

Our results also have implications for the sociology of science. Recently a range of authors have argued that increased research collaboration between corporations and universities is perverting the aims (and perhaps the purity) of scientific research (Krimsky, 2003; Press & Washburn, 2000). This work highlights the increasing commercial aims of university research and the role that this plays in eroding Mertonian norms of disinterestedness, communism, incrementalism, and scepticism (Merton, 1973). Furthermore, Nowotny and colleagues (2001) have argued that intersectoral collaboration has enervated the pursuit of "normal" science, while advancing an applied research agenda geared toward novelty and speculation. Overall, the imagery is of unidirectional influence when corporations and universities come into contact; our results suggest that this is overly simplistic.

We find evidence that, although the targets of regional research may be shaped by financial concerns, this is overlaid on a base of university research that fundamentally shapes the knowledge creation culture of a region. Moreover, the character of corporate research in a community appears to owe its shape to norms that flow through interactions with universities. Thus, our results challenge the view of corporate research as a monolithic and uniform force. Additionally, while some have argued that the pursuit of IP by universities has eroded the distinction between "basic" and "applied" science (Powell & Owen-Smith, 1998), our findings suggest that the deeper cultures of knowledge creation within universities endure despite changes in research outputs. Furthermore, these norms appear to act within broader communities with profound effects on the types of knowledge created by proximate institutions.

CONCLUSION

Our focus on the role of local communities in shaping the development of technological knowledge helps address a blind-spot in institutional theory that separates technological and cultural forces. Examining IP development in the field of carbon nanotubes, we show that regions possess distinctive technological knowledge producing cultures that shape the types of patents that they produce. In particular, we find that regions dominated by elite universities are significantly more likely to contribute to gains in narrow technological domains in ways that are consistent with a culture of "basic" science. Conversely, regions dominated by second-tier universities tend to produce extensive knowledge, consistent with an "applied" research culture, which contributes to gains across multiple domains. Furthermore, we observe that the knowledge creation culture of these universities is amplified within their communities by the presence of corporate R&D and other, similar, universities. Moreover, local knowledge creation norms appear to play a considerable role shaping corporate research, calling into question some existing assumptions about the pernicious effects of commercial interests on university research. In sum, we find that community-level forces provide unique insight into the institutional context of techno-scientific knowledge creation and further illustrate how institutional theory may advance by reconsidering false bifurcations of cultural processes on the one hand and technological/material forces on the other.

NOTE

1. We also constructed unreported models using the top 15 and top 50 US institutions as our criteria for *elite universities*. These models returned results similar to our reported models.

REFERENCES

Adams, S. B. (2005). Stanford and Silicon Valley: Lessons on becoming a high-tech region. *California Management Review*, *18*, 29–51.

Barley, S. (1986). Technology as an occasion for structuring: Evidence from observations of CT scatters and the social order of radiology departments. *Administrative Science Quarterly*, *31*, 78–101.

Berube, D. (2006). *Nanohype: The truth behind the nanotechnology buzz*. Amherst, NY: Prometheus Books.

Bresnahan, T., Gambardella, A., & Saxenian, A. (2001). "Old economy" inputs for "new economy" outcomes: Cluster formation in the new Silicon Valleys. *Industrial and Corporate Change*, *10*, 835–860.

Cameron, A., & Trivedi, P. (1986). Econometric models based on count data: Comparisons and applications of some estimators and tests. *Journal of Applied Econometrics*, *1*, 29–53.

Carroll, G., & Hannan, M. (2000). *The demography of corporations and industries*. Princeton, NJ: Princeton University Press.

Cohen, J., Cohen, P., West, S., & Aiken, L. (2002). *Applied multiple regression/correlation analysis for the behavioral sciences*. New York: Lawrence Erlbaum.

Dacin, T. (1997). Review-institutions and organizations. *Administrative Science Quarterly*, *42*, 821–824.

Dasgupta, P., & David, P. (1987). Information disclosure and the economics of science and technology. In: G. Feiwel (Ed.), *Arrow at the ascent of modern economic theory*. New York: University Press.

Dasgupta, P., & David, P. (1994). Toward a new economics of science. *Research Policy*, *23*, 487–521.

Davis, E. (1964). *Pioneering with taconite*. St. Paul: Minnesota Historical Society.

Deephouse, D. (1996). Does isomorphism legitimate? *Academy of Management Journal*, *39*, 1024–1040.

Feldman, M. (2001). The entrepreneurial event revisited: Firm formation in a regional context. *Industrial and Corporate Change*, *10*, 861–891.

Galaskiewicz, J. (1997). An urban grants economy revisited: Corporate charitable contributions in the Twin Cities, 1979–1981, 1987–1989. *Administrative Science Quarterly*, *42*, 445–471.

Galaskiewicz, J., & Burt, R. (1991). Interorganization contagion in corporate philanthropy. *Administrative Science Quarterly*, *36*, 88–105.

Garud, R., & Kumaraswamy, A. (1996). Technological designs for retention and reuse. *International Journal of Technology Management*, *7/8*, 883–892.

Garud, R., & Rappa, M. (1994). A socio-cognitive model of technology evolution: The case of cochlear implants. *Organization Science*, *5*, 344–362.

Goldberger, M., et al. (1995). *Research-doctorate programs in the United States: Continuity and change*. Washington, DC: National Research Council.

Guthrie, D. (2003). *Survey on corporate-community relations*. New York: Social Sciences Research Council.

Hargadon, A. B., & Douglas, Y. (2001). When innovations meet institutions: Edison and the design of the electric light. *Administrative Science Quarterly*, *46*, 476–501.

Harrison, B. (1992). Industrial districts: Old wine in new bottles? *Regional Studies*, *26*, 469–483.

Hirsch, P. M., & Lounsbury, M. (1997). Ending the family quarrel: Towards a reconciliation of "old" and 'new' institutionalism. *American Behavioral Scientist*, *40*, 406–418.

Hoffman, M., et al. (2006). *The nanotech report: Investment overview and market research for nanotechnology* (4th ed.). New York: Lux Research.

Iijima, S. (1991). Helical microtubules of graphitic carbon. *Nature*, *354*, 56.

Krimsky, S. (2003). *Science in the private interest*. New York: Rowman-Littlefield Publishing Co.

Kuhn, T. (1962). *The structure of scientific revolutions*. Chicago: University of Chicago Press.

Laudon, L. (1986). *Science and values: The aims of science and their role in scientific debate*. Berkely: University of California Press.

Lounsbury, M. (2007). A tale of two cities: Competing logics and practice variation in the professionalizing of mutual funds. *Academy of Management Journal*, *50*, 289–307.

Lounsbury, M., Jennings, D., & Wry, T. (2007). *Structuring intellectual property: The case of carbon nanotubes*. Working paper presented at Paths of Developing Complex Technologies: Insights from Different Industries Workshop, Berlin, September.

Lounsbury, M., Ventresca, M., & Hirsch, P. (2003). Social movements, field frames and industry emergence. *Socio-Economic Review*, *1*, 71–104.

Mansfield, E. (1991). Academic research and industrial innovation. *Research Policy*, *1*, 1–12.

Mansfield, E., & Lee, J. (1996). The modern university: Contributor to industrial innovation and recipient of industrial support. *Research Policy*, *25*, 1047–1058.

Markysen, A. (1996). Sticky places in slippery space: A typology of industrial districts. *Economic Geography*, *72*, 293–314.

Marquis, C., Glynn, M. A., & Davis, G. (2007). Community isomorphism and corporate social action. *Academy of Management Review*, *32*, 925–945.

Marquis, C., & Lounsbury, M. (2007). Vive la resistance: Competing logics and the consolidation of US community banking. *Academy of Management Journal*, *50*, 799–820.

Martin, R., & Sunley, P. (2003). Deconstructing clusters: Chaotic concept or policy panacea? *Journal of Economic Geography*, *3*, 5–35.

Merton, R. (1973). *Sociology of science*. Chicago: University of Chicago Press.

Meyer, M. (2000). Patent citations in a novel field of technology: What can they tell about interactions of emerging communities of science and technology? *Scientometrics*, *48*, 151–178.

Munir, K., & Phillips, N. (2005). The birth of the 'Kodak Moment': Institutional entrepreneurship and the adoption of new technologies. *Organization Studies*, *26*, 1165–1687.

NNI. (2007). NNI centers, networks, and facilities. Available at http://www.nano.gov/html/centers/nnicenters.html. Retrieved on September 2007.

Nowotny, H., Scott, P., & Gibbons, M. (2001). *Re-thinking science: Knowledge and the public in the age of uncertainty*. Cambridge: Polity Press.

OMB. (2006). OMB bulletin No. 07-01: Update of statistical area definitions and guidance on their uses (PDF). United States Office of Management and Budget (December 18, 2006). Retrieved on April 10, 2007.

Orlikowski, W. (2000). Using technology and constituting structure: A practice lens for studying technology in organizations. *Organization Science*, *12*, 404–428.

Owen-Smith, J., & Powell, W. W. (2004). Knowledge networks as channels and conduits: The effects of spillovers in the Boston biotechnology community. *Organization Science*, *15*(1), 5–21.

Paniccia, I. (1998). One, a hundred, thousands of industrial districts: Organizational variety in local networks of small and medium-sized enterprises. *Organization Studies*, *19*, 667–699.

Porter, M. (1998). Clusters and the new economic of competition. *Harvard Business Review* (November-December), 77–90.

Powell, W. (1996). Interorganizational collaboration in the biotechnology industry. *Journal of Institutional and Theoretical Economics*, *151*, 197–216.

Powell, W., & DiMaggio, P. (1991). *The new institutionalism in organizational analysis*. Chicago: University of Chicago Press.

Powell, W., Koput, D., & Owen-Smith, J. (2005). Network dynamics and field evolution: The growth of interorganizational collaboration in the life sciences. *American Journal of Sociology*, *110*, 1132–1205.

Powell, W., Koput, K., & Smith-Doerr, L. (1996). Interorganizational collaboration and the locus of innovation: Networks of learning in biotechnology. *Administrative Science Quarterly*, *41*, 116–145.

Powell, W., & Owen-Smith, J. (1998). Universities and the market for intellectual property in the life sciences. *Journal of Policy Analysis and Management*, *17*, 253–277.

Powell, W., & Snellman, K. (2004). The knowledge economy. *Annual Review of Sociology, 30*, 199–220.

Press, E., & Washburn, J. (2000). The kept university. *Atlantic Monthly*, *285*, 39–54.

Rhoten, D., & Powell, W. (2007). The frontiers of intellectual property: Expanded protection vs. new models of open science. *Annual Review of Law and Social Science*, *3*, 345–373.

Rosenberg, N., & Nelson, R. (1994). American universities and technical advance in industry. *Research Policy*, *23*, 323–348.

Saxenian, A. (1994). *Regional advantage: Culture and competition in Silicon Valley and Route 128*. Cambridge, MA: Harvard University Press.

Saxenian, A. L. (2001). Regional networks and the resurgence of Silicon Valley. *California Management Review* (Fall), 89–112.

Schummer, J. (2004). Interdisciplinary issues in nanoscale research. In: D. Baird, A. Nordmann & J. Schummer (Eds), *Discovering the nanoscale*. Amsterdam: IOS Press.

Scott, W. R. (2001). *Institutions and organizations* (2nd ed.). Newbury Park, CA: Sage.

Scott, W. R. (2008). Approaching adulthood: The maturing of institutional theory. *Theory and Society*, *37*, 427–442.

Selznick, P. (1949). *TVA and the grassroots*. Berkeley: University of California Press.

Shanghai Jiao Tong University. (2004). The academic rankings of world universities. Available at http://ed.sjtu.edu.cn/rank/2004/2004Main.htm. Retrieved on May 2007.

Sorenson, O., & Fleming, L. (2004). Science and the diffusion of knowledge. *Research Policy*, *33*, 1615–1634.

Stine, R. (1995). Statistical graphical interpretation of variance inflation factors. *Journal of the American Statistical Association*, *49*, 53–56.

Storper, M. (1997). *The regional world: Territorial development in a global economy*. New York: Guilford Press.

Strang, D., & Macy, M. (2001). In search of excellence: Fads, success stories, and adaptive emulation. *American Journal of Sociology*, *107*, 147–182.

Swann, P., & Prevezer, M. (1996). A comparison of the dynamics of industrial clustering in computing and biotechnology. *Research Policy*, *25*, 1139–1157.

Thomas, R. (1994). *What machines can't do: Politics and technology in the industrial enterprise*. Berkeley: University of California Press.

Thompson, J. (1967). *Organizations in action: Social science bases of administrative theory*. New York: McGraw-Hill.

Tolbert, P., & Zucker, L. (1983). Institutional sources of change in the formal structure of organizations: The diffusion of civil service reform, 1880–1935. *Administrative Science Quarterly*, *28*, 22–39.

USPTO. (2005). *Overview of the classification system*. Washington, DC: United States Patent and Trademark Office.

Uzzi, B. (1997). Social structure and competition in interfirm networks: The paradox of embeddedness. *Administrative Science Quarterly*, *42*, 35–67.

Vallas, S. P. & Kleinman, D. L. (2008). Contradiction, convergence and the knowledge economy: The confluence of academic and commercial biotechnology. *Socio-Economic Review*, *6*, 283–311.

Westphal, J., Gulati, R., & Shortell, S. (1997). Customization or conformity? An institutional and network perspective on the content and consequences of TQM adoption. *Administrative Science Quarterly*, *42*, 366–394.

Wollridge, A. (2005). The brains business. *The Economist*, September 8.

Woodward, J. (1965). *Industrial organization: Theory and practice*. Oxford: Oxford University Press.

Zald, M. (1970). *Organizational change: The political economy of the YMCA*. Chicago: University of Chicago Press.

Zhou, X. (1993). Occupational power, state capacities, and the diffusion of licensing in the American states: 1890 to 1950. *American Sociological Review*, *58*, 536–552.

Zucker, L., & Darby, M. (2007). Nanobank data description, release 1.0 (beta test). Los Angeles, CA: UCLA Center for International Science, Technology, and Cultural Policy and Nanobank.

APPENDIX. NAICS CODES RELEVANT TO NANOTECHNOLOGY R&D

Code	Label
211	Oil and gas extraction
313	Textile mills
314	Textile product mills
315	Apparel manufacturing
324	Petroleum and coal product manufacturing
325	Chemical manufacturing
326	Plastics and rubber manufacturing
327	Nonmetallic mineral production
331	Primary metal manufacturing
332	Fabricated metal product manufacturing
334	Computer and electronics manufacturing
335	Electrical equipment, appliance, and component manufacturing
336	Transportation equipment manufacturing
339	Miscellaneous manufacturing
517	Telecommunications
518	Internet service providers, web search portals and data processing service
541	Chemical manufacturing
927	Space research and technology
999977	Conglomerate firms

PROJECT-BASED INNOVATION: THE WORLD AFTER WOODWARD

Andrew Davies and Lars Frederiksen

ABSTRACT

This chapter develops a conceptual framework to help us position and understand the increasing importance of project-based innovation for industrial organization in the 21st century. It builds on and extends Joan Woodward's (1958 and 1965) pioneering research, which classifies industrial organizations according to the complexity of production technology and volume of output. We suggest that a radical revision of Woodward's framework is required to account for the extensive use of project-based organizations to gain competitive advantage through accelerated innovation and growth in new technologies and markets.

INTRODUCTION

It is well known that certain industries – such as defence, construction, film making, and software – are entirely project-based and that firms in all industries use projects for research and commercial product development. But several authors have recently claimed that the share of projects undertaken by all types of organizations is actually increasing (Ekstedt, Lundin, Söderholm, & Wirdenius, 1999; Pinto, 2007; Shenhar & Dvir, 2007).

Technology and Organization: Essays in Honour of Joan Woodward
Research in the Sociology of Organizations, Volume 29, 177–215

ISSN: 0733-558X/doi:10.1108/S0733-558X(2010)0000029015

The growth of the project form of organizing can be seen as wider industrial transition. During the 20th century, many firms focused on improving the performance of productive operations, rather than projects (Shenhar & Dvir, 2007). However, further efforts to improve or refine high-volume production processes may now be reaching their limits. Mass producers of cars, clothes, computers, and other consumer goods are outsourcing standardized production operations to low-cost locations and turning to projects to open up new sources of innovation and competitive advantage (Davies & Hobday, 2005). Some authors suggest that an industrial era of mass production when functional, divisional, and matrix organizational forms prevailed is giving way to a new period of innovation associated with dynamic and adaptable project-based organizations (Peters & Waterman, 1982; Miles, Snow, Mathews, Miles, & Coleman, 1997).

This trend towards so-called projectification (Midler, 1995) is driven by various pressures to innovate and produce highly customized outputs such as shortening product life cycles (PLC), customer demands for outsourcing solutions, the need for flexible organizations in the face of risk and uncertainty, and global demand for major infrastructure projects (Pinto & Kharbanda, 1995). Yet despite the growing body of empirical evidence and literature on the project organization, we still lack a comprehensive framework for understanding different types of projects within the modern firm, how projects represent a particular stage or system of production and how projects are used to promote innovation.

This chapter seeks to develop such a conceptual framework to help us position and understand the increasing importance of project-based production and innovation. To achieve this aim, the chapter builds on and extends Joan Woodward's (1958 and 1965) pioneering research, which classifies industrial organizations according to the complexity of production technology and volume of output. Woodward identified three main systems or modes of production: unit and small batch, large batch and mass production, and continuous process. She argues that each system of production requires a particular mix of technology and organization. Her classification shows how a firm can improve its productive performance through innovation. These can be achieved in two ways. The first is by adopting and refining the most advanced innovations in technology and organization appropriate for a given system of production. The second way is introducing the technologies required to progress from low- to high-volume systems of production in pursuit of larger markets and reductions in unit costs.

Over the past four decades since the publication of Woodward's research, her schema and recent versions of it have been widely used by scholars and practitioners to categorize firms and industries. It has been particularly helpful in showing how the project-based organization is the most efficient and effective structure to undertake unit and small batch production (Mintzberg, 1983; Mintzberg & McHugh, 1985; Hayes & Wheelwright, 1984; Hobday, 1998). However, Woodward's contribution must be seen as the product of the mid-20th century when efforts to achieve competitive advantage focused on improvements in productive efficiency associated with high-volume production, capacity utilization, and economies of scale.

We suggest that a radical revision of her framework is required to account for the extensive use of project-based organizations in the 21st century to gain competitive advantage through accelerated innovation and growth in new technologies and markets. Our revised schema draws upon a review of selected conceptual literature on the project form going back to the late 1950s and our own research on project-based firms and industries conducted over the past decade or so. By incorporating the project form into Woodward's original schema, we aspire to introduce a "project business" perspective to a wider audience concerned with innovation management and organization studies. The term "project" refers to a temporary organization that brings together and co-ordinates the specialized knowledge, skills, and resources required to complete the project goal within time, cost, quality, and other business constraints. In this chapter, we focus on project-based organizations established to:

- produce unique or highly customized products and services (e.g., trains, aircraft, and films)
- develop innovative new products and services, or improve existing ones
- exploring radical departures from a firm's existing business

Project organization is very different to the organization of repetitive and ongoing operations (Shenhar & Dvir, 2007) such as high-volume manufacturing and services (e.g., cars, MP3 players, and fast food restaurants). A project organization is required to perform many nonroutine tasks such as solving specific customer problems, responding to new business opportunities, and promoting innovation. This temporary form can be contrasted with a traditional bureaucratic structure set up as a permanent organization to undertake routine functional tasks involved in high-volume production of standardized products (Mintzberg, 1983; Stinchcombe & Heimer, 1985).

The chapter argues that three main modifications to Woodward's industrial classification are required to account for the following observations:

- The project form of organic and adaptive structure is the core organizing principle used in unit (Hunt, 1970; Hayes & Wheelwright, 1984; Mintzberg & McHugh, 1985) and small batch production (Hobday, 1998).
- The commercial development tasks undertaken by firms in all types of industries (unit, small and large batch, mass production, and continuous process) are organized as individual projects or portfolios of projects (Wheelwright & Clark, 1992b; Eisenhardt & Tabrizi, 1995).
- A special type of organization – a breakthrough project – is used to create radical product and process innovations, which can enable firms to explore new avenues of growth within an existing production system or move into an entirely new system of production (O'Reilly & Tushman, 2004).

The chapter is divided into three main sections. The following section provides an overview of Woodward's research on technology and production systems. The next section provides a summary of Woodward's analysis of organizational forms and identifies an important limitation of her work: the neglect of the project form as an alternative to functional and divisional structures. Then, the next section presents our revised framework, based on a modification and extension of the Woodward's schema, to account for increasing role of projects in modern industrial organization, innovation, and production. The concluding section summarizes our contribution and proposes some fruitful lines of future research based on our revised version of the production systems framework.

WOODWARD'S TYPOLOGY OF PRODUCTION SYSTEMS

This section introduces Woodward's original analysis of the technology of production systems and places her contribution in its historical context. It is worth spending some time reiterating the main features of Woodward's schema because some of the subtleties of her analysis are often neglected or misunderstood and because it continues to provide the basis of a simple and robust framework for analyzing new and emerging species of industrial organization in the 21st century.

Production Systems

Woodward's ambitious research project challenged the prevailing view held by classical management scholars in the 1950s and early 1960s that there is a "one best way" of organizing, which could be studied independently of technology. Building on organizational theory going back to Thorstein Veblen, Woodward argued that technology was the major explanatory variable in determining industrial organization. As an early proponent of what later became known as contingency theory, Woodward helped to clarify the link – or fit – between production technology and variations in organizational structure. Her core contribution is to show that industrial organizations can be classified in "technological terms" according to the volume of output and complexity of production systems and positioned along a continuum from "one-off" customized products to the high-volume production of standardized products.

Rather than adopt the "very broad headings" of jobbing, batch, and mass production traditionally used by production engineers or Drucker's (1954) three systems of production (unique-product, mass production, and process production), Woodward developed a more fine-grained 11-point scale of production systems, which she groups into three main systems of production:

- Unit and small batch production: one-off, unique products (e.g., a complex weapons system or a bespoke suit) or customised products made in small tailored batches (e.g., a fleet of locomotives) to meet customers' individual orders.
- Large batch and mass production: standardized products produced in high volumes (e.g., the mass production of computers or cars) to meet long-term plans made on the basis of orders and sales forecasts.
- Process production: "dimensional products" measured by weight, capacity, or volume (e.g., a chemical plant or an oil refinery) produced in high volumes on an intermittent or continuous flow basis.

These three modes of production are seen to be a "direct expression of the technology" (Hunt, 1970). Technology is defined as a "system" for producing a product or range of products. A production system consists of process and management levels: (1) the tools, machines, instruments, and technical formulas and methods of each production process and (2) how the process is controlled by policies (or what Drucker (1954) calls "management principles"), which determine the goals, functions, and rationale for the adoption of production techniques and methods.

Productive Performance and Innovation

Woodward's schema is used to show that a firm can improve its productive performance in two ways in pursuit of what she calls the modern manufacturing ideals of "standardization, specification and simplification" (Woodward, 1965, p. 43). This understanding of performance is grounded in Adam Smith's proposition that improvements in productivity are enabled by the division of labor (or specialization associated with the subdivision of functional tasks) and limited by the extent of the market (or volume of output) (Smith, 1776).

First, a firm can improve its performance within a given stage by applying consistently the most advanced technological innovations – techniques, methods, and management principles – of that particular system. Each production system has its own technical characteristics, requirements, and limitations and imposes its own logic on management systems, organizational structures, and behavior. To remain competitive in mass production, for example, today's producers of consumer goods such as cars, personal computers (PCs), and mobile phones have adopted and continue to perfect lean production techniques (Womack, Jones, & Roos, 1990; Womack & Jones, 1997) and other process innovations.

Second, a firm can improve its performance by moving between stages, from low volume to higher volume and progressively standardized production systems. At the same time, a firm faces a key innovation management challenge as it moves into higher volume production because as Drucker explains, it must "learn how to do new things rather than learn how to do the old things better" (Drucker, 1954, p. 45). The drive to innovate and achieve higher volumes of output by moving between stages is the dynamic explaining the growth of the firm in many influential accounts such as the role of economies of scale and scope in shaping the emergence of the modern corporation (Chandler, 1990) and the evolution of the PLC (Abernathy & Utterback, 1975; Utterback, 1994). The PLC model of innovation shows how firms progress from a low-volume stage emphasizing product innovation and many customized product designs to a high-volume stage focusing on process innovation and a few standardized products.

Technological Complexity

As well as an indicator of production volume, Woodward's scale of production systems is listed in order of historical progress and technological complexity. Whereas unit production is considered the oldest and most simple process, mass production and continuous flow processes at the high-volume end of the spectrum are considered the most advanced and most technically complex systems. As a firm moves from unit to more complex high-volume stages, it becomes easier to predict the results and to control the physical limitations of production (Drucker, 1954; Woodward, 1965).

According to Hunt (1970) in his review of Woodward's work, "complexity" is the critical technological element to which all types of organizational structures must respond. But he suggests that the technology variable in Woodward's typology is ambiguous (Hunt, 1970). As he puts it, unit producers of one-of-a-kind products such as those produced by the American space program may be as technically complex as a continuous flow process. As Hunt suggests, this anomaly could be resolved by acknowledging Harvey's (1968) argument that the technical complexity of production could also run in reverse.

Harvey's (1968) modification of Woodward's typology groups firms along a complexity continuum from "technical diffuseness" to "technical specificity." The technically diffuse mode refers to firms that operate a number of technical processes to produce a wide range of products. It corresponds to unit production in Woodward's typology because firms have to cope with demands for custom-made products, rapid product development, changes in production processes, and high rates of innovation. The move in the direction of technical specificity refers to firms that produce only one or a limited number of products. It corresponds to the process end of Woodward's typology, such as oil refineries, which are subject to fewer changes in products and processes. Harvey (1968) argues that this typology is needed to account for different systems of technology, but also changes in the scope or range of products produced within a given system. For example, a unit production firm can vary its output of products most of the time (technically diffuse) or produce the same product most of the time (technically specific). To clarify this point using modern terminology, we suggest that whereas Woodward emphasized the advantages of process innovation and economies of scale in high-volume production, Harvey helps to draw attention to innovation in product variety and economies of scope in low-volume production.

LINKING TECHNOLOGY AND ORGANIZATION

This section provides a summary of Woodward's analysis of the relationship between organizational forms and technology (or production systems).

Woodward's research is valuable because it identifies the precise ways in which both the functions and the forms of organization differ across each production system. However, we suggest that Woodward fails to recognize the project as an alternative to functional and divisional structures. Her framework needs to be modified to account for the growing importance of project organization as a production system in its own right and as the core principle for organizing modern innovation processes.

Functional Tasks

Each production system performs different combinations of the same three basic functional tasks in the connected cycle of tasks or activities involved in the production and sale of a product or range of products:

- *development* activities to create a new product or prototype.
- *production* activities involved in manufacturing a product or range of products.
- *marketing* activities involved in understanding varying market requirements, addressing customer needs, and selling a product or range of products.

In each production system, one of the function tasks is more "critical and central" to a firm's competitive success and survival than others (Woodward, 1965, p. 131). The precise sequence and importance of the three functional tasks in the cycle depends on characteristics of the production system:

- *Unit and small batch production:* The sequence is marketing, development, and production. Product development is the central and critical activity because the product is typically only developed after a customer's order is obtained and the product design is modified during production to a meet a customer's specific needs (Woodward, 1958).
- *Large batch and mass production:* Development is followed by production and then marketing. Production is the central and critical activity because differences in the performance of firms depend on the extent to which advanced technologies are used to standardize and rationalize production processes.
- *Process production:* The sequence moves from development through marketing to production. Marketing is the central and critical activity because a decision to make the large investment in capital intensive production systems depends crucially on first finding a market for the newly developed product.

It is essential to emphasize the role of development tasks in all stages and systems of production, because during the 1960s and 1970s, the project gradually replaced the functional organization as the main structure used to perform the development function (Allen, 1977), including Research and Development (R&D) and commercial product development undertaken by all types of firms.

Organizational Forms

Woodward's research also found that forms of organization differ across production systems. The form of organization refers to the formal and informal framework within which "the organization's tasks are specified, interrelated, performed and controlled" (Hunt, 1970). Woodward refers to two main types of functional structure:

- *Functional organization:* a structure based on specialized functions – tasks and skills – rather than people, organized into functional departments.[1]
- *Divisional organization:* a decentralized structure composed of autonomous product divisions performing all the functional activities required for effective operation.

Although she claimed that similar production systems have similar organizational structures, she did not identify a general trend linking specific varieties of functional structures to the different systems of production. A clearer pattern emerges when Woodward considers Burns and Stalker's (1961) distinction between "mechanistic" and "organic" management systems (Burns & Stalker, 1961). A mechanistic organization is characterized by rigid breakdown of jobs into functional specialisms, a hierarchical management structure, and vertical chain of command. An organic organization is the polar opposite and is characterized by a flexible organization, high degree of delegation of authority and responsibility of decision making, and a less formal definition of jobs. Although organic structures have subsequently been associated with the project form, Burns and Stalker (1961) do not make this connection. Hunt (1970) makes a similar distinction between "performance" (mechanistic) and "problem-solving" (organic) modes of organizing.

Woodward's research found that firms in batch (small and large) and mass production firms in the middle of the spectrum have mechanistic structures, which focus on improving productive performance and perfecting standardized routines in a stable environment. By contrast, unit and continuous process firms (at the extreme ends of the production system scale) have organic and flexible structures, which are geared to solving customers' individual problems, innovation, and rapidly changing conditions.

Incorporating the Missing Form – The Project Organization

As we have shown, Woodward's research helped to explore the precise relationship between technology and different forms of functional organization. She emphasized the importance of innovation in terms of achieving within-stage and volume-based improvements in productive performance. But there are two main limitations to Woodward's framework: (1) she underemphasized the wider role of "innovation" in creating and sustaining competitive advantage through rapid changes in technology, products, processes, and services and (2) she neglected to consider emergence of "the project" as an alternative to the functional form of organization (Hunt, 1970) and the preferred structure for managing the innovation process.

Projects have always been used to manage the construction of large infrastructure investments (e.g., canals, telephones, and railways). The project as a modern form of organization and industrial management was pioneered by unit producers in the US military and aerospace industries during the 1950s and 1960s. These organizations devised different forms of project structures to co-ordinate the diverse specialist knowledge and skills required to develop new and complex technology and systems such as military aircraft, intercontinental ballistic missiles, radar-based air defence, space exploration systems, and the Internet (Gaddis, 1959; Marquis & Straight, 1965; Middleton, 1967; Galbraith, 1971; Davis & Lawrence, 1977; Morris, 1994; Hughes, 1998).[2] As some of Woodward's contemporaries recognized, compared with the traditional functional bureaucracy, the project organization is an organic-adaptive (Bennis, 1966; Bennis & Slater, 1968) and problem-solving structure (Hunt, 1970), which is highly responsive to individual customer demands and rapidly changing technologies and markets. Whereas a project organization focuses outwardly on solving customer problems and promoting innovation, a functional organization is a performance-based structure that focuses inwardly on standardizing tasks and making repetitive decisions in a stable environment. As Stinchcombe explains, a project is a dynamic structure because every aspect of it "must be administered as if it were an innovation or a response to an unusual happening," whereas volume production is predictable, repetitive, and programed (Stinchcombe & Heimer, 1985, p. 26).

Mintzberg (1983) recognized that the project form could be incorporated into Woodward's schema in two ways. (1) A project is the preferred organization of unit producers – capital goods suppliers, construction firms, consultancies, film producers, and government bodies (e.g., NASA) – which custom-make each product to order. (2) Project organizations perform product development by all types of firms including high-volume producers of consumer goods (Mintzberg, 1983; Mintzberg & McHugh, 1985). He argued that firms in all industries are using project organizations to cope with the dynamic conditions associated with frequent changes in products.

TOWARDS A NEW FRAMEWORK

Informed by Mintzberg's original insights, this section revises and extends Woodward's schema to help classify, analyze, and understand the role of the project in contemporary forms of industrial organization. Referring to more recent research, it introduces a framework for examining production systems along two dimensions within a matrix: innovation in processes and products. The project is identified as the first stage or system within the matrix at the low-volume and complex product end of the spectrum. It then shows how projects are the engine of product development across all stages of production. Finally, it identifies a special type of breakthrough project is that is used to promote disruptive innovation, in a shift from one production system to another. A summary of the types of projects discussed in this section is provided in Table 1.

The Process and Product Matrix

Woodward was primarily concerned with differences between different production processes rather than products. In a brief discussion, she distinguishes between integral products produced by manufacturing firms and dimensional products produced by process producers (e.g., chemical plants) (Woodward, 1965). However, the primary distinction in her schema is the movement from customized or bespoke products produced in low volumes to standardized products produced in large volumes.

In subsequent research by Hayes and Wheelwright (1984), an explicit and useful distinction is made between process and product innovation. These authors developed a product-process matrix, which can be used to examine the co-evolution of production stages and PLC phases. Hayes and

Table 1. Projects and the Innovation Process.

Innovation Category	Project Type and Characteristics	Key Literature
Project production	Low-tech project – No new technology incorporated in the product Medium-tech project – Mostly based on existing technologies but incorporates limited new technology in a mature product High-tech project – Uses many new and recently developed technologies Super-high-tech project – Technologies incorporated in the product do not exist at the time of project initiation	Shenhar (1993) and Shenhar and Dvir (2007)
	Assembly project – An assembly product (a single component or device within a complete assembly), which performs a function in larger system or a self-contained product that performs a single function System project – A complete system including capital goods or new generation of consumer products Array (system of systems) project – A diverse collection of systems that function together to achieve a common goal	Shenhar (2001) and Shenhar and Dvir (2007)
	Unique project – Performs a large proportion of nonroutine tasks to produce a one-of-a-kind product Standardized project – Performs a high proportion of project routines that will be repeated across many projects	Stinchcombe and Heimer (1985), Lundin and Söderholm (1995) and Davies and Hobday (2005)
Commercial product development	Breakthrough project[a] – Radical innovation in products and processes such as new products incorporating new technologies or radically new manufacturing processes Platform project – Core common components and process for reuse across product development projects, more product or process changes than derivative projects, but without incorporating new technologies Derivative project – Incremental innovation in products and processes such as cost-reduced versions of existing products or modifications to existing production processes	Wheelwright and Clark (1992a and 1992b) and Shenhar and Dvir (2007)

Table 1. (*Continued*)

Innovation Category	Project Type and Characteristics	Key Literature
Disruptive innovation	Functional design within a firm's existing organizational structure Cross-function team operating within the established organization but outside the management hierarchy Unsupported team set up as an independent unit outside the established organization and managerial hierarchy Ambidextrous organization established as a structurally independent unit with its own processes, structures, and cultures, but integrated into the existing strategic management hierarchy	O'Reilly and Tushman (2004)
Exploration vs. exploitation	Mainstream projects support the momentum behind a company's established technology and markets within a given production system	Kanter (1990)
	Newstream projects have no such experience base and are used to create breakthrough innovations, explore new business ventures, and develop and test new business models	Davies and Hobday (2005)

[a]Breakthrough project that requires specific organizational structures.

Wheelwright's classification of production stages is similar to Woodward's typology of production systems, but they used different terminology and identified the "project" (equivalent to Woodward's unit production) as the first of five stages of production. These five stages or processes include the following:

- Project (or unit) production
- Small batch
- Large batch
- Mass production
- Continuous process

In Hayes and Wheelwright's matrix, these production stage processes are linked to changes in life cycle of products based on research originally conducted by Abernathy and Utterback (1978). The PLC refers to the evolution of a product from birth through a period of great product variety associated with a product's initial introduction to a mature phase of

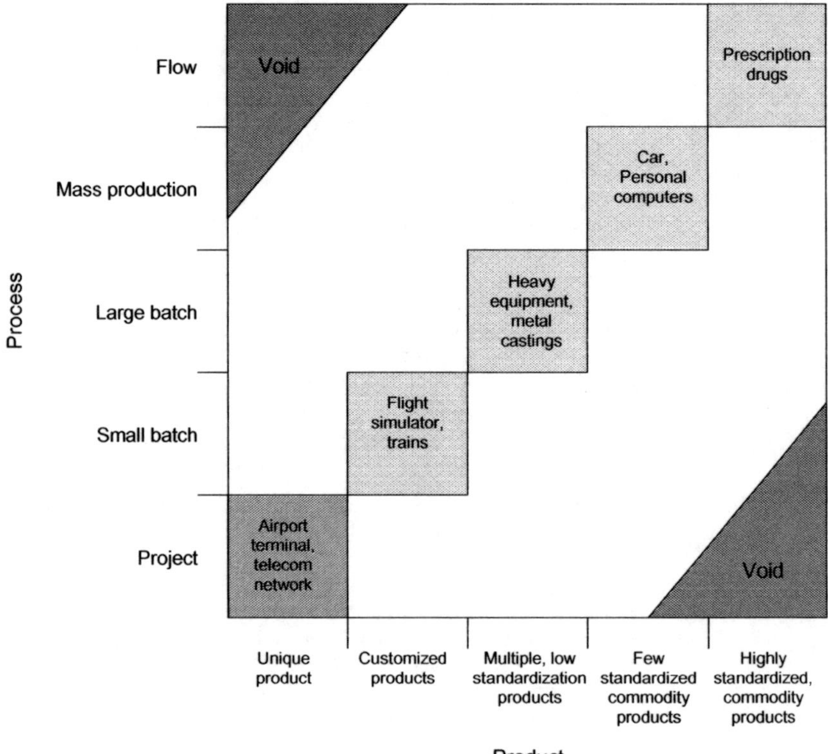

Fig. 1. Product-Process Matrix.

standardized commodity products and shift in focus from product to process innovation. Building on Hayes and Wheelwright's (1984) observation that the matrix can equally apply to services, Leon and Davies (2008) apply the matrix to IT and related services. Although Woodward's classification applied solely to manufacturing, we should emphasize that the use of the term "product" in our revised framework refers to outcomes composed of tangible physical products or intangible knowledge-based services. In our matrix shown in Fig. 1, we have modified Hayes and Wheelwright's product-process matrix to include the project as a distinct process and product stage in its own right. The specific product life stages in our matrix include the following:

- Unique or one-of-a-kind product
- Customized products

- Multiple low-standardization products
- Few major standardized commodity products
- High-standardization commodity products

As we have seen in our discussion of Woodard, a firm can innovate and achieve improvements in performance within a given stage in the matrix or by moving from lower to higher volume stages. As a firm progresses towards the production of standardized products in high volumes, the focus of competitive advantage shifts from production flexibility (or technical diffuseness) and product customization to production stability (or technical specificity) and product standardization.

Building on the pioneering research by Woodward (1958, 1965) and Hayes and Wheelwright (1984), Hobday (1998) considers the relationship between the product complexity and the production processes ranging from unit to mass production. There are many dimensions of product complexity, but some of the critical ones are the number of components that have to be integrated in the product or system, the degree of customization at the component and product levels, and the technological novelty of the product. The product complexity schema is the reverse of Woodward's production complexity scale. The most complex products are produced in projects by unit and small batch firms at the low-volume end of the complex-simple spectrum. Standardized commodity goods are produced at the high-volume, mass production end of the spectrum. A whole category of high-cost, engineering and software-intensive, complex products and systems produced on a project basis as one-offs or in small customized batches (Davies & Hobday, 2005). This category of pure project producers is located in the bottom left in the matrix in Fig. 1. But it is important to recognize a large proportion of small batch production is undertaken in projects, such as flight simulator production.

Project Production

Project production is an important and distinct stage or system of production in its own right. A large proportion of the activities performed by project producers are geared towards innovation to solve individual customer problems, respond rapidly to new technological opportunities and market demands, and cope with unexpected events. The innovative outputs of this stage of production include unique or highly customized products (e.g., commercial buildings, aircraft, IT systems, high-speed trains and telecom networks, and product prototypes) and services (e.g., film making, consultancy, and IT systems integration).[3]

There are two main types of project producers: (1) project-based organizations, ranging from stand-alone project structures within a single firm to large multi-firm project consortiums (Hobday, 2000; Davies & Hobday, 2005); and (2) project-based firms that use projects to perform the majority of their productive activities (DeFillippi & Arthur, 1998; Gann & Salter, 2000; Keegan & Turner, 2002; Whitley, 2006).

Each customer order initiates a new project that lasts for the time taken to achieve the final output. Project management is required to co-ordinate and control the input of the diverse functional skills, knowledge, and resources needed to produce a unique output on time, within budget, and to the required performance specifications. A project's performance is traditionally measured by the "triple constraints" of time, cost, and quality. However, it also depends on solutions that provide "customer satisfaction" (Pinto & Kharbanda, 1995) and added value during and after project execution (Shenhar & Dvir, 2007).

In many low-volume industries – such as military and commercial aircraft, trains, large turbine generators and flight simulators – project producers rarely achieve improvements in performance and innovation by moving "between stages" to higher volume, automated and process innovation–driven stages in the PLC and most innovation is product-oriented (Porter, 1985; Miller, Hobday, Leroux-Demers, & Olleros, 1995). The project form prevails in industries where unique outputs are not produced in sufficiently large volumes to achieve high levels of process standardization or in industries where changes in product development are too rapid to allow for product standardization. Project-based organizations and firms must therefore search to improve their performance by innovating in products and process "within this stage" of production. The same logic applies to unique services such as technical consultancy, advertizing, and professional services.

Process Innovation in Project Production

The difficulties of improving performance are substantial within this stage of production because projects involve many nonroutine processes, uncertain decisions at different levels of authority, and have less predictable performance outcomes than standardized, high-volume production (Stinchcombe & Heimer, 1985). However, the ability to master highly uncertain and non-routine processes has been aided by advances in project management as a systematic discipline based on highly structured processes (Pinto, 2007). Project management is the set of managerial skills, knowledge, tools, processes, and activities for organizing, controlling, and directing a project to a successful goal. Project activities and resources have to be managed in a time-sequenced way through the four main stages of the project life cycle: proposal and initiation, design, project execution, and commissioning stages. Scheduling of the diverse tasks is aided by project management tools (e.g., critical path analysis, PERT charts, and critical chain), which link them into a network to show the timing and interdependent relationships that must be managed to achieve a successful final outcome.

Although each project results in a unique output and requires a unique combination of resources, some firms have developed their core business around developing the project capabilities (skills, knowledge, and experience) needed to manage and successfully execute many projects, often on a repeat basis (Davies & Brady, 2000; Gann & Salter, 2000; Davies & Hobday, 2005). For example, construction firms such as Laing O'Rourke and design consultancies such as Arup specialize in different aspects of large infrastructure projects. Their competitive advantage lies in the capabilities they have developed and honed over years to manage a large portfolio of projects more effectively and efficiently than less experienced firms.

Product Innovation in Project Production

There is a strong emphasis on product innovation within the project stage of production because of the fundamental requirement that each complex product or outcome must be designed and produced to address a specific customer's requirements (Hobday, 1998). Such innovative efforts are strongly influenced by two of the dimensions used by Shenhar and Dvir (2007) to distinguish between different types of projects: (1) technological uncertainty: the problem of integrating new technology into the product; and (2) systems complexity: the challenge of integrating many components or subsystems into the product (Shenhar, 1993; Shenhar, 2001; Shenhar & Dvir, 2007). A third dimension – product novelty – is discussed below under product development projects.

Technological uncertainty is determined by the amount of new technology incorporated into the product. It is possible to identify four different types of projects according to the degree of technological uncertainty:

- *Low-tech projects*: with no new technology (e.g., construction of bridge or road).

- *Medium-tech projects*: the most common type of projects that are mostly based on existing technologies but incorporate limited new technology in a mature product (e.g., incremental improvements to an existing generation of aircraft or trains).
- *High-tech projects*: involving the integration of several new technologies that already existing in-house or can be acquired from external sources before the project's initiation (e.g., radically new generation of mobile communications or new military systems).
- *Super high-tech projects*: these are exceptionally rare projects that combine several new technologies that do not exist before the project's inception (e.g., NASA's Apollo moon landing project and the ARPANET project, which developed Internet protocol technology).

The degree of product innovation in each project increases in direct proportion to the degree of technological uncertainty. The higher the technological uncertainty, the greater the risk that the project will fail to achieve its objectives. Each project type requires its own style of project management and approach to the product design phase. In low-tech projects incorporating well-known and well-established technologies, the initial design and specifications for a product can be set very early, often before the project is initiated. In high-tech projects, by contrast, the integration of new advanced technologies and components into a system increases the uncertainties and risks of project overruns. The freezing point for the product design and specifications must be flexible and set at a much later date during development.

The complexity of the product is based on a hierarchy of systems. Each project results in a product that is composed of many components, subsystems, and systems. There are three different types of projects associated with increasing levels of system complexity:

- *Assembly projects*: A project responsible for producing an assembly product (a single component or device within a complete assembly), which performs a function in a larger system (e.g., computer hard drive) or is a self-contained product that performs a single function (e.g., LCD projector).
- *System projects*: A project that designs and produces complete systems including capital goods (e.g., aircraft, missiles, buildings, and telecommunications systems) and new generations of consumer products (e.g., automobiles, computers, or MP3 players).
- *Array (or "system of systems") projects*: A project that produces a diverse collection of systems that function together to achieve a common goal (e.g., city subway, airport, high-speed train, and new urban infrastructures).

This hierarchy of increasingly complex projects identifies the challenges involved in co-ordinating and integrating components and subsystems into a functioning system. Complexity affects the type and scale of organization required to manage a project. Whereas as an assembly project can be undertaken by a small project team working in a single location, an array project requires a large central organization to co-ordinate numerous subsystem projects (which are often geographically dispersed) and deal with financial, legal, and planning issues.

The Dynamics of Process and Product Standardization

We suggest that Woodward's thinking about progressive stages from low-volume to high-volume production systems applies within the project stage, as a project-based schema nested within the broader classification of products and processes. By opening up and looking inside the project production box in the matrix shown in Fig. 2, it is possible to identify different types of projects according to the co-evolving dynamics of process and product standardization. As Woodward (1965, p. 45) recognized, firms can improve their performance within unit production by searching for innovative ways to standardize, simplify, and specify their processes and products. Even if the final product produced on a project basis cannot be standardized, the production of its component parts – if manufactured in large volumes – can be standardized, thus providing the "best of two production worlds – reducing production costs and still continuing to satisfy individual customers" (Woodward, 1965, p. 45).

A project can be located on a spectrum of processes ranging from (a) one-off and unique to (b) repetitive and standardized tasks (Lundin & Söderholm, 1995). Whereas a unique task involves uncertain and unpredictable behavior, a repetitive task involves recurring project roles and institutional routines. When an organization performs a unique task, members of the project have little or no knowledge or experience how to proceed. Because of the high risks of failure, project managers have to be willing to abandon existing routines and be creative in their efforts to explore novel ways to achieve the project's goals.

When a project organization performs a repetitive task, members of the project use existing "project routines" – repetitive processes and institutionalized procedures – to guide their actions (Stinchcombe & Heimer, 1985). Project routines are often codified in a firm's in-house project management manual, such as Ericsson's PROPS guide, which lays out a set of

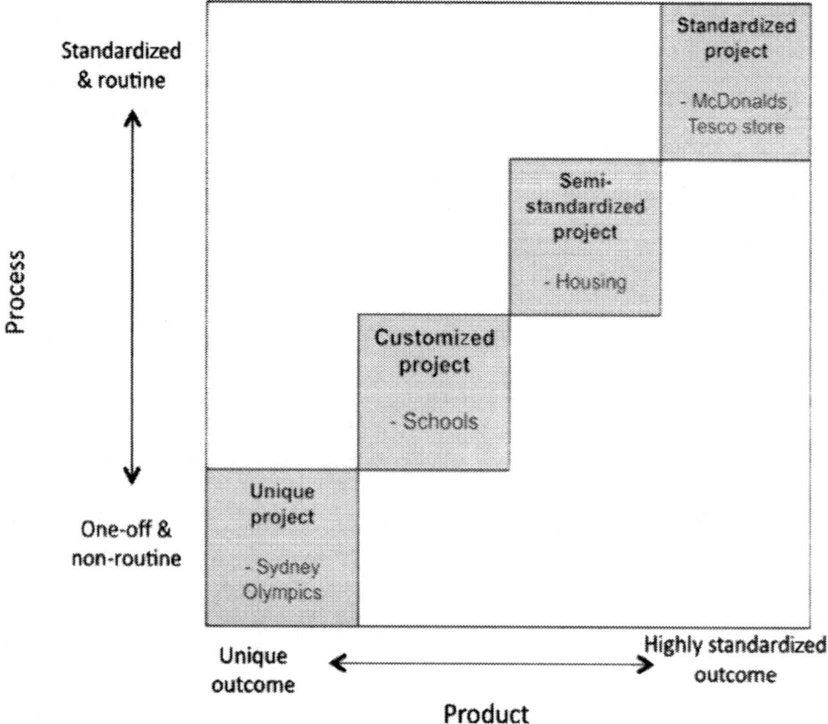

Fig. 2. Product-Process Dynamics within Project Production.

standardized processes, milestones, and stage-gates for managing projects. Roles and responsibilities are clearly defined at the outset and project managers "know what to do, and why and by whom it should be done" (Lundin & Söderholm, 1995). They share similar experiences and a common perception of the project management challenge involved because they have performed similar tasks on projects in the past.

Projects also differ along the product dimension according to the degree of customization or standardization of the final product. By developing a standardized product design based on modular components that can easily be configured and reconfigured for various customer needs, project producers can combine the cost advantages of standardized component production with high flexibility in product design. Components of a product can be standardized and the interfaces linking components into a system made compatible so that multiple components can be specified, adjusted, and integrated in various pre-determined ways to the meet the individual needs of each customer (Mattson, 1973; Hanniford, 1976; Page & Siemplenski, 1983). Product modularity and platforms approaches are now widely used to standardize the components that form parts of products from low- to high-volume industries (Baldwin & Clark, 2000; Gawer & Cusumano, 2002). For example, IBM's System/360 introduced in 1964 was the first computer based on a modular design, composed of standardized components that could easily be integrated into a customized product as long as they conformed to the pre-determined design (Baldwin & Clark, 2000). The unique or highly customized output of each project is a customized adaptation of the basic modular system and its standardized components. Component standardization enables the producer to benefit from economies of scale and scope in production, while providing each customer with a product produced on a project basis.

Many project-based organizations and firms have developed a capability in systems integration to design, integrate, and configure highly customized final products composed of standardized and modular components (Prencipe, Davies, & Hobday, 2003; Davies, Brady, & Hobday, 2007). Strong in-house systems integration knowledge and experience is needed to co-ordinate a network of in-house and external component suppliers. However, there are limits to component standardization based on modularity because the need to customize the final product often requires a high degree of customization at the component and interface levels, as in the case of chemical plants and aero-engines (Brusoni, Prencipe, & Pavitt, 2001).

Some project producers have attempted to improve their performance by standardizing, simplifying, and specifying project-based processes and products to achieve an efficient, predictable, and replicable approach to project design and delivery. Take for example BAA (formerly British Airports Authority). In the 1990s, under an initiative led by Sir John Egan, BAA's CEO at the time, the company introduced successful practices found in the car industry to improve the performance of its large program of routine capital projects based on a typical value of £15 m (Davies, Gann, & Douglas, 2009).[4] BAA created a project management guide used in-house and by supply chain partners called "Continuous Improvement Project Process" (CIPP). The CIPP guide laid out a set of standardized and repeatable processes for delivering cost-effective and profitable projects. It introduced product innovations so that BAA's projects used standardized product designs (e.g., car parks and office buildings) repeated across many projects at less cost, time, and effort; standardized components ranging from individual modules to complete buildings; and concurrent engineering, enabling the fabrication and construction to proceed concurrently with the design. By exploiting the learning curve advantages of "design it once, build it multiple times," BAA was able to achieve significant cost reductions in routine capital project delivery. Standardized product designs and modular components could be combined and recombined across repeat projects at lower cost than bespoke solutions.

Further research is required to analyze, identify, and elaborate on the different stages within the project production. However, a useful starting point is to consider the essential differences between a unique project (e.g., the Channel Tunnel and the London Olympics 2012) and standardized project (e.g., roll-out mobile network projects based on a mature product and standardized design). A unique project performs a large proportion of nonroutine tasks to produce a one-of-a-kind product such as the Sydney Opera House (Pitsis, Clegg, Marosszeky, & Rura-Polley, 2003). In this extreme case, both the final product and its component parts are often heavily customized. However, recent research has shown that in the case of some large, complex, and highly unique megaprojects, such as London's Heathrow Terminal 5 (an example of an array project), there are opportunities to improve performance by standardizing a large proportion of project tasks and components that enter into the final unique outcome (Davies et al., 2009).

In the top right quadrant of the project schema, a standardized project performs a high proportion of routine tasks that will be repeated across many projects. In this case, the product, its components, and processes are standardized as far as possible, as in the case of the standardized product design template for a MacDonald's restaurant or Tesco superstore, which is repeated throughout the firm's global retailing operations. Most projects lie between the two extremes and involve different combinations of standardized and unique elements.

Innovation plays a less important role in the top right quadrant because processes and the final product are largely based on routine tasks and replicable processes. Innovation becomes more central and critical in project production as one moves towards the bottom left quadrant where project producers undertake complex product design, perform systems integration involving new technologies, and have to manage many non-routine processes within tight constraints.

PRODUCT DEVELOPMENT PROJECTS: THE ENGINE OF INNOVATION ACROSS INDUSTRIES

Development projects are undertaken to drive innovation in products and processes to improve a firm's market position, create new markets, and promote organizational renewal (Allen, 1977; Bowen, Clark, Holloway, & Wheelwright, 1994). The long-term growth, profitability, and competitive advantage of the modern firm depends on its product development capabilities (Wheelwright & Clark, 1992b) and adaptive processes (Eisenhardt & Tabrizi, 1995). This section shows that the project organization is now widely used to undertake the product development tasks by firms operating in all systems of production.

Development Projects and Innovation

As previously discussed, development is one of three main functional tasks performed to design, produce, and sell products in all systems of production. Woodward (1965) emphasizes that the division of labor applies progressively at the task level, because the three main functions are more easily separated and independent of one another (i.e., organized in specialized functional or project groups) as one moves towards the high-volume end of the spectrum. The development task itself is further subdivided into distinct innovation phases of R&D and commercial development, each undertaken by stand-alone organizations:

- *R&D projects* are undertaken to explore the possibilities of existing technologies and to create new ideas and knowledge about the frontier of new technologies.
- *Commercial development projects* are undertaken to convert stable technology (the output of R&D) into new or modified products and processes that satisfy business, market, or customer needs.

Traditionally, R&D and product development projects were distinct stages in a linear innovation process, with different types of organizations and management approaches. However, in modern large research-intensive firms such as Nokia and IBM, commercial development is often tightly coupled to R&D by a process of mutual adaptation, involving close communication and interactions between upstream technology creators and downstream product and process developers.

In the 1960s and 1970s, various functional, project, and matrix organizations were used to accomplish R&D and commercial development tasks (Allen, 1977). However, subsequent improvements in the performance of these tasks since the 1980s have been linked to the widespread adoption of project organizations to co-ordinate interdependent tasks and promote cross-functional interactions in product design (Clark & Fujimoto, 1991; Wheelwright & Clark, 1992b; Cusumano & Nobeoka, 1998). In mobile handset markets, for example, Nokia's new product development process brings together a team of people with different technological knowledge and functional expertise (e.g., handset design, wireless engineering, multimedia applications, manufacturing, and finance) to work in each handset design project. When a new handset model is designed and goes into production and marketing, the project is finished and the team disbanded, and its members move on to other development projects. This circulation of people from project to project fosters cross-functional learning and knowledge transfer, which helps to build and maintain a firm's product development capability.

Development Projects and Systems of Production

As shown in Fig. 3, development projects cut across all types of production systems, but the sequence of functional tasks varies depending on characteristics of each production system. Unit production is the only system in Woodward's schema where marketing, development, and production are performed together as a project. In higher volume stages, the development task is undertaken by stand-alone project organizations and is increasingly independent from production and marketing. This point can be illustrated by comparing the contrasting role of development in project and mass production systems.

In project production, the development task is positioned between marketing and production. The three overlapping and closely connected tasks are performed as time-sequenced activities within the life cycle of a single project. Marketing is initiated by a customer's order during an invitation to tender or bid phase, and in many cases, it is "the idea" rather than a product that has to be sold to the customer (Woodward, 1958). Each customer order constitutes a new project organization (Mintzberg, 1983). The product is typically only developed after a customer's order is obtained and the design is often modified to a meet a customer's changing needs even during late stages of production. Unlike other systems, the production phase

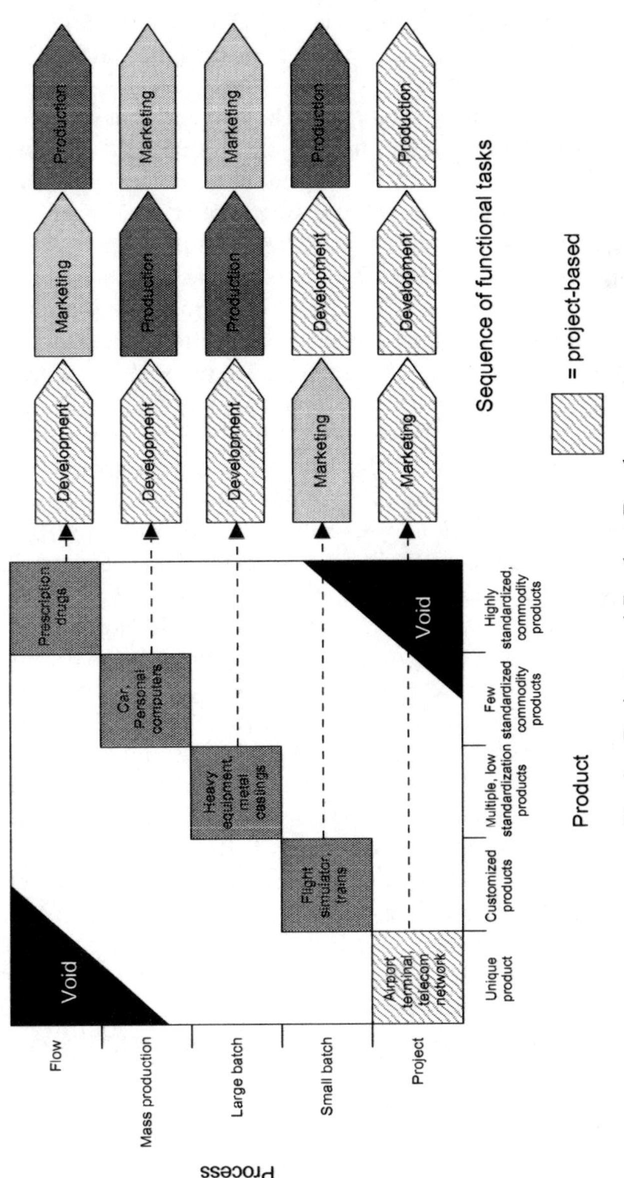

Fig. 3. Projects and Product Development.

itself is governed by an "ethos of research" (Woodward, 1965). Product developers work closely with production managers in the final phase of the project life cycle during product or system integration, testing, verification, and hand over to the customer.

In some cases of project production, however, the development task is becoming more loosely connected to marketing and production and internally subdivided into R&D and commercial development projects. While not moving into high-volume stages of standardized production, some large-scale project producers in global capital goods markets – such as mobile communications networks, trains, and commercial airlines – undertake a sufficiently large number of projects to partition their innovation process into distinct phases. For example, Ericsson – the world's largest producer of mobile communications networks – conducts three different types of projects, corresponding to the R&D, commercial development, and project production phases of the innovation process. First, Ericsson undertakes a few high-profile "research projects" to develop each new generation of mobile communications technology, based on various standards and technologies such as GSM, wideband CDMA, and Internet protocol technologies. Second, Ericsson launches "product development projects" to adapt each generation of technology for the specific requirements of mobile operators and generic market applications. Third, Ericsson undertakes numerous "implementation projects" to design, produce, install, and roll out mature products (low-tech projects based on existing mobile communications technology), which are designed, integrated, and configured to each mobile operator's specific needs and priorities.

The customer – usually a large business or government organization – plays a leading and active role as lead user in all phases of the innovation process in project production (Gardiner & Rothwell, 1985; Von Hippel, 1988). The supplier must remain in close contact with the adaptation processes taking place in lead customer organizations and incorporate user-initiated modifications to the design. For example, Ericsson participates in large development projects – called First Office Application (FOA) – with lead mobile operator customers to create a new line of products based on each generation of technology. In 1996, Ericsson completed a three-year FOA project with three lead users – Telia (now TeliaSonera), Vodafone, and Mannesmann (now owned by Vodafone) – to create a new mobile base station product for second generation networks, which subsequently became part of Ericsson's mature product line in the roll-out of literally hundreds of implementation projects for mobile operators around the world (Davies, 1997).

In the mass production of consumer goods such as MP3 players, laptop computers, cars, and digital cameras, development is undertaken by autonomous project organizations. The marketing department is responsible for articulating the needs of target customers during development. Development is responsible for creating the product plan, freezing the product design, and working out precise specifications for each component before incurring the heavy capital expenditures needed to produce and sell the new product in high volumes. The function of marketing is to convince mass markets of final consumers to buy the new product. In contrast with project production, the customer appears only at the downstream end of the innovation process in mass production industries. As Woodward (1965) pointed out, a key challenge facing mass producers is the need to maintain an effective channel of communication between the product development task and production and marketing departments.

The development process in high-volume manufacturing is more clearly delineated from production and marketing tasks than in project production. Take for example the development of a new car design. The adoption of highly successful Japanese lean production techniques pioneered by companies such as Honda and Toyota in the 1980s and 1990s encouraged car manufacturers in the United States and Europe to used stand-alone project organizations for product design and development (Womack et al., 1990; Clark & Fujimoto, 1991). The development of the Honda Accord 1990 model, for example, was based on a totally self-contained project organization. Members of the project team were borrowed from relevant departments and assigned to the Accord project for its life. A heavyweight project manager was responsible for managing resources and directing the efforts of the team over a number of years until the project was completed.

Commercial Development Projects

Commercial development activities can be subdivided further into three main types of projects (Wheelwright & Clark, 1992a, 1992b):

- *Derivative projects:* Based on incremental innovation in products and processes such as cost-reduced versions of existing products or modifications to existing production processes.
- *Platform projects:* Core common components and process for reuse across development projects, based on more product or process changes than derivative projects, but without incorporating new technologies.

- *Breakthrough projects:* Based on radical innovation in products and processes such as new products incorporating new technologies or radically new manufacturing processes.

These three types of development projects apply to firms operating in all stages of production. The three-part distinction continues to provide a useful schema for identifying how "novel" a product is to customers, users or the market in general (Shenhar & Dvir, 2007). It also helps to identify the special role that breakthrough projects play in the shift from one production system into an entirely new one, based on new technologies or new customer needs.

Derivative projects are the most common type of development project. They are usually completed within a few months and require limited resources to undertake minor design changes. These projects undertake three types of development tasks: first, incremental changes to existing products, such as new packaging or features, with little or no changes in process; second, incremental changes to existing processes, such as a reduction in production costs, with little or no changes to existing products; and third, incremental changes on both dimensions.

Platform projects occur much less frequently than derivative projects. They are difficult to define because they lie in the middle of the development spectrum (Wheelwright & Clark, 1992a). A product platform is based on a standardized design consisting of modular components, standardized interfaces, and common parts that can be recombined, reused, and shared at lower cost across subsequent derivative projects. A product platform is designed for a well-defined customer group or core market, which can be modified slightly to address the needs of other customers. The product and its standardized components are designed for easy modification into derivative products and processes, through the addition, replacement, or removal of components and features. A well-designed platform enables a smooth transition from one product generation to the next. The Honda 1990 Accord product line, discussed above, is an early example of a new platform approach to car design, now used by all of the world's leading car manufacturers such as BMW, Ford, and General Motors. Honda developed the Accord product design and manufacturing process, without incorporating new technologies. This platform model formed the basis of numerous derivative projects to create slightly modified versions of the car (e.g., two-door and four-door models) for different market demands in different parts of the world.

Breakthrough projects are a "rare breed" of projects. They create pioneering new products or processes within a given production system. But in exceptional cases, they can create an entirely new production system and define a new market that lies beyond the current customer base, but has yet to be clearly defined. This type of project can take a number of years to complete and requires large resources to incorporate new technologies into the product and to develop new processes. Although firms can achieve profitability and successful growth by understanding their current customers' needs and by integrating existing technologies into their new products, they often fail when faced with breakthrough innovations – or disruptive technologies that represent a fundamental change in product design or purpose (Christensen, 1997; Hargadon, 2003). Concerned with the integration of new technologies and creating new market demands, breakthrough projects involve much greater risk and have more uncertain outcomes than other types of projects.

Such novel initiatives with unforeseeable uncertainty lie outside a firm's existing capabilities. They often require new procedures and organizational approaches to proceed successfully (De Meyer, Loch, & Pich, 2002; Pich, Loch, & De Meyer, 2002). Because breakthrough projects also represent a challenge to a firm's traditional organization and business practices, they require the creation of new project-based units to overcome organizational inertia and enforce the changes required to promote radical innovation. Four structures for organizing breakthrough projects include (O'Reilly & Tushman, 2004) the following:

- A *functional design* within a firm's existing organizational structure.
- A *cross-functional team* operating within the established organization but outside the management hierarchy.
- An *unsupported team* set up as an independent unit outside the established organization and managerial hierarchy.
- An *ambidextrous organization* established as a structurally independent unit with its own processes, structures, and cultures, but integrated into the existing strategic management hierarchy.

Firms face a difficult challenge of deciding how to allocate their resources to different types of development projects. Each project plays a different role, requires a different mix of resources and management style, and produces different results. In a shift away from the development of isolated products, some firms have built multi-project management capabilities to harness core common components, technologies, and knowledge across a co-ordinated stream of new products, permitting reductions in development and production costs (Cusumano & Nobeoka, 1998). Wheelwright and

Clark (1992a) developed an "aggregate project plan" to help firms: categorize and map their development projects into the types discussed above (derivative, platform, and breakthrough), sequence their development projects over time, and ensure that the set of projects contributes towards the firm's overall business strategy. This portfolio management technique is used to help firms manage the development task by planning the developing of new and existing products or processes and building product development capabilities.

Breakthrough to a New Production System

Woodward's research emphasizes the improvements in performance obtained by adopting the most advanced technologies and organizational structures appropriate to a particular stage of production or by moving to more "advanced" higher volume stages of production. The PLC, discussed earlier, shows how organizational structures evolve over time within a given production system from the organic structures associated with a product's initial introduction towards a high-volume stage when the mechanistic structures are established for high-volume production routines (Utterback, 1994). Similarly, Galbraith (1982) developed a model of organizational growth beginning with a venture project and resulting in high-volume, functional organization.

Like many of her contemporaries, Woodward emphasized the "advantages of size" gained by standardization, specialization, and scale economies within a given production system. She did not consider the process of growth and diversification that enables some highly innovative firms to use technology, knowledge, and practices developed and perfected in one production system and recombine them in new ways to move into – or create – an entirely new market and production system (Hargadon, 2003). A breakthrough project is the organizational vehicle for achieving such innovative recombinations. As early as the 1960s, the project form was being used in this way by firms as flexible means of exploring highly risky and uncertain "departures from their traditional business" (Middleton, 1967). In a growing market, Middleton (1967) recognized that an initial breakthrough project could lead to a dynamic process of organizational change and growth in a new business base:

> A project organization can also be the beginning of an organizational cycle. The project may become a long term or permanent effort that eventually becomes a program or branch organization. The latter in turn may become separated from the parent

> organization and be established as a fully-fledged product division, functionally organized. Then management may create a series of new project organizations within the new product division, starting the cycle over again. (Middleton, 1967, p. 76)

In this way, a project tends to be associated with youth and the early stages of organizational development (Mintzberg, 1983, p. 272). Today, project structures are widely used to achieve breakthrough or "disruptive innovations" as pioneering firms seek to break free from the preferences and demands of existing customers and establish projects to create and experiment with radically new products, markets, business models, and customer demands (Christensen, 1997; Chesbrough, 2003; Hargadon, 2003; Thomke, 2003). Over time, forces of standardization and economies of scale drive a firm to move from the ad hoc, organic-adaptive project structure set up to nurture the breakthrough innovation towards more stable, bureaucratic and functionally organized mechanistic structures appropriate for high-volume production.

The process of growth from breakthrough project to far-reaching organizational change is illustrated by Ericsson's shift from manufacturing physical products to systems integration and service provision since the mid-1990s (Davies & Brady, 2000; Brady & Davies, 2004). The process was initiated by a breakthrough project in the United Kingdom in 1995 to design, integrate, and deliver a system and provide operational and maintenance support. The process was followed by the creation of a new organizational group to support the UK business. But it soon culminated in the creation of Ericsson Global Services in 2000, which created a new services division to support Ericsson's strategic move into systems integration and services. IBM experienced a similar transformation in the journey from its first major IT outsourcing project with Eastman Kodak in 1989 to the creation of IBM Global Services in the mid-1990s.

The challenge of allocating scarce resources to projects can be seen in terms of the more fundamental trade-off between the exploitation of current technologies, products, and markets or exploration of new ones (March, 1991). Building on a similar theme, Kanter (1985) has suggested that the pressure to innovate encourages firms to maintain two very different types of projects: mainstream and newstream projects. Mainstream projects support the momentum behind a company's established technology and markets within a given production system. These exploitative activities are focused on understanding existing customers' needs and integrating established technologies into their products and processes. They are driven by performance criteria and predictability. A project-based organization in a firm's existing business develops a reputation for "doing what it does best," encouraging it to repeat certain types of projects by exploiting specific products, contingencies, and programs (Mintzberg, 1983, p. 27).

Newstream projects have no such experience base and are used to create breakthrough innovations, to explore new business ventures (Galbraith, 1982; Burgelman, 1984; Kanter, 1985), and to develop and test new business models. Such exploratory efforts can produce a breakthrough innovation leading to the creation of an entirely new production system. Take, for example, IBM's PC that was brought to market in 1981 (Cringely, 1992). One of the IBM's so-called renegade independent business units (the Entry Systems division based in Florida) created a separate project organization called Project Chess that developed the PC in one year. At the same time, an IBM mainstream project responsible for developing the PC using internally developed components was in its fourth year with no end in sight. The willingness of Project Chess to break the rules by buying components helped to accelerate product development time.

These two types of projects are often in conflict with each other. Firms are confronted with a difficult balancing act of maintaining the momentum of their mainstream activities, while starting breakthrough projects that will create future business. If the industry technology and market conditions are relatively stable, managers are more likely to show a preference for initiating predictable mainstream projects. Whereas in turbulent and uncertain industry environments, managers are more willing to risk launching a large number of breakthrough projects that are outside the firm's existing productive system.

CONCLUSIONS

More than four decades have passed since the publication of Woodward's classification of production systems, yet her work continues to inform and shape our understanding of technology and organization. She drew attention to the role of innovation in generating improvements in the performance of production processes – within a given stage of production or by moving to higher volume stages. However, there are limitations to her model. She neglected to consider the project form of organization, which was already becoming important in the 1960s as an alternative to traditional bureaucratic structure. We suggested that a radical rethink of Woodward's schema is necessary and presented a revised framework that takes into account three essential features of the project-based innovation:

- Project production: ranging from (a) unique projects to create innovative products and services to (b) standardized projects using common processes and components to achieve improvements in performance.
- Project-based development: to organize R&D and commercial product development across all stages and systems of production.
- Breakthrough projects: to support disruptive innovative moves into an entirely new production system.

First, the project is the initial stage of low volume (unit and some forms of small batch production) in our revised schema, which compares the standardization of both products and processes. This stage refers to a large category of project-based organizations and project-based firms that design and deliver complex, one-off or highly customized products and services. Project producers depend on strong project management and systems integration capabilities to complete projects within time, cost, quality, and other constraints. We suggested that project production can be opened up and examined in a more fine-grained way as series of stages, ranging from unique to standardized projects. However, more research is required to explore and classify different types of projects. There is also need to study how innovation occurs in different types of projects (ranging from megaprojects to routine capital projects) and whether improvements in project performance can be obtained by standardizing and simplifying project processes (e.g., modularity and standardized project management processes). Davies et al. (2009) use the framework outlined in an earlier version of this chapter to analyze the types of process innovation in a megaproject.

Second, the project structure is used to organize and manage development tasks – including R&D and various commercial development projects – across all stages and systems of production. Launching successful development projects is increasingly central to achieving and sustaining competitive advantage in global markets as firms focus on R&D, commercial development to create new sources of innovation, growth, and profitability. Although project producers continue to perform tightly-coupled sales, development and production tasks on each project (e.g., aircraft, aircraft engines, trains, and telecom switching manufacturers), firms in higher volume consumer goods industries are outsourcing standardized high-volume production tasks to low-cost locations such as China, India and Eastern Europe and relying on rapid and effective product development to achieve competitive advantage. Today, many mass producers in the

United States and Europe are more like "project coordinators" of product development tasks rather than producers of goods and services:

> The "business-as-usual" bits of their operations have been outsourced, leaving them free to design and orchestrate ideas. Nike, for instance, does not make shoes any more; it manages footwear projects. Coca-Cola, which hands most of bottling and marketing of its drinks to others, is little more than a collection of projects, run by people it calls "orchestrators." Germany's BMW treats each new car "platform," which is the basis of new vehicle ranges, as a separate project. (*Economist*, 2005)

Third, a special type of structure – a breakthrough project – is used to initiate pioneering moves into a new production system. This organization is designed to support, promote, and nurture disruptive innovations in products, services, processes, and business models as firms seek to break free from the demands of existing customers and create entirely new markets. In growing markets, a breakthrough project is the first stage in a process of organizational growth and transformation as a firm builds its business in the new production system.

The organic-adaptive project organization has come of age since the publication of Woodward's classic study of industrial organization. It is the structure most capable of solving a customer's specific problems, coping with uncertainty and risks, and driving innovation in technologies, products and services. Project-based organizing and managing is now a core capability and source of competitive advantage for the modern firm in both manufacturing and services. Our chapter represents an attempt to create a conceptual framework that can account for these changes by placing the project organization at the center of our analysis of industrial organization and innovation.

A fruitful strand of future theoretical research could seek to extend Woodward's model by considering how organizations are shaped not just by their technology but also by their institutional context. Although Woodward helped to overcome the one-size-fits-all approach to organizational development, her analysis tends to assume that various types of organizational forms are or should be selected to fit the requirements of a particular technology (or productive system). However, there are other factors involved in the evolution and selection of organizational forms. Institutional theory helps to draw attention to the role of isomorphism in creating homogeneity of organizational forms (see, e.g., DiMaggio & Powell, 1983; Hargrave & Van de Ven, 2006). For example, mimetic isomorphism refers to a standard response to uncertainty when organizations model themselves on what they perceive to be successful organizations or practices (DiMaggio & Powell, 1983, p. 151). It occurs when a large population of firms adopt organizational forms and practices – such as particular project management structures and processes – because they are believed to be successful or because the adoption of these innovations enhances their legitimacy by demonstrating that they are trying to improve performance (Meyer & Rowan, 1977). In other words, we should end on a note of caution: While technology plays a key role in determining variation among organizations, institutional factors can work in the opposite direction by encouraging homogeneity in organizational fields.

NOTES

1. Two variations of the functional structure discussed by Woodward (1965) include the line organization (people with different functional skills are placed under the authority of a single manager) and line-staff organization (functional specialists to provide support and service to a line organization under the control of a single authority).

2. The matrix form was also emerging at this time. A matrix organization lies between the project and the functional in the spectrum of organizational forms. In this two-dimensional structure, each member reports to a functional and project manager and is associated with a functional unit composed of fellow specialists and co-workers.

3. In her discussion of one-off, unit production, Woodward (1965, p. 37) distinguishes between "simple products" (e.g., bespoke suit) and "complex products" (e.g., electronic equipment). While the making of a bespoke suit could be organized as a project, here we focus on unique/highly customized complex products and services that are always produced as projects.

4. This new thinking was embodied in a government-sponsored report called Rethinking Construction (1998) written by Sir John Egan – which became a manifesto for the transformation of the UK construction industry (Egan, 1998). The report recommended that clients should abandon competitive tendering and embrace long-term partnerships with suppliers, based on clear measures of performance, and that suppliers should focus more strongly on customer needs, integrating project processes and teams, and on quality rather than cost.

ACKNOWLEDGMENTS

The chapter is part of a program of current research and teaching on "innovation in project business" by the EPSRC Innovation Studies Centre (ISC), Imperial College Business School. It drew upon previous research undertaken by the authors on project-based firms and industries including Andrew Davies's studies of complex products and systems (1994–2005) at SPRU, Sussex University, and Lars Frederiksen's work on the music industry undertaken (2001–2006) at Copenhagen Business School. We thank Nelson Phillips, Graham Sewell, Sara Kaplan, James Barlow, David Gann and Mark Dodgson for useful comments on previous versions of the chapter.

REFERENCES

Abernathy, W. J., & Utterback, J. M. (1975). A dynamic model of process and product innovation. *Omega*, *3*(6), 639–656.

Abernathy, W. J., & Utterback, J. M. (1978). Patterns of industrial innovation. *Technology Review*, *80*(7), 40–47.

Allen, T. (1977). *Managing the flow of technology: Technology transfer and the dissemination of technological information within the R and D Organization*. Cambridge, MA: The MIT Press.

Baldwin, C., & Clark, K. (2000). *Design rules: The power of modularity*. Cambridge, MA: The MIT Press.

Bennis, W. G. (1966). *Beyond bureaucracy: Essays on the development and evolution of human organization*. San Francisco: Jossey-Bass Publishers.

Bennis, W. G., & Slater, P. L. (1968). *The temporary society*. New York: Harper and Row.

Bowen, H. K., Clark, K. B., Holloway, C. A., & Wheelwright, S. C. (1994). Development projects: The engine of renewal. *Harvard Business Review*, *5*(September–October), 110–120.

Brady, T., & Davies, A. (2004). Building project capabilities: From exploratory to exploitative learning. *Organization Studies*, *26*(9), 1601–1621.

Brusoni, S., Prencipe, A., & Pavitt, K. (2001). Knowledge specialization, organizational coupling, and the boundaries of the firm: Why do firms know more than they make? *Administrative Science Quarterly*, *46*(4), 597–621.

Burgelman, R. A. (1984). Managing internal corporate venturing. *Sloan Management Review*, *1984*(Winter), 33–48.

Burns, T., & Stalker, G. M. (1961). *The management of innovation*. London: Tavistock Publications.

Chandler, A. D. (1990). *Scale and scope: The dynamics of industrial capitalism*. Cambridge, MA: The Belknap Press of Harvard University Press.

Chesbrough, H. (2003). *Open innovation: The new imperative for creating and profiting from technology*. Boston, MA: Harvard Business School Press.

Christensen, C. M. (1997). *The innovator's dilemma: When new technologies cause great firms to fail*. Boston, MA: Harvard Business School Press.

Clark, K. B., & Fujimoto, T. (1991). *Product development performance: Strategy, organization and management in the world auto industry*. Boston, MA: Harvard Business School Press.

Cringely, R. X. (1992). *Accidental empires: How the boys of Silicon Valley make their millions, battle foreign competition, still can't get a date*. London: Penguin Books.

Cusumano, M., & Nobeoka, K. (1998). *Thinking beyond lean: How multi-project management is transforming product development at Toyota and other companies*. New York: The Free Press.

Davies, A. (1997). *Ericsson CME R5A Project*. SPRU-CENTRIM CoPS Working Paper. Sussex University.

Davies, A., & Brady, T. (2000). Organizational capabilities and learning in complex product systems: Towards repeatable solutions. *Research Policy*, *29*(7–8), 931–953.

Davies, A., Gann, D., & Douglas, T. (2009). Innovation in megaprojects: Systems integration at London Heathrow Terminal 5. *California Management Review*, *51*(2), 101–125.

Davies, A., & Hobday, M. (2005). *The business of projects: Managing innovation in complex products and systems*. Cambridge, MA: Cambridge University Press.

Davies, A., Brady, T., & Hobday, M. (2007). Organizing for solutions: Systems seller vs systems integrator. *Industrial Marketing Management*, *36*, 183–193 (Special Issue 'Project marketing and marketing solutions').

Davis, S. M., & Lawrence, P. R. (1977). *Matrix*. Reading, MA: Addison-Wesley Publishing Company. Inc.

DeFillippi, R. J., & Arthur, M. B. (1998). Paradox in project-based enterprise: The case of film making. *California Management Review*, *40*(2), 125–139.

De Meyer, A., Loch, C. H., & Pich, M. T. (2002). Managing project uncertainty: From variation to chaos. *MIT Sloan Management Review*, *2002*(Winter), 60–67.

DiMaggio, P. J., & Powell, W. W. (1983). The iron cage revisited: Institutional isomorphism and collective rationality in organizational fields. *American Sociological Review*, *48*, 147–160.

Drucker, P. (1954). *The practice of management*. New York: Harper and Row.

Economist. (2005). Project management: Overdue and over budget, over and over again. *Economist*, June 11, pp. 65–66.

Egan, J. (1998). *Rethinking construction*. London: Department of Environment, Transport and the Regions.

Eisenhardt, K. M., & Tabrizi, B. N. (1995). Accelerating adaptive processes: Product innovation in the global computer industry. *Administrative Science Quarterly*, *40*(1), 84–110.

Ekstedt, E., Lundin, R., Söderholm, A., & Wirdenius, H. (1999). *Neo-industrial organizing – Renewal by action and knowledge in a project-intensive economy*. London: Routledge.

Gaddis, P. O. (1959). The project manager. *Harvard Business Review* (May–June), 89–97.

Galbraith, J. R. (1971). Matrix organization designs: How to combine functional and project forms. *Business Horizons*, *14*(1), 29–40.

Galbraith, J. R. (1982). The stages of growth. *Journal of Business Strategy*, *3*(1), 70–79.

Gann, D., & Salter, A. (2000). Innovation in project-based, service-enhanced firms: The construction of complex products and systems. *Research Policy*, *29*(7–8), 955–972.

Gardiner, P., & Rothwell, R. (1985). Tough customers: Good designs. *Design Studies*, *6*(1), 7–17.

Gawer, A., & Cusumano, M. A. (2002). *Platform leadership: How Intel, Microsoft, and Cisco drive industry innovation*. Cambridge, MA: Harvard Business School Press.

Hanniford, W. J. (1976). Systems selling: Problems and benefits for buyers and sellers. *Industrial Marketing Management*, *5*, 139–145.

Hargadon, A. (2003). *How breakthroughs happen: The surprising truth about how companies innovate*. Boston, MA: Harvard Business School Press.

Hargrave, T. J., & Van de Ven, A. H. (2006). A collective action model of institutional innovation. *Academy of Management Review*, *31*(4), 864–888.

Harvey, E. (1968). Technology and the structure of organizations. *American Sociological Review*, *33*, 247–259.

Hayes, R. H., & Wheelwright, S. C. (1984). *Restoring our competitive edge: Competing through manufacturing*. New York: Wiley.

Hobday, M. (1998). Product complexity, innovation and industrial organization. *Research Policy*, *26*(6), 689–710.

Hobday, M. (2000). The project-based organization: An ideal form for managing complex products and systems. *Research Policy*, *27*(7–8), 871–893.

Hughes, T. P. (1998). *Rescuing Prometheus*. New York: Pantheon Books.

Hunt, R. G. (1970). Technology and organization. *Academy of Management Journal* (September), 235–252.

Kanter, M. I. (1985). Supporting innovation and venture development in established companies. *Journal of Business Venturing*, *1*, 47–60.

Kanter, R. M. (1990). *When elephants learn to dance: mastering the challenges of strategy, management, and careers in the 1990s*. London: Unwin Paperbacks.

Keegan, A., & Turner, R. J. (2002). The management of innovation in project-based firms. *Long Range Planning*, *35*(4), 367–388.

Leon, N., & Davies, A. (2008). The managed service paradox. *IBM Systems Journal, Special Issue on Services Science, Management and Engineering*, *47*(1), 153–166.

Lundin, R., & Söderholm, A. (1995). A theory of the temporary organization. *Scandinavian Journal of Management*, *11*(4), 437–455.

March, J. G. (1991). Exploration and exploitation in organization learning. *Organization Science*, *2*(1), 71–87.

Marquis, D. G., & Straight, D. M. (1965). Organizational factors in project performance. Paper presented at the Second Conference on Research Program Effectiveness, sponsored by Office of Naval Research.

Mattson, L. G. (1973). Systems selling as a strategy on industrial markets. *Industrial Marketing Management*, *3*, 107–120.

Meyer, J. W., & Rowan, B. (1977). Institutionalized organizations: Formal structure as myth and ceremony. *American Journal of Sociology*, *83*(2), 340–363.

Middleton, C. J. (1967). How to set up an organization. *Harvard Business Review* (March–April), 73–82.

Midler, C. (1995). Projectification of the firm: The Renault case. *Scandinavian Journal of Management*, *11*, 363–375.

Miles, R., Snow, C., Mathews, J., Miles, G., & Coleman, H. (1997). Organizing in the knowledge age: Anticipating the cellular form. *Academy of Management Executive*, *11*(4), 7–24.

Miller, R., Hobday, M., Leroux-Demers, T., & Olleros, X. (1995). Innovation in complex systems industries: The case of flight simulators. *Industrial and Corporate Change*, *4*(1), 363–400.

Mintzberg, H. (1983). *Structures in fives: Designing effective organizations*. Englewood Cliffs, NY: Prentice Hall.

Mintzberg, H., & McHugh, A. (1985). Strategy formulation in an adhocracy. *Administrative Science Quarterly*, *30*, 160–197.

Morris, P. W. G. (1994). *The management of projects*. London: Thomas Telford.

O'Reilly, C. A., & Tushman, M. L. (2004). The ambidextrous organization. *Harvard Business Review*, *5*(April), 74–81.

Page, A. L., & Siemplenski, M. (1983). Product systems marketing. *Industrial Marketing Management*, *12*, 89–99.

Peters, T., & Waterman, R. H. (1982). *In search of excellence: Lessons from America's best run companies*. London: Profile Books.

Pich, M. T., Loch, C. H., & De Meyer, A. D. (2002). On uncertainty, ambiguity, and complexity in project management. *Management Science*, *48*(8), 1008–1023.

Pinto, J. K. (2007). *Project management: Achieving competitive advantage*. New Jersey: Pearson Education.

Pinto, J. K., & Kharbanda, O. P. (1995). Lessons for an accidental profession. *Business Horizons*, *5*(March–April), 41–50.

Pitsis, T. S., Clegg, S. R., Marosszeky, M., & Rura-Polley, T. (2003). Constructing the Olympic dream: A future perfect strategy for project management. *Organization Science*, *14*(5), 574–590.

Porter, M. E. (1985). *Competitive advantage: Creating and sustaining superior performance*. New York: Free Press.

Prencipe, A., Davies, A., & Hobday, M. (2003). *The business of systems integration*. Oxford: Oxford University Press.

Shenhar, A. J. (1993). From low- to high-tech project management. *R&D Management*, *23*(3), 199–214.

Shenhar, A. J. (2001). One size does not fit all projects: Exploring classical contingency domains. *Management Science*, *47*(3), 394–414.

Shenhar, A. J., & Dvir, D. (2007). *Reinventing project management: The diamond approach to successful growth and innovation*. Boston, MA: Harvard Business School Press.

Smith, A. (1776). *The wealth of nations*. Harmondsworth: Penguin Books.

Stinchcombe, A. L., & Heimer, C. A. (1985). *Organization theory and project management: Administering uncertainty in Norwegian offshore oil*. Oslo: Norwegian University Press.

Thomke, S. H. (2003). *Experimentation matters*. Boston, MA: Harvard Business School Press.

Utterback, J. M. (1994). *Mastering the dynamics of innovation*. Cambridge, MA: Harvard Business School Press.

Von Hippel, E. (1988). *The sources of innovation*. New York: Oxford University Press.

Wheelwright, S. C., & Clark, K. B. (1992a). Creating project plans to focus product development. *Harvard Business Review*, *5*(March–April), 70–82.

Wheelwright, S. C., & Clark, K. B. (1992b). *Revolutionizing product development*. New York: Free Press.

Whitley, R. (2006). Project-based firms: New organizational form or variations on a theme? *Industrial and Corporate Change*, *15*(1), 77–99.

Womack, J., & Jones, D. (1997). *Lean thinking: Banish waste and create wealth in your corporation*. New York: Free Press.

Womack, J. P., Jones, D. T., & Roos, D. (1990). *The machine that changed the world*. New York: Maxwell Macmillan International.

Woodward, J. (1958). *Management and technology*. London: Her Majesty's Stationery Office.

Woodward, J. (1965). *Industry and organization: Theory and practice*. Oxford: Oxford University Press.

TAKING TIME TO UNDERSTAND: ARTICULATING RELATIONSHIPS BETWEEN TECHNOLOGIES AND ORGANIZATIONS

Jennifer Whyte

ABSTRACT

Dynamic relationships between technologies and organizations are investigated through research on digital visualization technologies and their use in the construction sector. Theoretical work highlights mutual adaptation between technologies and organizations but does not explain instances of sustained, sudden, or increasing maladaptation. By focusing on the technological field, I draw attention to hierarchical structuring around inter-dependent levels of technology; technological priorities of diverse groups; power asymmetries and disjunctures between contexts of development and use. For complex technologies, such as digital technologies, I argue these field-level features explain why organizations peripheral to the field may experience difficulty using emerging technology.

Technology and Organization: Essays in Honour of Joan Woodward
Research in the Sociology of Organizations, Volume 29, 217–236

ISSN: 0733-558X/doi:10.1108/S0733-558X(2010)0000029016

INTRODUCTION

Since Joan Woodward's (1980 [1965]) seminal work, there has been considerable interest in exploring and explaining inter-relationships between technologies and organizations. However, in the trajectory of work inspired by Woodward, the approach of modern scholars differs from hers in important ways. Woodward's work is grounded in detailed empirical study of 1950s' manufacturing firms in Essex, United Kingdom, and looks at inter-relationships between the technologies of production and the management within the firm. Recent literature on organizations and institutions (e.g., Scott, 2001) shifts the focus to inter-relationships at the level of the field. This literature locates organizational practices in a broader institutional context, not only within the firm itself but also in practices that span firm boundaries (Orlikowski & Barley, 2001).

This change in focus is an important step in a "post-Woodward" world. It allows us to acknowledge the nested nature of organizational structures within a society and provides a strong sociological basis for inquiry. Technologies become seen as potent means of making durable, transporting, and replicating social structures, and the work of changing technologies takes on significant social and political dimensions (Garud, Jain, & Kumaraswamy, 2002; Munir & Phillips, 2005). Recent authors distinguish the technological field (Garud & Karnøe, 2003; Granqvist, 2007) as a social structure that brings together the range of organizations interested in the development of a set of artefacts and techniques and use it to address questions about technological change. According to Granqvist (2007, p. 9), the technological field:

> refers to those organizations that, in aggregate, are engaged in development, use, regulation or exploitation of a technology or set of technologies, share a common meaning system and are in regular contact with one another.

The technological field is broader than the industry, including all the organizations that affect performance. The idea focuses attention on the social organization of technology development and use. It provides a context for understanding how firms are embedded or engaged within a wider social structure, how some organizations may be more central and powerful than others, and how these power positions may be in flux.

In this chapter, I draw on this concept of the "technological field" to explore and contextualize inter-relationships between technologies and organizations. In the next section, I return to and provide a close reading of Orlikowski's classic description of these relationships, raising questions about the limits of mutual adaptation. The following section describes the setting and method of the empirical work. The findings highlight uses of digital visualization technologies within construction firms and discuss these in the context of the broader history of the technological field. Attention is drawn to disjunctures between development and use across the field and the implications of these disjunctures for sensemaking and decision-making within the user organizations. In conclusion, I highlight power asymmetries across the technological field and the varying status and access of different firms as they face disjunctures between design and use.

DEVELOPMENT AND USE OF TECHNOLOGIES

The starting point for this study of relationships between technology and organization is the idea of mutual adaptation highlighted in the literatures (e.g., Leonard-Barton, 1988; Orlikowski, 1992). In her classic work on duality of technology, Orlikowski (1992) frames design and use as ongoing modes of action, thus reconciling previous descriptions of technology as either socially constructed in its design or fixed in its use. She writes, "Rather than positing design and use as disconnected moments or stages in a technology's lifecycle, the structuration model of technology posits artefacts as potentially modifiable throughout their existence" (Orlikowski, 1992, p. 408). Hence, the co-existence of design and use is important to her model of technology and organization.

Orlikowski (1992) argues that the traditional divisions of labor between the technology designers and the technology users blur in the case of computer-based artefacts. This allows her to emphasize the mutual constitution of technology and organization. However, revisiting the empirical case used in this classic chapter, I notice disjunctures between the contexts of design and the contexts of use that are involved. In the case, Beta Corporation is a large multi-national software consulting firm from the North East of the United States, studied in 1987. Here functional consultants act as users and designers of different technology. They are *users* of productivity tools, which were developed by their colleagues, the technical consultants. They are *designers* of customized applications for the firm's clients. They play a mediating role and are simultaneously both users and designers, but of different technologies.

Thus, development and use cross firm boundaries. The functional consultants' working practices become inscribed into the practices of its client organizations through the technological solutions (customized applications) that they design. Orlikowski (1992, p. 411) writes that "Technology is built and used within certain social and historical circumstances and its form and function will bear the imprint of these conditions." This raises questions about the circulation of technology from contexts of design into its contexts of use that are under-explored in the discussion of technology and organization. Orlikowski's (1992, p. 417) focus in the paper is on how technologies become a more local "mechanism for technical control, delimiting the ways consultants perceive and interact with their work." However, tools developed in Beta Corporation not only contribute to Beta Corporation's structures of signification but also contribute to those of their client organizations.

Uses of technologies depend also on the types of users and skills, but crucially here, there is mutual adaptation across the boundaries of the organization. Although this wider adaptation is not commented on by Orlikowski, it is noted by one of her informants:

> In the front-end when we were designing with the screen and report design editors, we found we were leading clients on to accept the screens and reports in certain formats, because that's the way the design tool wants it done. So sometimes the client was forced to accept designs because of our technical environment. (reported speech of a functional consultant, from Orlikowski, 1992, p. 416)

There is an interesting power relationship suggested by this consultant's explanation. The users within the client organization are forced to accept designs because of the technical environment at Beta Corporation. This deserves further theoretical attention as it implies disjunctures between contexts of technology design and contexts of use that are not fully theorized within this model of technology and organization.

As I will discuss further using the empirical data, the proliferation of mediating roles is a part of the history of information technology in general, and digital visualization technologies in particular. The functional consultants that Orlikowski studied play a mediating role within the software consultant. Friedman (1994, p. 382) notes how, from the 1960s onwards, the typical IT specialist comes to occupy a mediating position between bought-in computer systems and non-IT specialist users within the user organization, and there is a massive increase in wider computer literacy. The changes to technologies through these mediating roles and the questions about how developments across firm boundaries affect the potential for mutual adaptation and use within the firm lead to the research question: "How does the locus of development and use across a technological field pattern inter-relationships between complex technologies and organizations?"

Before addressing this question through the empirical work, I want to clarify use of the terms "technology" and "organization" as scholarship has had to contend with widely varying definitions. Woodward's study takes a broad and inclusive definition of technology as the configuration of the firm's production system, but more recent work focuses on technology *as artefact* – focusing on particular material objects that are used to achieve tasks within an organization, or technology *as a bundle of techniques* – focusing on the capabilities and priorities that become embodied within such an artefact. Both approaches have merits, but here, I use the latter definition of technology to articulate the various features (Griffith, 1999) of complex technologies and the priorities in the associated technological fields. I also treat the term "organization" not as synonymous with "firm" but as referring more broadly to purposeful social structures that involve co-ordination, both co-operative and antagonistic, in a routine manner. Organizations include the firms, government departments, voluntary associations, and clubs across the technological field.

RESEARCH SETTING AND METHOD

To illustrate and extend the above discussion, I consider the use of visualization technologies in the UK construction sector. I use the term "digital visualization technologies" to indicate software applications that show 3D models and allow for real-time interaction. These include a range of simulation and prototyping technologies. Digital visualization technologies are important applications as they affect the way we see and comprehend the world, and ultimately, in the case of construction sector users, the way that it is built. On the personal computer (PC), a range of interactive, real-time, 3D applications were beginning to be commercialized in the late 1990s, when I started researching the technological field in the United Kingdom, and the construction sector was seen as a major potential market. A survey in the United Kingdom found a broad range of graphical systems that were being used in work described as "virtual reality" (VR):

> The other striking thing is the broad range of software in use. Much of this cannot be classed by any stretch of the imagination as VR software, suggesting that many groups are still developing their own solutions to problems using underlying graphic systems. As in last year's report this may imply quite a large degree of duplication of effort. (Howard, Hubbold, Murta, & West, 1995)

In the United Kingdom, virtual reality was being portrayed as an important new technology awaiting a "dominant design" (Swann & Watts, 2000;

Watts, Swann, & Pandit, 1998). A UK government initiative, the Department of Trade and Industry (DTI)'s VR Awareness Programme (DTI, 2000), identified construction as one of five key sectors for VR use along with automotive, aerospace/defence, oil and gas, and major engineering contractors. The report states,

> Of the five Key Sectors, the Construction industry professionals and trade organizations have been the most receptive to the DTI Awareness Programme, a promising indicator for future growth in this important market sector. (DTI, 2000)

The United Kingdom made a substantial contribution to the development of this technological field during the 1990s. It had related software and hardware industries, with virtual reality firms either headquartered (e.g., division and virtuality) or with regional offices in the United Kingdom. Research laboratories in the private sector, particularly those in recently privatized utilities, were conducting substantial VR research, for example, the British telecommunications firm BT was active and involved in standards development. Both the UK government and the European Union (EU) put substantial funding into research in this area. (By 2001, the EU had funded 105 projects that used "virtual reality as a descriptor" and 24 of those were ongoing.) There were also active VR associations. The UK VR Special Interest Group (SIG) was active from 1993 to 1999, and it co-existed with regional groups such as the London VR SIG, which was active from 1996 to 2000, and the UK-based Virtual Reality Education Foundation (VeRGe), which was active from 1992 to 1999.

These data were collected between 1997 and 2007, across a number of studies focused on aspects of the development and use of digital visualization technologies in this context. The approach here is to seek longitudinal and contextual understanding (Pettigrew, 1985) using these empirical data to develop and extend theories about conceptual relationships. I collected data using semistructured interviews, participant observation, and archival analysis, maintaining ongoing relationships with developers of visualization technologies and with their users in the construction sector. For example, I conducted interviews in 11 construction firms and 6 virtual reality suppliers in 2001. I also participated in the organizations within the technological field, for example, attending most of the meetings of the London VR SIG from 1997 to 2000, where I often met with technology specialists from construction organizations. The London VR SIG had brought together people from high-end immersive VR labs and the games industry with researchers from particular industrial applications.

I conducted further interviews as part of cross-sectoral analysis of the use of digital visualization technologies conducted in 2005 and 2006, in some instances re-interviewing firms and individuals that I had first interviewed in 2001. This provided a context for hearing their reflections on the success and failure of previous implementation strategies. Building on previous work (Whyte, 2002, 2003), I use these data here to examine the dynamic inter-relationships between technologies and organizations in this setting.

In discussing the findings, the next section provides examples of uses of digital visualization technologies within construction firms and raises questions about why these firms are not able to mutually adapt technologies and organizations, rather facing a range of sustained, sudden, or increasing maladaptation. The following section discusses the broader history of the technological field. It provides a broader context by describing the early developments within the field and the hierarchical structures within the field because of the complex nature of visualization technologies. Then the heterogeneous priorities of users across the field and the disjunctures between development and use are discussed.

CONSTRUCTION SECTOR USERS

The inter-relationships between technology and organization are difficult to understand by focusing solely on the construction sector user organization. The construction sector users that were the focus of my research were enthusiastic users of technologies that then became obsolete, either because they were based on standards that stopped being developed or because the firms that supplied them changed their strategic direction.

There was a significant research community developing solutions for the construction sector, with investment from the EU and UK research councils and a number of university-based VR laboratories for use in built environment applications. Many of these companies and others that I visited around this time were working closely with universities on projects in this area. My conversations with IT specialists across the construction sector revealed a range of different strategies and priorities associated with using interactive real-time 3D software. Five examples are given in Table 1.

Although most of this commercial use of interactive real-time 3D applications was at the "proof-of-concept" stage, some firms had well-developed visualization facilities and teams and significant investment in activities in this area. For example, the computer-aided design (CAD) and visualization group of construction contractor B, given in Table 1, had five

Table 1. Five Examples of Discussions about Interactive Real-Time 3D in Different Architectural, Engineering and Construction Firms.[a]

Type of Company	Visualization activities
Construction contractor A	The firm has a "positive drive towards a 3D single data environment;" they are interested in "how to control our projects using a system." There are 16 people who work in visualization in different parts of the company with 13 of those in central office. They use both the major CAD packages, and my conversation was with the senior CAD consultant and another CAD consultant.
Consultant engineer	This firm has a particular "proof-of-concept" virtual reality tool that they had developed following a number of highway projects on which it had used virtual reality. The R&D manager and IT manager demonstrated the tool's use on a railway project. They felt that this would "produce better and safer designs in a shorter time." Animations can be generated from the models to evaluate signal visibility as well as checking the clearances to new platforms.
Architect	There are computer visualization specialists, and a CAD tool on every designer's desk, with a large model shop with tools for making CAD-generated models. The head of IT is sceptical about allowing the client to fly around a model in real time: "Buildings don't get designed by pushing walls around;" "There is a naïve view that the client should be showed what they will experience every day, however this is actually one aspect of a building."
Construction contractor B	The emphasis is on the single project model rather than the single building model as they are interested in all the data that are not 3D as well as the geometric information. The head of design and the visualization manager explained that "They are interested in virtual reality as a browser of the project or object model." They are interested in selling a product and feel there may be problems when VR becomes a contractual document.
Project manager	In the United Kingdom, there is a team of three visualization specialists, with another person embedded in a major project. Here, data for VR models come from various CAD packages. They showed a five-minute clip of a model that took 200 hours of work to create. In the United States, there is a team that started in 1995 and had peaked at six people. Unusually for a firm in the construction sector, this team uses workstations. This team had recently become part of the firm's R&D department.

[a]In all of these companies, the interviews were conducted in 2001, comments in quotations are taken from notes of the meetings.

to six full-time members of staff providing support to engineers on a wide range of projects. The visualization manager explained to me that the firm had a long history of using CAD tools having obtained a mainframe computer in the early 1970s when he was a new member of staff. The office was full of PCs and the team acted as a technology broker, learning about the newest and best technologies, and introducing them to the wider firm. It had a particular focus on integrating data from multiple applications.

As the technology champions within the firm (construction contractor B), this team mediates between the users within the firm and the developers of technologies outside the firm. They also identified areas in which they believe that restructuring industrial practice around the process of developing models would lead to significant productivity improvements. For example, the team were convinced that using this software saved money by reducing the need to introduce costly or unsatisfactory "work-arounds" at a late stage in the detailing process or on site. It made ensuring spatial compatibility between different engineering systems easier. However, they expressed frustration that other members of the industry did not use these models. They felt that if the architect designed in 3D, then they would not have to be developing the model at such a late stage in the process.

What the strategies of these five firms have in common is the combination of development work in-house with externally sourced software; the interest in combining interactive real-time 3D applications with CAD and animation packages and the strong interest in integration of data from a number of professional sources and software packages. All five firms are champions of real-time interactive 3D, but the extent to which they use packages with these capabilities varies.

Yet the success of implementing these technologies was partial: These data suggest instances of sustained, sudden, or increasing maladaptation as well as mutual adaptation. Construction contractor A does not have a real-time interactive package but has a strong emphasis on 3D modeling. The consultant engineer has developed his/her own "proof-of-concept" tool using a 3D standard [Virtual Reality Modelling Language (VRML)], which, discussed in the next section, then stops being developed. Both of the members of staff interviewed had left in 2005. The architect is relatively sceptical of the need for real-time interaction, although they have specialists who create highly rendered realistic images that have less emphasis on interaction. Construction contractor B is trialling a new software as discussed above; however, the company is sold and this group is disbanded even before this software stops being developed. The project manager works with a CAD firm to develop visualizations for a later project. I argue that this maladaptation and the adaptation of technology and organizations are best explained by theoretical work at the level of the technological field.

A HISTORY OF THE TECHNOLOGICAL FIELD

In a technological field, organizational activity focuses on a shared set of technologies or technological visions (Granqvist, 2007, p. 9). Central players within the computer visualization field that emerged in the late 20th century include the US government that provided substantial research funding, the military, advanced manufacturing, and entertainment firms that provided major user bases, the growing computer industry in the United States that spawned some of the related industries and firms, and SIGGRAPH, a special interest group for people working with computer-generated images. There is a shared vision of interactive, real-time, 3D visualization. Interaction means that there is a commitment to direct manipulation techniques. Real time means that user input needs to be responded to seemingly instantly; 3D visualization means that a model needs to be shown. Common underlying graphic technologies became shared across a range of flight simulation, urban warfare simulation, film production, and CAD solutions, with built environment applications such as real-time architectural walk-throughs discussed as potential applications of the emerging technology from the early days of the field.

Users and Developers through the Early History of the Field

The technological field has its infancy in the 1950s, when the potential to achieve interactive, real-time, 3D visualizations on the computer is first understood. Real-time interaction is developed through military research from the 1940s onwards. The computer, "Whirlwind," is a flight simulator developed as part of Project SAGE to create a computer-based air-defence system against long-range bombers. Although it was quite different to what we think of as a "computer" today, with substantial physical mass, 10 tons weight and 150 kW power consumption (for only 1,024 bytes × 2 banks of memory), it was the first computer designed to respond instantly to the user's input at the console. At this point in the history of the information technology field, users and developers were often the same people (Friedman, 1994, pp. 376–377).

Whereas computers such as Whirlwind were transforming computing from a "batch-process" operation to real-time interaction, it is through the 1960s' projects with manufacturing application that the potential for 3D visualization became realized (at least in the civilian context). The graphical system, "Sketchpad," was developed at MIT to allow drawing of vector lines on a computer screen with a light-pen. Other early examples of CAD packages include commercial packages such as DAC-1, used by General Motors in 1963. The US government continued to fund most of this early research and was the single most sustained source of funding for visualization technologies. A Special Interest Committee on Graphics was formed within the Association for Computing Machinery (ACM) in 1963 forming the basis for the later Special Interest Group (SIGGRAPH) in 1969.

The technological field expanded and to some extent matured through the 1970s and 1980s. The first interactive architectural walk-through system was developed at UNC Chapel Hill where researchers used networks of high-end computers to get more processing power for complex 3D graphics and developed techniques for the addition of colors, textures, lights, and shading. During this period, SIGGRAPH focused its efforts on standard development (Brown & Cunningham, 2007). The development and use of visualization technologies began to become more disaggregated across the field.

Then in the 1980s, basic real-time, interactive, 3D visualization began to become possible on personal home computers as well as on high-end systems. As the processing power, graphic capabilities, and versatility of low-end systems became sufficiently developed for widespread use, games on personal home computers became popular. For example, the game "Elite" shows a basic line-based 3D universe on 8-bit machines. CAD packages are commercialized for use on PCs, with Autodesk Inc starting in 1982 and Bentley Systems starting in 1985. Here, there is a significant shift from dedicated machines with dedicated applications to commercial software packages and computers that can be used for multiple applications. It is in the late 1980s that the term "virtual reality" was coined and that virtual reality software applications were first commercialized. Autodesk, for example, demonstrated a PC-based virtual reality CAD package "Cyberspace" at the major US graphics conference SIGGRAPH in 1989.

The idea of "virtual reality" became a focal point for development in the 1990s, although this focus is not uncontested. On "high-end" hardware involving dedicated immersive facilities and UNIX-based workstations, there are a range of virtual reality applications available. Many of these applications prioritize calculating and updating images to represent speed and movement rather than accurate geometry and scale within an environment. They are well suited for flight simulation, urban warfare, and entertainment applications but not for built environment and manufacturing uses where geometric accuracy is crucial. At the same time, as developments in immersive virtual reality, the games industry drove the development of a range of graphics cards for "low-end" PC hardware. Open standards for a

VRML were developed for wider web-based applications. Although potential uses for designing buildings and cities continued to be part of the rhetoric of the field, construction industry users were not presented with clear technological options but rather had to make sense, interpreting the various dynamics of the field to decide about their own investments in technology.

Hierarchical Structure of the Field

By the 1990s, digital visualization technologies were complex technologies, and the field was socially structured and organized around different aspects of these increasingly complex computer-based artefacts that needed to be articulated. Hardware and operating systems are relatively standard, and the computer visualization field as a whole uses these generic components. However, within the field, development work focuses on formats and standards, software applications, and the add-on packages or macros that customize software applications to particular uses. This involves a hierarchical structuring of the field that patterns the power positions of different organizations around:

1. *Hardware:* Workstations and PCs;
2. *Operating systems:* Unix on the workstation and MS Dos and then Windows on the PC;
3. *Formats and standards:* open standards (e.g., Open GL on Unix; VRML on Windows) and proprietary standards (e.g., Performer on Unix; Direct 3D and Java 3D on Windows);
4. *Applications:* these include a wide range of applications for virtual reality authoring, military simulation, gaming, film production, and so on; and
5. *Add-on packages:* include software that adds visualization capabilities onto other packages such as CAD and Geographic Information Systems (GIS).

The development of each item in the above list usually depends on the use of technology at the preceding level. Developments across the field are interconnected, and changes involved at the lower levels (hardware, operating system, formats, and standards) often cascade out into further changes involved at the higher levels (applications, add-on packages). Hence, the pattern of interdependencies and changing power relations are inter-related with the articulated elements of the technology. A new hardware platform or operating system will require new activities in tailoring formats and standards and rewritten applications and add-on packages. Although they are omitted from the above list, most digital visualization systems also involve some peripherals – from the mouse and light-pen to haptic gloves, immersive displays, and stereoscopic glasses. These were particularly important to many users of virtual reality and were sometimes also hardware- or software-dependent.

DISJUNCTURES BETWEEN TECHNOLOGY DEVELOPMENT AND USE

Heterogeneous Priorities across the Field

Generating high-quality real-time 3D graphics continues to require substantial high-end computing resources. Hence, ongoing development within the technological field becomes structured around different sets of priorities: for real-time viewing, for geometric accuracy, and for high-quality graphics. In flight simulation and warfare simulation, the priority is often given to *real-time* viewing, and geometries are shown in less detail or with less accuracy where the computer does not have time to update a scene. In manufacturing and built environment applications, the priority is often given to *geometric accuracy*, and the view may slow where there are insufficient computational resources. In games, the priority is often given to *high-quality graphics*; real-time interaction is also important, but geometric accuracy is less, and hence, models are not fully detailed and may be one-sided or re-used within a scene to save computational power.

The priorities and interests of different sub-groups within the technological field are visible in interactions and strategic actions around formats and standards at the field level. In the mid-1990s, the VRML was developed by independent programers (based on Open Inventor) with the aim of developing networked virtual worlds. It became an open standard in 1997. The workstation supplier Silicon Graphics championed this standard and employed an early advocate of virtual reality as a "VR evangelist" from 1995 to 2001. However, Microsoft brought out Direct3D as a proprietary standard for Windows and Sun Microstation brought out Java 3D. Garud et al. (2002) trace the journey of the latter technology, but by the end of the 1990s, it was the Microsoft proprietary standard that was most widely used by PC-based games and hardware developers.

Associated with the diversity of technological priorities are disjunctures between development and use. These disjunctures have a geographic dimension. Despite an input of public money, the overall (UK-based) technological field became less rather than more coherent during the period studied. The disintegration of the self-organized researcher-led associations came at the same time as the government's VR Awareness Programme, which aimed to disseminate the use of technology into the industry. The committee of the London VR SIG, for example, agreed unanimously that the changes in the technology, markets and the group required a "reframing," to broaden its outlook from conventional VR, be it immersive or desktop. In the email they circulated, they suggested terms such as "virtualized realities" and "changing realities" to try to capture the wider feel; however, no further meetings were then held and this group ceased to exist. The main disjunctures I focus on below, however, have a strong sectoral dimension.

Disjunctures between Technology Developers and Users

During the period in which fieldwork was conducted, construction sector users found themselves facing significant uncertainties as the customers and users for technologies that were in the process of disruptive and non-cumulative change. There was a significant question around what hardware should be involved: whether advanced visualization should be a PC-based or workstation-based activity. High-end software firms were rewriting the software so that it would run on PCs as well as workstations. This involved a transition from a UNIX-based operating system to a Windows-based system – a transition out of the high-end market in which users were themselves trained computer scientists comfortable setting up visualization through text-based commands into a growing consumer market in which users expected more graphical modes of interactions in setting up as well as in viewing visualizations. The incumbent software providers found themselves ill-prepared for this wider market, in which they found themselves competing and also having to collaborate with a range of CAD, GIS, and animation suppliers.

The high-end software suppliers were seeking to diversify away from military and flight simulation and training applications and establish themselves as more generic visualization products. One of the major suppliers, interviewed in early 2001, was based in Los Angeles and had about 15 years of experience developing modelling and visualization software. Up until the late 1990s, they had produced applications exclusively for SGI Workstations.

> Now today we can take the same techniques that we do on the high end and deliver them on common PC hardware which is directly attributable to all the wonderful advances in processing speed but more importantly graphic card architecture and that is being driven ... by kids! The gaming industry, I mean it's wonderful.

Their firm had identified the built environment as a key area in which their software could provide benefit, but they were finding it a difficult market. They dedicated staff to developing customized urban simulations although they had little domain-specific knowledge of the market in planning and construction. Their background was in military training applications, particularly flight simulation, and they found the needs of construction sector firms for data exchange with CAD problematic. An interviewee described the experience of the practices of construction users as follows:

> when they turn on the computer they are turning on their CAD program ... and CAD programs and virtual reality sometimes don't mix well, at least from our perspective they don't because we are into real-time visualization and that's a whole very focused discipline in 3D visualization.

During this period, significant research effort was going into virtual reality in construction. At the same time, wary of the "hype" surrounding the term "virtual reality," high-profile suppliers removed it from their literature, with Multi-Gen, for example, re-branding themselves as suppliers of "visual simulation."

The enthusiastic use of technologies that then became obsolete by construction sector organizations is illustrated through a UK survey (Howard et al., 1995), in which the most widely used PC-based VR software package was used for fire simulation and for engineering simulation by the two construction sector firms that replied. Interest in the technology had brought together engineers and software developers from an unlikely mix of industries (including the porn industry), and in the late 1990s, this package was used to build stand-alone 3D applications and to author 3D web pages (it included VRML authoring capabilities). However, the developers of the software packages were themselves making decisions about which industry to be in as well as which technologies to use. I attended the rather heated user group meeting in which the software firm announced its new strategy, which effectively abandoned their existing user base to follow a web-based e-commerce route (the firm now describes itself as a mobile games publisher of 3D wireless games).

DISCUSSION: IMPLICATIONS FOR USER SENSEMAKING

In the previous sections, I have considered the dynamics across the various technological levels and the disjunctures between technology development and use, to understand how the locus of development and use across a technological field pattern inter-relationships between complex technologies and organizations. The levels I discuss – hardware, operating systems, formats and standards, applications, and add-on packages – are described in the practitioner literatures and are easily recognizable to the people I interviewed. They are used here to begin to articulate the hierarchical structure of the technological field and to articulate and disaggregate different contexts of development and contexts of use to theorize about their inter-relationships.

A challenge for organizations participating within a technological field is that it takes time to understand the dynamics across different levels. Individuals and organizations are constantly engaged in retroactive sensemaking to guide their future actions (Emirbayer & Mische, 1998; Weick, 1995). Competing technological systems may exist together for some time in a relation of dialectical tension (Hughes, 1983), and it may be unclear to the majority of users which system will be durable. This is clearly a challenge to the construction user firms that were the focus of my investigations, and the sustained, sudden, and increasing maladaptation that they experienced is only explainable in the context of these wider dynamics. Previous academic work has described the kind of disruptive innovation (Christensen, 2000) within the development industries that are involved. What have not been previously described are the difficulties this creates for users. More broadly, the dynamics across a technological field have implications for our understandings of relationships between technologies and organizations.

I have used Orlikowski's (1992) classic study on the mutual adaptation of technology and organization as a starting point for this investigation of relationships between technologies and organization. By introducing the concept of the technological field, I shift attention to adaptations across organizational boundaries; to hierarchical structuring around inter-dependent levels of technology; technological priorities of diverse groups; power asymmetries; and disjunctures between contexts of development and use. The understanding that technology and knowledge circulates across such contexts is elaborated in a trajectory of theorizing in the sociology of technology that has sensitized organizational theorists to such circulation across networks and contexts (e.g., Gherardi & Nicolini, 2000).

However, rather than focusing on the thing that circulates, in this chapter, I have sought to theorize about inter-relationships.

In this, the idea of the technological field has been crucial. It allows the mediating roles to be made visible. This is particularly important as digital technologies have become more complex and their complexity structures relationships across a field, suggesting limits to the mutual adaptation of technology and organization. The close relationship between development and use described in Orlikowski (1992) may be seen as a special case, enjoyed by central actors with good connections. In her case, the functional consultants she studied were users of software developed in-house by the technical consultants. However, modern organizations are often users of software that is developed elsewhere: there are spatial and temporal disjunctures between development and use. The idea of a technological field provides a context for understanding the "idiosyncratic strategies of individual organizations" (Hung & Whittington, 1997) as firms engage in strategic choices across pluralistic local contexts relating to technology and business.

A further implication of this study is the importance of taking time to understand. Just as it has taken me considerable time to analyze and interpret the data thus far (significantly more than I would have hoped), it takes organizations within the technological field significant time to make sense of their positions and to change their strategies. In seeking to understand the inter-relationships between complex technologies and organizations, a longitudinal and contextual approach to understanding the field seems to yield particular insight. The concept of the technological field used here is different from concepts such as "technology trajectories" and "dominant designs" in the economic literatures as these pay little attention to the character of the users, the uses to which IT is put, and the labor market for IT specialists (Friedman, 1994). As technology becomes more complex, I argue that we need such broad sociological approaches that articulate and situate studies within the particular historical patterns of technology development and use.

CONCLUSIONS

The above data and discussion show the limitations of a model of mutual constitution of technology and organization and its neglect of issues of competition and power. I find that what looks like mutual adaptation from the center of a technological field may be maladaptation for those on the edge. Across a technological field, organizations vary in their status, access and ability to mutually adapt technology and organization, with less central and powerful organizations often experiencing sustained, sudden, or increasing maladaptation. Thus, in answering the question, "How does the locus of development and use of technology pattern inter-relationships between complex technologies and organizations?," there are a number of disjunctures, which may be spatial and sectoral, but are in essence to do with different sets of priorities for further technological development. For example, there are disjunctures between construction industry users and the designers of virtual reality systems. Generic VR suppliers and resellers conceived of virtual reality as an entirely separate application creating a sense of presence, but for construction industry users, the access to engineering data, and connectivity of CAD and VR were major issues.

This work has a number of implications. Most importantly, it implies that our theoretical understanding of the relationships between technology and organization cannot escape a consideration of the position of the organization within the technological field. It implies the need for longitudinal and contextual studies. The work also has practical implications for organizations that are looking to implement and use new technologies. Conceiving of technology strategies in relation to their position and power within a technological field and the potential moves and outcomes that may be possible from that position will allow for more realistic strategizing and help firms to make sense of maladaptation. It also suggests a number of areas for further research.

Further research is needed to contextualize these findings within the wider academic literatures on information systems and organizations, to develop wider understandings of users, outside of those centrally located within technological fields, and to develop practical strategies for such firms. Despite substantial differences between my definitions and approach and that of Woodward, in seeking to develop theory that differentiates across organizations rather than providing a more singular theoretical approach, I find myself returning to and re-enjoying a key contribution of her work.

ACKNOWLEDGMENT

I would like to thank Nelson Phillips, Graham Sewell, Libby Schweber, and Nina Granqvist for helpful comments on earlier versions.

REFERENCES

Brown, J., & Cunningham, S. (2007). A history of ACM SIGGRAPH. *Communications of the ACM Archive, 50*, 54–61.

Christensen, C. M. (2000). *The innovator's dilemma*. New York: Harper Business.

DTI. (2000). *UK business potential for virtual reality, a market survey conducted by Cydata limited on behalf of the Department of Trade and Industry*. London: Department of Trade and Industry.

Emirbayer, M., & Mische, A. (1998). What is agency? *American Journal of Sociology, 103*, 962–1023.

Friedman, A. L. (1994). The information technology field: Using fields and paradigms for analysing technological change. *Human Relations, 47*, 367–392.

Garud, R., Jain, S., & Kumaraswamy, A. (2002). Institutional entrepreneurship in the sponsorship of common technological standards: The case of Sun Microsystems and Java. *Academy of Management Journal, 45*, 196–214.

Garud, R., & Karnøe, P. (2003). Bricolage versus breakthrough: Distributed and embedded agency in technology entrepreneurship. *Research Policy, 32*, 277–300.

Gherardi, S., & Nicolini, D. (2000). To transfer is to transform: The circulation of safety knowledge. *Organization, 7*, 329–348.

Granqvist, N. (2007). *Nanotechnology and nanolabeling: Essays on the emergence of new technological fields*. Helsinki: HSI.

Griffith, T. L. (1999). Technology features as triggers for sensemaking. *Academy of Management Review, 24*, 472–488.

Howard, T. L. J., Hubbold, R. J., Murta, A. D., & West, A. J. (1995). *1995 survey of virtual reality activity in the UK: The Advanced Interfaces Group*. SIMA Report.

Hughes, T. P. (1983). *Networks of power: Electrification in western society, 1880–1930*. Baltimore and London: John Hopkins University Press.

Hung, H., & Whittington, R. (1997). Strategies and institutions: A pluralistic account of strategies in the Taiwanese computer industry. *Organization Studies, 18*(4), 551–576.

Leonard-Barton, D. (1988). Implementation as mutual adaptation of technology and organization. *Research Policy, 17*, 251–267.

Munir, K., & Phillips, N. (2005). The birth of the Kodak moment: Institutional entrepreneurship and the adoption of new technologies. *Organization Studies, 26*, 1665–1687.

Orlikowski, W. J. (1992). The duality of technology: Rethinking the concept of technology in organizations. *Organization Science, 3*, 398–427.

Orlikowski, W. J., & Barley, S. R. (2001). Technology and institutions: What can research on information technology and research on organizations learn from each other? *MIS Quarterly, 25*, 145–165.

Pettigrew, A. M. (1985). Contextualist research and the study of organizational change process. In: E. Mumford, R. Hirschheim, G. Fitzgerald & A. T. Wood-Harper (Eds), *Research methods in information systems: Proceedings of the IFIP WG 8.2 colloquium* (pp. 53–78). Amsterdam, New York, Oxford: New Holland.

Scott, R. W. (2001). *Institutions and organizations*. Thousand Oaks, CA: Sage.

Swann, G. M. P., & Watts, T. P. (2000). Visualisation needs vision: The pre-paradigmatic character of virtual reality. In: S. Woolgar (Ed.), *Virtual society?: Technology, cyberbole, reality*. Oxford: Oxford University Press.

Watts, T., Swann, G. M. P., & Pandit, N. R. (1998). Virtual reality and innovation potential. *Business Strategy Review*, *9*, 45–54.

Weick, K. E. (1995). *Sensemaking in organizations*. London: Sage.

Whyte, J. K. (2002). *Virtual reality and the built environment*. Oxford: Architectural Press.

Whyte, J. K. (2003). Innovation and users: Virtual reality in the construction sector. *Construction Management and Economics*, *21*, 565–572.

Woodward, J. (1980 [1965]). *Industrial organization: Theory and practice*. Oxford: Oxford University Press.

SECTION 4 – SHORT ESSAYS IN TECHNOLOGY AND ORGANIZATION

TECHNOLOGY AND ORGANIZATION: CONTINGENCY ALL THE WAY DOWN

Wanda J. Orlikowski

The influence of Joan Woodward on studies of technology in organizations has been profound – not only did she launch a series of research investigations (her own and that of others) into the relationship between technology and organization structure, but her findings laid the groundwork for what came to be known as contingency theory (Klein, 2006). I want to take the opportunity provided by this short reflection piece to highlight some entailments of Woodward's important insights and trace out the various ways that contingencies matter in matters of organizing.

CONTINGENCY – TAKE I

In her research studies, Woodward (1958) found that those firms that were organized according to the logic of their production technologies were more successful (on a set of economic measures) than those that did not. On the conceptual front, this acknowledgment of contingency in organizational life was particularly valuable in helping management scholars shift away from assumptions and expectations of "one best way to organize."[1] It also helped to counter reductionist claims of technological determinism, the view that

Technology and Organization: Essays in Honour of Joan Woodward
Research in the Sociology of Organizations, Volume 29, 239–246

ISSN: 0733-558X/doi:10.1108/S0733-558X(2010)0000029017

technology is an independent force that has determinant and universal social impacts.

On the empirical front, contingency theory helped to spawn a stream of research studies into the range of contingencies that influence the relationship between technology and organization (Blau, Falbe, McKinley, & Tracy, 1976; Carter, 1984; Galbraith, 1977; Kelley, 1990; Perrow, 1967; Pfeffer & Leblebici, 1977; Schoonhoven, 1981). Contingency approaches continue to inform contemporary investigations into the impacts of information technology on organizations, for example, in research on media richness (Trevino, Lengel, & Daft, 1987; Trevino, Webster, & Stein, 2000), decision making (Huber, 1990), information processing and coordination (Dewett & Jones, 2001), network power (Burkhardt & Brass, 1990), and firm performance (Aral & Weill, 2007; Brynjolfsson & Hitt, 1996).

Technology studies done under the auspices of contingency theory typically pursue a variance logic (Mohr, 1982), and on this view, contingencies take the form of contextual variables (e.g., market, size, uncertainty, culture, capabilities) that moderate the relationship between technology and organization design or organizational effectiveness. Some studies adopt a voluntaristic version of this account, positing the contextual variables less as strong constraints than as contingencies to be manipulated by managerial action (in the form of strategic choice, intervention, or decision making). In either case, the contingencies are assumed to be contextual factors distinct from the technology, the organization and the relationship they moderate. Or to invoke Latour's (1987) terminology, contingency in this stream of research is located outside the black box that is the relationship between technology and organization.

CONTINGENCY – TAKE II

A different treatment of contingencies is evident in an alternative stream of technology research, broadly characterized by Markus and Robey (1988) as "the emergent perspective." Employing a process logic (Mohr, 1982) to understand the relationship between technology and organization, researchers in this stream view technologies and organizations as interacting in complex and indeterminant ways, reflecting various cultural, institutional, and temporal influences. Contingencies are now framed as complex social processes entailing meanings, interests, and history.

Influential research in this genre includes social constructivist studies of science and technology (Pinch & Bijker, 1984; Woolgar & Grint, 1991), where scholars find that a technology may have multiple meanings depending on the social groups that interact with it. This notion of contingent meanings – or what is termed "interpretive flexibility" – is seen to arise most frequently during the development and early use of a technology where there is often considerable uncertainty and contestation over meanings. In organizational studies, Barley's (1986, p. 106) research into the implementation of CT scanning technology in two separate hospitals found that "identical technologies" occasioned different structural changes within the two hospitals "because they became social objects whose meanings were defined by the context of their use."

The highly contingent ways in which technologies interact with organizations are now centre stage, as scholars develop various ways to theorize the social processes through which specific technological capacities are associated with particular organizational outcomes. Examples of such conceptual developments include notions of articulation (Gerson & Star, 1986), informating (Zuboff, 1988), appropriation (DeSanctis & Poole, 1994), equivoque (Weick, 1990), formative contexts (Ciborra & Lanzara, 1994), boundary objects (Bechky, 2003; Carlile, 2002), technologies-in-practice (Orlikowski, 2000), improvized learning (Boudreau & Robey, 2005), and affordances (Hutchby, 2001; Zammuto, Griffith, Majchrzak, Dougherty, & Faraj, 2007). In this stream of research, the black box is opened and contingency is located within the processes seen to characterize the relationship between technology and organization.

CONTINGENCY – TAKE III

A third stream of technology research presses the notion of contingency further, and although this work is largely being done in science and technology studies, it is slowly beginning to influence organizational research. Scholars in this stream challenge the received view that "technology" and "organization" are separate entities, reconceptualizing these as heterogeneous, shifting, and contingent associations (Latour, 2005) that participate in "the ongoing, contingent coproduction of a shared sociomaterial world" (Suchman, 2007, p. 23). Multiple approaches to articulate these ideas have been developed, including such notions as actor-network (Callon, 1986; Scott & Wagner, 2003; Walsham & Sahay, 1999), object-centred sociality (Knorr Cetina, 1997), mangle of practice (Pickering, 1995; Jones, 1998), fluidity (de Laet & Mol, 2000), practice-order bundles (Schatzki, 2002), and sociomaterial assemblages (Suchman, 2007).

As is evident from these examples, the vocabulary has shifted – away from discrete, pre-given entities (technology and organization), and their relationship (impacts or interactions) – to human and nonhuman agencies dynamically ordered in emergent and contingent configurations. As Suchman (2007, p. 242) explains: "Capacities for action are recast here from inherent capabilities to possibilities generated and reiterated through specific sociomaterial assemblages and enactments. These approaches shift the frame of reference from the autonomous human individual to arrangements that produce effective forms of agency within ramifying networks of social and material relations."

Examples of studies in this genre include Pickering's (1995) empirical examination of the construction of a scientific instrument – the bubble chamber in particle physics – and Suchman's (2005) investigation of how a particular Xerox photocopier technology was (re)configured in multiple trajectories of interest and action, contingent on the different disciplinary practices of the various communities. In social studies of economics (Beunza & Stark, 2004; Callon & Muniesa, 2005; MacKenzie, 2006), scholars examine how financial models and economic theories produce the market conditions they attempt to represent and explain. For example, MacKenzie (2006) explains how the Black-Scholes options pricing model first described the world of options pricing, but then through being integrated into traders' knowledge and routines on the exchange floor, and subsequently inscribed in computer algorithms, it came to produce that world over time. In this third stream of research, the black box is effectively deconstructed, and contingency is now located in the very constitution of people, things, and associations, as these are enacted dynamically in practice.

CONTINGENCY – GOING FORWARD

We have traveled a far way from Woodward's early insight into the importance of contingency in explaining the relationship between technology and organization structure. We now see contingency everywhere: not just in factors external to the organization, or in emergent processes of technology innovation, implementation, and use, but in the very constitution of what we call organizing. Going forward, what are some of the implications of these multiple takes on contingency in organizational life?

For certain kinds of questions, the first two takes on contingency (locating it within contextual factors or social processes) may serve organizational scholars well. For some other questions, however, these two views on contingency may be less helpful – particularly for those studies seeking to explore the emergent, fluid, distributed, networked, and virtual worlds of organizing (Law & Mol, 2002; Law & Urry, 2004; Girard & Stark, 2002; Zammuto et al., 2007). For these kinds of investigations, the third take on contingency may be more useful, focusing as it does on how "new agencies and accountabilities" are reconfigured through the "real-time contingency of performance" (Suchman, 2007, p. xii).

These investigations would seem to be particularly relevant in such dynamic, cross-disciplinary, contemporary contexts as biotech ventures, nanotechnology projects, web-based start-ups, global sourcing, financial trading, and new media production. In such contexts, operations are emergent and fluid, goods and services are intangible and informational, authority is distributed and diverse, and accountability is multiple and shifting (Child & McGrath, 2001; Rindova & Kotha, 2001; Stark, 2001). Consider a simple example – the now commonplace task of information search. For a good number of people in many organizations, this activity will involve accessing the Internet through a technology known as a web browser that provides access to a web search engine. Given the algorithmic configuration (Callon & Muniesa, 2005) of a search engine such as Google with its patented PageRank algorithm (Brin & Page, 1998), web search entails the performance of millions of lines of computer code written by software engineers, executing on multiple computers (configured with particular hardware and software elements and designed and built by computer engineers and production workers), whose operation depends on the millions of distributed people who use computers to create and update web pages every day, and the millions of people around the world who enter particular search criteria into their web browsers running on still other computers designed and built by yet other people.

In this description, the performance of a search engine and the results it produces are not primarily dependent on the impacts of some fixed technical capacity on some particular human behavior or organizational outcome *(Contingency – Take I)*. Neither do they depend primarily on an identifiable socio-historic process of interaction between particular human users and specific technological artifacts *(Contingency – Take II)*. Instead, the operation of web search may be better understood as the enactment of a sociomaterial configuration constituted dynamically by the dense entangling of human and material agencies in many different practices, places, and times *(Contingency – Take III)*.

In conclusion, the idea of contingency has helped us move beyond notions of singular determinism and optimal organization forms. It has also helped us recognize the situated pragmatics of socio-technical processes and the open-ended possibilities of emergent technological interactions. It is now poised to help us challenge and reconceptualize deeply embedded notions of technological and organizational realities. Fifty years on from Woodward's appreciation of the power of contingency, we may be set to realize that in matters of technology and organization, it is contingency all the way down.

NOTE

1. Although not entirely, as a variant of the latter has crept back into managerial rhetoric under the guise of "best practices" (Wagner, Scott, & Galliers, 2006).

REFERENCES

Aral, S., & Weill, P. (2007). IT Assets, organizational capabilities and firm performance. *Organization Science*, *18*(5), 763–780.

Barley, S. R. (1986). Technology as an occasion for structuring: Evidence from observation of CT scanners and the social order of radiology departments. *Administrative Science Quarterly*, *31*, 78–108.

Bechky, B. A. (2003). Object lessons: Workplace artifacts as representations of occupational jurisdiction. *American Journal of Sociology*, *109*(3), 720–752.

Beunza, D., & Stark, D. (2004). Tools of the trade: The socio-technology of arbitrage in a Wall Street trading room. *Industrial and Corporate Change*, *13*(2), 369–400.

Blau, P. M., Falbe, C. M., McKinley, W., & Tracy, P. K. (1976). Technology and organization in manufacturing. *Administrative Science Quarterly*, *21*, 20–40.

Boudreau, M.-C., & Robey, D. (2005). Enacting integrated information technology: A human agency perspective. *Organization Science*, *16*(1), 3–18.

Brin, S., & Page, L. (1998). The anatomy of a large-scale hypertextual web search engine. *Computer Networks and ISDN Systems*, *30*, 107–117.

Brynjolfsson, E., & Hitt, L. (1996). Paradox lost? Firm-level evidence on the returns to information systems spending. *Management Science*, *42*(4), 541–558.

Burkhardt, M. E., & Brass, D. J. (1990). Changing patterns or patterns of change: The effects of a change in technology on social network structure and power. *Administrative Science Quarterly*, *35*, 104–127.

Callon, M. (1986). Some elements of a sociology of translations: Domestication of the scallops and the fishermen in St Brieuc Bay. In: J. Law (Ed.), *Power, action, and belief: A new sociology of knowledge*. London: Routledge.

Callon, M., & Muniesa, F. (2005). Economic markets as calculative collective devices. *Organization Studies*, *26*(8), 1229–1250.

Carlile, P. R. (2002). A pragmatic view of knowledge and boundaries: Boundary objects in new product development. *Organization Science*, *13*(4), 442–455.

Carter, N. M. (1984). Computerization as a predominate technology: Its influence on the structure of newspaper organizations. *Academy of Management Journal, 27*, 247–270.

Child, J., & McGrath, R. G. (2001). Organizations unfettered: Organizational form in an information-intensive economy. *Academy of Management Journal, 44*(6), 1135–1148.

Ciborra, C., & Lanzara, G. F. (1994). Formative contexts and ICT: Understanding the dynamics of innovation in organizations. *Accounting, Management and Information Technology, 4*(2), 61–86.

de Laet, M., & Mol, A. (2000). The Zimbabwe bush pump: Mechanics of a fluid technology. *Social Studies of Science, 30*(2), 225–263.

DeSanctis, G., & Poole, M. S. (1994). Capturing the complexity in advanced technology use: Adaptive structuration theory. *Organization Science, 5*(2), 121–147.

Dewett, T., & Jones, G. R. (2001). The role of information technology in the organization: A review, model, and assessment. *Journal of Management, 27*(3), 313–346.

Galbraith, J. (1977). *Organization design*. Reading, MA: Addison-Wesley.

Gerson, E. M., & Star, S. L. (1986). Analyzing due process in the workplace. *ACM Transactions on Information Systems, 4*(3), 257–270.

Girard, M., & Stark, D. (2002). Distributing intelligence and organizing diversity in new media projects. *Environment and Planning A, 34*(11), 1927–1949.

Huber, G. P. (1990). A theory of the effects of advanced information technologies on organizational design, intelligence, and decision making. *Academy of Management Review, 15*(1), 47–71.

Hutchby, I. (2001). Technologies, texts and affordances. *Sociology, 35*(2), 441–456.

Jones, M. R. (1998). Information systems and the double mangle: Steering a course between the scylla of embedded structure and the charybdis of material agency. In: T. Larsen, L. Levine & J. I. DeGross (Eds), *Information systems: Current issues and future challenges* (pp. 287–302). Laxenburg: International Federation for Information Processing.

Kelley, M. R. (1990). New process technology, job design, and work organization: A contingency model. *American Sociological Review, 55*(2), 191–208.

Klein, L. (2006). Applied social science: Is it just common sense? *Human Relations, 59*(8), 1155–1172.

Knorr Cetina, K. (1997). Sociality with objects: Social relations in postsocial knowledge societies. *Theory, Culture and Society, 14*(4), 1–30.

Latour, B. (1987). *Science in action*. Boston: Harvard University Press.

Latour, B. (2005). *Reassembling the social: An introduction to actor-network-theory*. Oxford: Oxford University Press.

Law, J., & Mol, A. (Eds). (2002). *Complexities: Social studies of knowledge practices*. Durham, NC: Duke University Press.

Law, J., & Urry, J. (2004). Enacting the social. *Economy and Society, 33*(3), 390–410.

MacKenzie, D. (2006). *An engine not a camera: How financial models shape markets*. Cambridge, MA: MIT Press.

Markus, M. L., & Robey, D. (1988). Information technology and organizational change: Causal structure in theory and research. *Management Science, 34*(5), 583–598.

Mohr, L. B. (1982). *Explaining organizational behavior*. San Francisco, CA: Jossey-Bass.

Orlikowski, W. J. (2000). Using technology and constituting structures. *Organization Science, 11*(4), 404–428.

Perrow, C. (1967). Framework for the comparative analysis of organizations. *American Sociological Review, 32*, 194–208.

Pfeffer, J., & Leblebici, H. (1977). Information technology and organizational structure. *Pacific Sociological Review, 20*(2), 241–261.

Pickering, A. (1995). *The mangle of practice: time, agency and science*. Chicago, IL: University of Chicago Press.

Pinch, T. J., & Bijker, W. E. (1984). The social construction of facts and artefacts: Or how the sociology of science and the sociology of technology might benefit each other. *Social Studies of Science, 14*(3), 399–441.

Rindova, V. P., & Kotha, S. (2001). Continuous "morphing": Competing through dynamic capabilities, form, and function. *Academy of Management Journal, 44*(6), 1263–1280.

Schatzki, T. R. (2002). *The site of the social: A philosophical account of the constitution of social life and change*. University Park, PA: Pennsylvania State University Press.

Schoonhoven, C. B. (1981). Problems with contingency theory: Testing assumptions hidden within the language of contingency theory. *Administrative Science Quarterly, 26*, 349–377.

Scott, S. V., & Wagner, E. L. (2003). Networks, negotiations, and new times: The implementation of enterprise resource planning into an academic administration. *Information and Organization, 13*(4), 285–313.

Stark, D. (2001). Ambiguous assets for uncertain environments: Heterarchy in postsocialist firms. In: P. DiMaggio (Ed.), *The twenty-first century firm: Changing economic organization in international perspective*. Princeton, NJ: Princeton University Press.

Suchman, L. A. (2005). Affiliative objects. *Organization, 12*(3), 379–399.

Suchman, L. A. (2007). *Human-machine reconfigurations: Plans and situated actions*. Cambridge, UK: Cambridge University Press.

Trevino, L. K., Lengel, R. H., & Daft, R. L. (1987). Media symbolism, media richness, and media choice in organizations: A symbolic interactionist perspective. *Communication Research, 14*(5), 553–574.

Trevino, L. K., Webster, J., & Stein, E. W. (2000). Making connections: Complementary influences on communication media choices, attitudes, and use. *Organization Science, 11*(2), 163–182.

Wagner, E., Scott, S., & Galliers, R. D. (2006). The creation of 'best practice' software: Myth, reality and ethics. *Information and Organization, 16*(3), 251–275.

Walsham, G., & Sahay, S. (1999). GIS for district-level administration in India: Problems and opportunities. *MIS Quarterly, 23*(1), 39–65.

Weick, K. E. (1990). Technology as equivoque. In: P. Goodman, L. Sproull, & Associates (Eds), *Technology and organizations* (pp. 1–44). San Francisco, CA: Jossey-Bass.

Woodward, J. (1958). *Management and technology*. London: HMSO.

Woolgar, S., & Grint, K. (1991). Computers and the transformation of social analysis. *Science, Technology, and Human Values, 16*(3), 368–381.

Zammuto, R. F., Griffith, T. L., Majchrzak, A., Dougherty, D. J., & Faraj, S. (2007). Information technology and the changing fabric of organization. *Organization Science, 18*(5), 749–762.

Zuboff, S. (1988). *In the age of the smart machine*. New York: Basic Books.

TEXTUALIZING TECHNOLOGY: KNOWLEDGE, ARTIFACT, AND PRACTICE

Cynthia Hardy

This chapter argues that by conceptualizing technologies as texts (cf. Grint & Woolgar, 1997), it becomes possible to open up studies of technology to greater use of organizational discourse theory and discourse analysis, which focus on the systematic examination of bodies of texts. There are three common definitions of technology: as knowledge, practice, and artifact (Garud & Rappa, 1994). This chapter shows how all three definitions are consistent with the idea of "textualization" and, furthermore, that opening up these conceptualizations offers the opportunity not only to learn more about technology in contemporary society but also to extend the range of methods currently used in organizational discourse theory.

Organizational discourse theory is a research approach based on "strong" social constructivist assumptions (Schwandt, 2000), which focuses attention on the processes whereby the social world is constructed and maintained (Phillips & Hardy, 2002). Discourse has been defined as a "recognizable collection of statements which cohere together" (Wetherell, 2001, p. 194) and a set of social practices that "make meaning" (Jaworski & Coupland, 1999, p. 7). It provides "a language for talking about a topic" and produces "a particular kind of knowledge about a topic" (du Gay, 1996, p. 43). In this way, discourse refers "both to the production of knowledge through language and representations and the way that knowledge is institutionalised, shaping

Technology and Organization: Essays in Honour of Joan Woodward
Research in the Sociology of Organizations, Volume 29, 247–258

ISSN: 0733-558X/doi:10.1108/S0733-558X(2010)0000029018

social practices and setting new practices into play" (du Gay, 1996, p. 43). Discourses define "who and what is "normal," standard and acceptable" (Meriläinen, Tienari, Thomas, & Davies, 2004, p. 544) and are constitutive, rather than descriptive, of reality "through the way they make sense of the world for its inhabitants, giving it meanings that generate particular experiences and practices" (Phillips, Lawrence, & Hardy, 2004, p. 636).

Social constructionist assumptions are not new in technology studies. For example, work on the social shaping of technology (MacKenzie & Wajcman, 1985) has sought to problematize the nature of technologies and their implications by emphasizing its negotiable nature (Williams & Edge, 1996). The sociology of scientific knowledge (Shapin, 1995) and the sociology of technology (Woolgar, 1991) have focused on the development of scientific fields, seeking to identify points of "interpretative flexibility" and to understand why one interpretation rather than another prevails (Williams & Edge, 1996). The work on the social construction of technology (Bijker, Hughes, & Pinch, 1987) has extended these ideas to the study of technological artifacts, arguing that "the meanings given by a relevant social group actually constitute the artifact" (Bijker, 1995, p. 77). Struggle over these meanings emerges as different social groups seek to "impose its definition as the 'universal' meaning of the technology and to define its practices as 'normal'" (Stahl, 1995, p. 236). Actor-network theory has adopted a more radical position in challenging essentialized notions of the social, by focusing on networks of human actors, technologies and objects, and according humans and technologies similar status (Munir & Jones, 2004). It examines how, through the process of "translation," a network can be made to appear more fixed and stable, as a result of which the scientific facts, technical artifacts and modes of thought that constitute it seem more "real" (e.g., Callon, 1986a; Latour, 1987).

Notwithstanding the debates that surround and permeate these various schools of thought, they are united by an "insistence that the "black-box" of technology must be opened" (Williams & Edge, 1996, p. 886). In other words, they recognize that broader social processes shape and permeate processes of knowledge production and technological change. As such, the study of technology is compatible with the social constructionist assumptions on which organizational discourse theory is based and thereby amenable to discourse analysis, which studies the ways in which texts "are made meaningful through their links to other texts, the ways in which they draw on different discourses, how and to whom they are disseminated, the methods of their production, and the manner in which they are received and consumed" (Phillips et al., 2004, p. 636).[1]

There is no a priori reason why technology cannot be considered as text. As symbols that affect how people interact (see Canato & Ravasi, this volume), technology is also textual. Texts are manufactured, durable products that allow multiple readings by different people. They have been defined as "any kind of symbolic expression requiring a physical medium and permitting of permanent storage" (Taylor & Van Every, 1993, p. 109), which includes technology. Equally, a text is also a form of technology: "there are technological skills involved in its production. More than that, it is itself a technology, a skill to be mastered and requiring tools for its production. Because it is a technology, it is susceptible to the elaboration of methods in a search for perfectibility, and it lends itself to specialization, and the acquiring of expertize by an elite trained in the procedures of its production" (Taylor & Van Every, 1993, p. 108).

In the remainder of this chapter, different views of technology – as knowledge, practice, and artifact – are examined. In the first of these areas – technology as knowledge – studies drawing on organizational discourse theory are relatively common, and the idea of technology as text is readily accepted. In the second area – technology as practice – researchers have tended to focus on action and interaction, even though action is informed by texts and takes place within a broader discursive context. In the third area – technology as artifact – researchers have been the most dismissive of the limitations of discourse and some have explicitly rejected the metaphor of text.

TECHNOLOGY AS KNOWLEDGE

One common view of technology is as knowledge. "Defining technology as knowledge has important implications for how we comprehend technology in the making because it conceivably includes not only what exists, but what individuals believe is possible" (Garud & Rappa, 1994, p. 346). If "all knowledge and all knowledge-claims are to be treated as being socially constructed" (Pinch & Bijker, 1984, p. 401), the importance of discourse to such a view of technology is clear.

For example, a study of the role of mass media in the advent of computer technology in the 1980s shows the dominance of discourses of magic and religion (Stahl, 1995, p. 235). The cover of *Time* (16 April 1984) proclaimed "Computer Software: The Magic inside the Machine." Computers "conjure up" programs (*Time*, 31 January 1983, p. 65); while "teen age sorcerers" use them to practice the "secret arts of the computer age" (*Time*, 3 May 1982, p. 54).[2] As these particular discourses were drawn upon to talk about technology, they influenced technological development: as "a magical black box, computers were portrayed as a source of hope amid fear" (Stahl, 1995, p. 252). They also had political consequences insofar as the way in which the anxieties caused by technological change were reduced tended to advantage those best able to appropriate the new technologies, that is, the entrepreneurs who developed and sold the machines (Stahl, 1995).

Discourses thus help to explain the entry and exit of technologies from the economy. Maguire (2004) argues that artifacts are held in place in the economy by arguments, which in turn are constructed within a broader discursive context. Toxic chemicals such as DDT exited the economy as marketing, technical, public, and policy discourses changed and problems to human and environmental health surfaced. Different discourses can thus construct the same technology in very different ways, as shown in a study comparing the discourses of sound science and precaution (Maguire & Hardy, 2006). Sound science constructs certain risk-generating technologies as safe until proven guilty, whereas the discourse of precaution constructs them as potentially dangerous. The different discourses also shape power relations among actors: sound science positions governments as reactive, marginalizes NGOs, and gives business more latitude to develop and continue to sell risky products. Precaution, on the contrary, empowers a wider range of actors, especially governments and NGOs, to play a role in the process whereby products are categorized as risky and removed from the economy.

Discourses do not, however, fully determine outcomes, and there is, as a result, room for actors to draw on particular discourses strategically through the authoring of texts (Munir, 2005). Munir and Phillips (2005, p. 1682) show how actors can use discursive strategies to institutionalize new technologies. The success of the Kodak camera "was not a result of any inherent attributes of the technology…but instead due to the intense institutional entrepreneurship of Kodak, as it produced thousands of texts that supported a very different idea of what a camera was, who should use it and for what." Other writers have focused less on the strategic actions of individual entrepreneurs and more on the multi-lateral political processes of negotiation and contestation that surround the technology. Spicer (2005, p. 883) shows how these processes shaped Australian Broadcasting Corporation (ABC) Online – the website of the ABC, which is Australia's largest public broadcaster. Depending on how the discursive struggle among the stakeholders stabilized at different points, ABC Online turned "into a quite different technology that would serve quite different purposes," including a tool for positioning the larger corporation in the global marketplace, a commercial enterprise, and a vehicle for advertizing.

TECHNOLOGY AS PRACTICE

Technology is also seen as practice: it "manifests itself in certain practices that become institutionalized within a community of researchers" (Garud & Rappa, 1994, p. 346). Technology may have an independent objective reality, but, according to this view, it can only be understood through the way in which it is enacted in practice.

> [T]echnology is, on the one hand, an identifiable, relatively durable entity, a physically, economically, politically, and socially organized phenomenon in space-time. It has material and cultural properties that transcend the experience of individuals and particular settings. In this aspect, it is what we may call a technological artifact, which appears in our lives as a specific machine, technique, appliance, device, or gadget. At the same time, use of the technology involves a repeatedly experienced, personally ordered and edited version of the technological artifact, being experienced differently by different individuals and differently by the same individuals depending on the time or circumstance. In this aspect it may be termed a technology-in-practice. (Orlikowski, 2000, p. 408)

This work adopts "a radically contextual view, in which objects and their positions are inseparable, subjects are always located, and subjects and objects mutually implicate each other" (Suchman, 2005, p. 394).

Schultze and Orlikowski (2004) use a practice perspective to examine employees' daily activities in a firm that implemented a network technology – in this case an Internet-based, self-serve technology – to mediate brokerage relations. By examining the work practices of customers and employees, as well as the interactions between them, these researchers found that the way in which the new technology was used undermined the ability of sales representatives to provide consulting services, changing the nature of the network relations between the firm and its clients in ways that contradicted the goals of the original implementation. Similarly, Dery, Hall, and Wailes (2006) found that the way in which branch managers engaged with a new Enterprise Resource Planning system introduced in a bank limited the ability of the technology to deliver the anticipated benefits. The material nature of the technology was less important in explaining the outcome than non-material factors related to the nature of work at the branch.

Technology as practice cannot, however, be completely divorced from technology as text. First, practices take place in relation to texts (e.g., marketing demonstrations, manuals, instructions, training workshops, and feedback sessions) that are located within a wider discursive context. As a result, practices are not enacted in a social vacuum within which anything is possible, but in a set of broader historically situated power–knowledge relations, as critics of the community of practice literature have already pointed out (Fox, 2000; Contu & Willmott, 2003). Material practices are thus always invested with meaning (Parker, 1992) and in producing acceptable ways to think and talk, discourse also produced acceptable ways to act (Hall, 2001; Reed, 1998). Only certain practical possibilities exist. Second, language itself is a practice; and bodily practices rarely occur in organizational settings without recourse to language. A discourse consists of a "complex configuration of systematic linkages between linguistic and material practices" (Reed, 1998, p. 196). Thus, critical discourse analysts such as Fairclough (1995, p. 132) study the relationships between discursive *and* non-discursive practices to understand how "practices, events and texts arise out of and are ideologically shaped by relations of power and struggles over power." Third, material practices "disappear" into the discursive realm as soon as they are performed, through the way representations of them are "textualized" for the purposes of communication to those who were not present or part of them. Thus, once "concrete" practices become resources for discursive practices of both research subjects and researchers – even practice researchers have to textualize embodied practices to publish their research.[3]

TECHNOLOGY AS ARTIFACT

Technology is also seen in the form of physical artifacts. This view highlights "the form and functional characteristics of a technology," including "dimensional shape and material of construction" (Garud & Rappa, 1994, p. 346). This work has directly challenged the discursive approach associated with technology as knowledge (Hutchby, 2001; Schwanen, 2007).

> After poststructuralism and constructivism had melted everything that was solid into air, it was perhaps time that we noticed once again the sensuous immediacy of the objects we live, work and converse with, in which we routinely place our trust, which we love and hate, which bind us as much as we bind them. High time perhaps also, after this panegyric of textuality and discursivity, to catch our theoretical sensibilities on the hard edges of our social world again, to feel the sheer force of things which strike back at us with unexpected violence, in the form of traffic jams, rail accidents, information overload, environmental pollution, or new technologies of terrorism. (Pels, Hetherington, & Vandenberghe, 2002, p. 1)

It also challenges the technology as practice approach because, while recognizing that "a technology's material properties influence agency" (Orlikowski & Barley, 2001, p. 149), it tends to privilege human agency. "Technologies-in-practice are only changed through human action, whether deliberately or inadvertently" (Orlikowski, 2000, pp. 411–412). Moreover, the practice approach rejects the idea that properties are intrinsic to the artifact and argues they are instead constructed through "the relations that they establish with humans, and their performance of a more or less active role in social life is due not to their properties but to the type of relation" (Bruni, 2005, p. 361).[4]

According to this view, agency is not confined to a capacity located within the human mind; artifacts also act as agents through the way in which they enable people to overcome capability constraints and make action possible (Schwanen, 2007). One example of technology as artifact is actor-network theory, which argues that artifacts do not function as simple intermediaries, but they potentially translate intentions and mediate relations (Pels et al., 2002; Schwanen, 2007). For example, Callon's (1986b) study of the attempt to develop the electric car in France shows that it floundered when one of the material objects – the catalyzer – failed to play its role in the network (see Hutchby, 2001). Accordingly, these researchers insist that technological artifacts exist "outside the interpretive work which humans engage in to establish what those artifacts 'actually are'" (Hutchby, 2001, pp. 442–443); and posses "affordances," which are "functional and relational aspects which frame, while not determining, the possibilities for agentic action in relation to an object" (Hutchby, 2001, p. 444). These affordances constrain and enable how different actors interpret the artifact in question.

It has been argued that this approach to technology is incompatible with the metaphor of text (Hutchby, 2001). However, there is no reason why this should be so, for a number of reasons. First, technological artifacts are often read indirectly *through* a range of texts, such as graphs from gas chromatography from which residues of DDT are inferred.[5] These texts can be analyzed in the same way as any other text. Second, many technological artifacts can be read directly as texts to ascertain their agency. Research has already been conducted on the agency of written texts (e.g., Cooren, 2004; Hardy, 2004). It has to be admitted that, so far, this research has focused on characteristics such as intertextuality, genre, and the linguistic devices employed in the text (e.g., Hardy & Phillips, 2004; Harley & Hardy, 2004; Phillips et al., 2004). For example intertextuality has been deemed important because it "is not just 'the text' that shapes interpretation" but also "those other texts which interpreters variably bring to the interpretation process" (Fairclough, 1992, p. 85). A text is therefore more likely to influence discourse if it evokes other texts and draws on meanings that are more broadly grounded. Genres are recognized types of communication characterized by particular conventions, for example, letters, memos, meetings, training seminars, resumes, and announcements (Yates & Orlikowski, 2002) and are "instruments and outcomes of organizational power" that is "exercised through the manipulation or selective application of existing genre rules" (Yates & Orlikowski, 1992, p. 321). Texts also enact various linguistic devices that help to shape meaning, for example, rhetoric (Suddaby & Greenwood, 2005), narrative (Ainsworth & Hardy, 2004), and metaphor (Oswick, Keenoy, & Grant, 2002).

Notwithstanding the current emphasis on written text – the opportunity to broaden the understanding of text to material features exists. Pablo (2007) has gone some way towards this in her systematic use of discourse analysis to "decompose" features of Web portals into three different types of text. In addition to examining written words, she also analyzes visual categories such as composition and modality (which includes saturation, differentiation, and color scheme) and interactivity (such as the use of tools like bulletin boards, drop-down menus, and radio buttons) using resources from the fields of marketing, visual design (e.g., McCracken, 1993; Kress & Van Leeuwen, 1996), and information systems (e.g., Singh, Zhao, & Hu, 2003; Hart-Davis, 2005). Building on these ideas, future research could examine how intertextuality helps us to understand compatibility and integration, for example in relation to computer technology; genre could be more fully informed by studies of aesthetics, perhaps in the case of mobile phones; and linguistic devices could translate into visual clarity of a range of technologies.

CONCLUSION

This chapter builds on the idea that technologies can be treated as texts. By examining three approaches it finds one approach – technology as knowledge – which is particularly amenable to textualization and the area where discourse studies are most common. A second area – technology as practice – seems ripe for research that breaks down the longstanding – and much lamented – dichotomy between discourse and practice. By adopting a broader idea of text – one consistent with definitions regularly promoted in organizational discourse theory, albeit a conceptualization less often applied in a field that still tends to focus on the written text – it becomes possible to extend discourse analytic methods to physical artifacts. It has been argued that texts become more powerful as, among other things, they are transcribed on to more permanent media that permits storage, as well as temporal and physical removal; and as they are transformed into materialized physical frames (Taylor, Cooren, Giroux, & Robichaud, 1996). This naturally takes us towards the idea of a physical artifact and offers promising new avenues of research for technology and discourse researchers alike.

NOTES

1. Since discourses are not found in their entirety – only clues to them can be found in texts (Parker, 1992) – texts are the discursive "unit" (Chalaby, 1996) on which the organizational discourse researcher focuses (Grant, Hardy, Oswick, & Putnam, 2004).
2. *Time* citations are quoted in Stahl (1995).
3. This discussion is not intended to suggest that practices somehow pre-exist discourse or exist apart from it. They can be conceptualized as objects (Hardy & Phillips, 1999), parts of the material world with ambiguous meaning; also see Taylor et al. (1996) on text and conversation.
4. Although Orlikowski (2007) has recently argued for greater attention to materiality within the practice approach in advocating a "position of constitutive entanglement" that does not privilege either humans or technology, she does not suggest that materiality alone has agentic properties. For example, in explaining patterns of use of the Blackberry, she states: "It is not a matter of the material features of the BlackBerry technology having certain social impacts, or the new affordances of mobile email devices making communication more efficient or effective. The performativity of the BlackBerrys is sociomaterial, shaped by the particular contingent way in which the BlackBerry service is designed, configured, and engaged in practice. For example, the 'push email' capability inscribed into the software running on the servers has become entangled with people's choices and activities to keep devices turned on, to carry them at all times, to glance at them repeatedly, and to respond to email regularly. Such activities are only relevant in the circumstance of messages being continually pushed to handheld devices, and of shifting interpretations and interests that become bound up with the constantly available electronic messages. It is not a matter of the technology interacting with the social, but of constitutive entanglement" (p. 1444).
5. Thanks to Steve Maguire for this example.

REFERENCES

Ainsworth, S., & Hardy, C. (2004). Discourse and identities. In: D. Grant, C. Hardy, C. Oswick & L. Putnam (Eds), *Handbook of organizational discourse* (pp. 153–174). London: Sage.

Bijker, W. E. (1995). *Of bicycles, bakelites and bulbs: Toward a theory of sociotechnical change*. Cambridge, MA: MIT Press.

Bijker, W. E., Hughes, T. P., & Pinch, T. (Eds). (1987). *The social construction of technological systems*. Cambridge, MA: MIT Press.

Bruni, A. (2005). Shadowing software and clinical records: On the ethnography of non-humans and heterogeneous contexts. *Organization, 12*(3), 357–378.

Callon, M. (1986a). Some elements of a sociology of translation: Domestication of the scallops and the fisherman of St. Briene Bay. In: J. Law (Ed.), *Power, action and belief: A sociology of knowledge*. London: Routledge.

Callon, M. (1986b). The sociology of an actor-network: The case of the electric vehicle. In: M. Callon, J. Law & A. Rip (Eds), *Mapping the dynamics of science and technology: Sociology of science in the real world.* London: MacMillan.

Chalaby, J. K. (1996). Beyond the prison-house of language: Discourse as a sociological concept. *British Journal of Sociology, 47*(4), 684–698.

Contu, A., & Willmott, H. (2003). Re-embedding situatedness: The importance of power relations in learning theory. *Organization Science, 14*(3), 283–296.

Cooren, F. (2004). Textual agency: How texts do things in organizational settings. *Organization, 11*(3), 373–393.

Dery, K., Hall, R., & Wailes, N. (2006). ERPs as "technologies-in-practice:" Social construction, materiality and the role of organisational factors. *New Technology, Work and Employment, 21*(3), 229–241.

Du Gay, P. (1996). *Consumption and identity at work*. London: Sage.

Fairclough, N. (1992). *Discourse and social change*. Cambridge: Polity Press.

Fairclough, N. (1995). *Critical discourse analysis: The critical study of language*. London: Longman.

Fox, S. (2000). Communities of practice, Foucault and actor network theory. *Journal of Management Studies, 37*(6), 853–857.

Garud, R., & Rappa, M. A. (1994). A socio-cognitive model of technology evolution: The case of cochlear implants. *Organization Science, 5*(3), 344–362.

Grant, D., Hardy, C., Oswick, C., & Putnam, L. (2004). Introduction. In: D. Grant, C. Hardy, C. Oswick & L. Putnam (Eds), *Handbook of organizational discourse* (pp. 1–36). London: Sage.

Grint, K., & Woolgar, S. (1997). *The machine at work*. Cambridge: Polity.

Hall, S. (2001). Foucault: power, knowledge and discourse. In: M. Wetherell, S. Taylor & S. Yates (Eds), *Discourse theory and practice: A reader* (pp. 72–81). London: Sage.

Hardy, C. (2004). Scaling up and bearing down in discourse analysis: Questions regarding textual agencies and their context. *Organization, 11*(3), 415–425.

Hardy, C., & Phillips, N. (1999). No joking matter: Discursive struggle in the Canadian refugee system. *Organization Studies, 20*(1), 1–24.

Hardy, C., & Phillips, N. (2004). Discourse and power. In: D. Grant, C. Hardy, C. Oswick & L. Putnam (Eds), *Handbook of organizational discourse* (pp. 219–318). London: Sage.

Harley, B., & Hardy, C. (2004). Firing blanks? An analysis of discursive struggle in HRM. *Journal of Management Studies, 41*(3), 377–400.

Hart-Davis, G. (2005). *HTML quicksteps*. California: McGraw-Hill.

Hutchby, I. (2001). Technologies, texts and affordances. *Sociology, 35*(2), 441–456.

Jaworski, A., & Coupland, N. (1999). Introduction: Perspectives on discourse analysis. In: A. Jaworski & N. Coupland (Eds), *The discourse reader* (pp. 1–44). London: Routledge.

Kress, G., & Van Leeuwen, T. (1996). *Reading images: The grammar of visual design*. London: Routledge.

Latour, B. (1987). *Science in action: How to follow scientists and engineers through society*. Cambridge, MA: Harvard University Press.

MacKenzie, D., & Wajcman, J. (Eds). (1985). *The social shaping of technology: How the refrigerator got its hum*. Milton Keynes: Open University Press.

Maguire, S. (2004). The coevolution of technology and discourse: A study of substitution processes for the insecticide DDT. *Organization Studies*, *25*(1), 113–134.

Maguire, S., & Hardy, C. (2006). The emergence of new global institutions: A discursive perspective. *Organization Studies*, *27*(1), 7–29.

McCracken, E. (1993). *Decoding women's magazines*. Houndmills, Basingstoke, Hampshire and London: Macmillan.

Meriläinen, S., Tienari, J., Thomas, R., & Davies, A. (2004). Management consultant talk: A cross-cultural comparison of normalizing discourse and resistance. *Organization*, *11*(4), 539–564.

Munir, K. A. (2005). The social construction of events: A study of institutional change in the photographic field. *Organization Studies*, *26*(1), 93–112.

Munir, K. A., & Jones, M. (2004). Discontinuity and after: The social dynamics of technology evolution and dominance. *Organization Studies*, *25*(4), 561–581.

Munir, K. A., & Phillips, N. (2005). The birth of the "Kodak moment": institutional entrepreneurship and the adoption of new technologies. *Organization Studies*, *26*(11), 1665–1687.

Orlikowski, W., & Barley, S. R. (2001). Technology and institutions: What information systems research and organization studies can learn from each other. *MIS Quarterly*, *25*, 145–165.

Orlikowski, W. J. (2000). Using technology and constituting structures: A practice lens for studying technology in organizations. *Organization Science*, *11*(4), 404–428.

Orlikowski, W. J. (2007). Sociomaterial practices: Exploring technology at work. *Organization Studies*, *28*, 1435–1448.

Oswick, C., Keenoy, T., & Grant, D. (2002). Metaphor and analogical reasoning in organization theory: Beyond orthodoxy. *Academy of Management Review*, *27*, 294–303.

Pablo, Z. (2007). *Shaping cyberspace: The discursive construction, dynamics, and implications of metaphors on internet-based portals*. Ph.D. thesis, Melbourne University, Melbourne.

Parker, I. (1992). *Discourse dynamics*. London: Routledge.

Pels, D., Hetherington, K., & Vandenberghe, F. (2002). The status of the object. *Theory, Culture and Society*, *19*(5/6), 1–21.

Phillips, N., & Hardy, C. (2002). *Understanding discourse analysis*. Thousand Oaks, CA: Sage.

Phillips, N., Lawrence, T., & Hardy, C. (2004). Discourse and institutions. *Academy of Management Review*, *29*(4), 1–18.

Pinch, T. J., & Bijker, W. E. (1984). The social construction of facts and artefacts: Or how the sociology of science and the sociology of technology might benefit each other. *Social Studies of Science*, *14*(3), 399–441.

Reed, M. (1998). Organizational analysis as discourse analysis: A critique. In: T. Keenoy, D. Grant & C. Oswick (Eds), *Discourse and organization* (pp. 193–213). London: Sage.

Schultze, U., & Orlikowski, W. J. (2004). A practice perspective on technology-mediated network relations: The use of internet-based self-serve technologies. *Information Systems Research*, *15*(1), 87–106.

Schwandt, T. A. (2000). Three epistemological stances for qualitative inquiry: Interpretivism, hermeneutics, and social constructionism. In: N. K. Denzin & Y. S. Lincoln (Eds), *Handbook of qualitative research* (pp. 189–213). Thousand Oaks: Sage.

Schwanen, T. (2007). Matter(s) of interest: Artefacts, spacing and timing. *Geography Annual, 89B*(1), 9–22.

Shapin, S. (1995). Here and everywhere: Sociology of scientific knowledge. *Annual Review of Sociology, 21*, 289–321.

Singh, N., Zhao, H., & Hu, X. (2003). Cultural adaptation on the web: A study of American companies' domestic and Chinese websites. *Journal of Global Information Management, 11*(3), 63–80.

Spicer, A. (2005). The political process of inscribing a new technology. *Human Relations, 58*(7), 867–890.

Stahl, W. A. (1995). Venerating the black box: Magic in media discourse on technology. *Science, Technology, and Human Values, 20*(2), 234–258.

Suchman, L. (2005). Affiliative objects. *Organization, 12*(3), 379–399.

Suddaby, R., & Greenwood, R. (2005). Rhetorical strategies of legitimacy. *Administrative Science Quarterly, 50*(1), 35–68.

Taylor, J. R., Cooren, F., Giroux, N., & Robichaud, D. (1996). The communicational basis of organization: Between the conversation and the text. *Communication Theory, 6*(1), 1–39.

Taylor, J. R., & Van Every, E. J. (1993). *The vulnerable fortress: Bureaucratic organization in the information age*. Toronto, Canada: University of Toronto.

Wetherell, M. (2001). Minds, selves and sense-making. In: M. Wetherell, S. Taylor & S. J. Yates (Eds), *Discourse theory and practice: A reader* (pp. 186–197). London: Sage and Open University.

Williams, R., & Edge, D. (1996). The social shaping of technology. *Research Policy, 25*, 865–899.

Woolgar, S. (1991). The turn to technology in social studies of science. *Science, Technology, and Human Values, 16*(I), 20–50.

Yates, J., & Orlikowski, W. J. (1992). Genres of organizational communication: A structurational approach to studying communication and media. *Academy of Management Review, 17*(2), 299–326.

Yates, J., & Orlikowski, W. (2002). Genre systems: Structuring interaction through communicative norms. *Journal of Business Communication, 39*(1), 13–35.

TECHNOLOGY, INSTITUTIONS, AND ENTROPY: UNDERSTANDING THE CRITICAL AND CREATIVE ROLE OF MAINTENANCE WORK

Graham Dover and Thomas B. Lawrence

As we write this chapter, in the autumn of 2008, the US financial sector is in crisis – major investment banks have gone bankrupt, others have lost most of their market value, and the US Congress is considering a bailout of some 700 million US dollars (*The Economist*, 2008). The situation represents a clear case of the extraordinary potential for breakdown in social systems that depend on complex layers of technology and institutionalized practice – a "logistical nightmare of fixing a market whose complexity is central to the crisis" (*The Economist*, 2008, p. 81). More generally, we argue that it challenges prevailing images of technology and institutions as stabilizing forces and points to the fundamentally important, but often neglected, work of maintaining technology and institutions.

The dominant image of technology and institutions in organization studies is as mechanisms through which patterns of behavior become embedded and thus more certain, stable, and predictable. Technology achieves stability by connecting human action to sets of unyielding mechanical and electronic mechanisms that guide behavior and constrain the range of choices available to individuals (Shaiken, 1984; Winner, 1986). Technology embeds in material objects assumptions about the ways in which individuals ought to behave

Technology and Organization: Essays in Honour of Joan Woodward
Research in the Sociology of Organizations, Volume 29, 259–264

ISSN: 0733-558X/doi:10.1108/S0733-558X(2010)0000029019

that both facilitate such behaviors and prohibit others (Lawrence, 2008). Similarly, institutions are commonly understood as constraining social mechanisms that alter the costs and benefits of certain practices and associate them with self-activating sets of rewards for compliance and punishments for non-compliance (Jepperson, 1991; Phillips, Lawrence, & Hardy, 2004; Scott, 2001). Through regulative, normative, and cognitive mechanisms, institutions control individuals and organizations within specific domains (Scott, 2001). Thus, much of the literature connecting technology and institutions has focused on the ways in which they interact to control human behavior and how individuals and organizations work to resist or transform technological–institutional regimes.

Largely missing in these discussions is the common tendency of both technology and institutions toward entropy. Technological entropy is a well-established pattern, associated with the gradual breakdown in performance and reliability of technical systems (Romer, 1990). Whether through use, overuse, or underuse, all physical systems tend toward decay and breakdown over time. Rail tracks need fixing; phone network cables need replacing; software needs updating, and so on. A similar character has been noted with respect to social institutions (Zucker, 1988) – mechanisms of social control will tend over time to decay in their efficacy unless intervention occurs that restores those controls or implements new mechanisms (Lawrence & Suddaby, 2006). Often portrayed as powerful, enduring forces, institutions may be more fragile and their persistence less inevitable than is typically acknowledged (Oliver, 1992). We argue that this shared tendency toward entropy may be exacerbated in social systems that depend on complex layers of technology and institutions because the entropic tendencies of each may interact in ways that multiply the potential for breakdown. Decaying technologies undermine the institutionalized practices that are built upon them, as any rail commuter who has experienced the delays and uncertainties associated with degraded tracks can attest. Decaying institutions can similarly weaken associated technologies, as a lack of use and attention can lead to neglect and disinvestment.

These dynamics point to the need to understand and appreciate forms of work aimed at maintaining technology, institutions, and the relationships between them. In the case of the US financial crisis, the sector seems to have been kept afloat, despite clearly dysfunctional policies and design principles, by the active, creative maintenance work of an army of financial actors shoring up institutional frameworks and technologies. And now, the work of the US administration and the Congress to construct a bailout represents an extraordinary instance of maintenance work aimed at propping up the social institutions and technologies that comprise the US financial sector. Despite the importance of maintaining technology and institutions illustrated by this exceptional case, a quick look at the scholarly and practical literatures reveals only a passing interest in the maintenance of technology and institutions, and a far greater fascination with effecting change. Technology research and writing is dominated by studies of innovation, creativity, and transformation. Even institutional research, with its roots in understanding social stability, now focuses primarily on the transformation of fields and industries, often through institutional entrepreneurship and innovation. In this context, the work of maintaining technology and institutions – individuals and organizations ensuring that existing physical and social systems remain intact and functional – is portrayed at best as relatively simple and mundane, and more often as a hindrance to progress.

In contrast, we argue that the work of maintaining technology and institutions involves creative and strategic sets of practices. In a review of research on institutional work, Lawrence and Suddaby (2006) identify a range of practices associated with maintaining institutions that illustrate a high degree of creativity on the part of actors but largely overlook the complex interplay of technology and institutions. This relationship, we argue, can present a range of distinctive challenges. Complex layers of technology and institutionalized practices can lead to situations in which the workings of social systems become nearly impenetrable even to most insiders, making detection of entropy difficult and maintenance highly problematic. Such a state describes many parts of the financial sector and may come to describe the national and international agreements around carbon taxing, trading, and offsetting. In addition, the interdependencies among multiple sets of technology and institutions can mean that entropy becomes dispersed, with minimal levels of local decay adding up to significant levels across systems. This dynamic can make the need for maintenance difficult to identify at close range, such that local actors may perceive systems as robust, whereas more distant actors may be better placed to detect potentials for collapse. Moreover, the ways in which institutional systems affect the distribution of power and resources may lead to situations in which the entropy of technology and institutions is deliberately hidden: some actors might intentionally facilitate decay in technology and institutions, either to reap the rewards of an existing system or to engender its collapse. Together, these challenges suggest the work of maintaining technology and institutions involves sophisticated skills, both diagnostic and strategic, and diverse interests and aims; it can require the abilities to identify often hidden instances of entropy, diagnose complex causes of decay, create new physical and social mechanisms to support existing systems and coordinate the efforts of large numbers of individuals and organizations.

The importance of this work can be demonstrated by exploring the relationship between maintaining technology and institutions, and the work associated with creating and disrupting them. Several points are worth noting here. First, in highly complex technological–institutional environments, as exemplified by the financial sector, the demands of maintaining technology and institutions may absorb the material and cognitive resources of an entire field, such that the problems of an institutional arrangement are overlooked or ignored until a crisis occurs. Similar dynamics occur in large organizations, which often employ small armies of individuals to maintain the operation of technologies and institutionalized practices and rules. Inertia in such contexts involves not mindless repetitive behavior, but the active, creative work of those whose identities and roles are tied to the continuity of existing systems. Whereas research on resistance to change has tended to focus on the ways in which new organizational arrangements threaten the skills and interests of members, conceptualizing maintenance work as active, interested, and coordinated suggests that resistance may be a more basic phenomenon, emerging regardless of the attractiveness or threats associated with proposed changes.

Second, studies of the creation of new technological–institutional arrangements have tended to focus primarily on the problem of establishing those arrangements (Garud, Jain, & Kumaraswamy, 2002; Maguire, Hardy, & Lawrence, 2004), with relatively little attention paid to the problem of maintaining them. An important lesson could be learned here from the research on quality in manufacturing and service contexts that points to the advantages of designing quality into products and processes, rather than attempting to correct deficiencies later. This logic would suggest that certain combinations of technology and institutions may engender complex and costly work to maintain them, whereas other combinations may be far more robust and enduring. Particularly important may be the role of feedback, such that actors capable of maintaining systems are aware of decay and breakdown as it occurs, rather than being isolated from it either technologically or socially. This points to the potentially paradoxical relationship between bricolage (Campbell, 2004) and the maintenance of technology and institutions. On the one hand, bricolage epitomizes solutions borne out of "tinkering" or "fiddling" that appear unstable, but on the other hand, its inherent and explicit messiness might create situations in which maintenance is expected and that expectation is incorporated into the social architecture associated with it. As such, systems based on bricolage may be more reliable than those that are extensively planned and designed, simply because they are less vulnerable to over-complexity and isolation from other systems.

Third, disrupting technological–institutional arrangements may be effectively and efficiently achieved by undermining the ability of actors to maintain those arrangements. This might occur intentionally, as exemplified by the Thatcher government's approach to prompting reform in the National Health Service in the United Kingdom (Illife, 1985). It might also happen unintentionally, as when a wide variety of relatively equally resourced actors attempt to manage the maintenance of technology and institutions, but with divergent aims and interests, and thus create a patchwork of unconnected and competing solutions. The general implication may be that change is likely to occur not only in cases of institutional entrepreneurship, but also when maintenance workers become overloaded and are simply unable to address the pace or scale of the entropy they face.

Having identified the interesting and important role of maintenance work in complex technological–institutional environments, we hope to encourage research that looks directly at the practices, roles, resources, and relationships of the actors who maintain those systems, both the operational workers responsible for fixing and cleaning, and the managers, planners, and architects who oversee and design that work. Such research, however, needs sets of theoretical frameworks that conceptualize maintenance work and its relationships to other phenomena. At present, we have only the beginning of a theoretical language to describe and understand how technological–institutional systems are maintained. One potentially fruitful approach might be to draw on the concrete language of technological maintenance: concepts such as maintenance cycles, shutdowns, cleanups, turnarounds, and backups point to intriguing possibilities when applied to social systems involving complex layers of technology and institutions. The concept of a "shutdown," for instance, resonates with Weick's (2000) arguments regarding the notion of "freezing" social systems to diagnose problematic relationships and vicious circles. We are not sure what it would look like to clean up or reboot an institution, but images such as those might energize organizational scholars interested in better understanding how naturally decaying social systems are maintained and with what consequences.

REFERENCES

Campbell, J. L. (2004). *Institutional change and globalization*. Princeton, NJ: University Press.

Garud, R., Jain, S., & Kumaraswamy, A. (2002). Institutional entrepreneurship in the sponsorship of common technological standards: The case of Sun Microsystems and Java. *Academy of Management Journal, 45*(1), 196–214.

Illife, S. (1985). The politics of health care: The NHS under Thatcher. *Critical Social Policy, 5*(14), 57–72.

Jepperson, R. L. (1991). Institutions, institutional effects, and institutionalism. In: W. W. Powell & P. J. DiMaggio (Eds), *The new institutionalism in organizational analysis* (pp. 143–163). Chicago: University of Chicago Press.

Lawrence, T. B. (2008). Power, institutions and organizations. In: R. Greenwood, C. Oliver, K. Sahlin & R. Suddaby (Eds), *Sage handbook of organizational institutionalism* (pp. 170–197). London: Sage.

Lawrence, T. B., & Suddaby, R. (2006). Institutions and institutional work. In: S. R. Clegg, C. Hardy, T. B. Lawrence & W. R. Nord (Eds), *Handbook of organization studies* (2nd ed., pp. 215–254). London: Sage.

Maguire, S., Hardy, C., & Lawrence, T. B. (2004). Institutional entrepreneurship in emerging fields: HIV/AIDS treatment advocacy in Canada. *Academy of Management Journal, 47*(5), 657–679.

Oliver, C. (1992). The antecedents of deinstitutionalization. *Organization Studies, 13*(4), 563–588.

Phillips, N., Lawrence, T. B., & Hardy, C. (2004). Discourse and institutions. *Academy of Management Review, 29*(4), 635–652.

Romer, P. M. (1990). Endogenous technological change. *The Journal of Political Economy, 98*(5), S71–S102.

Scott, W. R. (2001). *Institutions and organizations* (2nd ed.). Thousand Oaks, CA: Sage.

Shaiken, H. (1984). *Automation and labor in the computer age*. New York: Holt, Rinehart and Winston.

The Economist. (2008). The doctor's bill, *The Economist*, September 27, pp. 81–82.

Weick, K. E. (2000). Emergent change as universal in organizations. In: *Breaking the code of change* (pp. 223–241). Boston, MA: Harvard Business School Press.

Winner, L. (1986). *The whale and the reactor: A search for limits in an age of high technology*. Chicago, IL: University of Chicago Press.

Zucker, L. G. (1988). Where do institutional patterns come from? In: L. G. Zucker (Ed.), *Institutional patterns and organizations: Culture and environment*. Cambridge, MA: Ballinger.

WHAT ARE BUSINESS MODELS? DEVELOPING A THEORY OF PERFORMATIVE REPRESENTATIONS

Markus Perkmann and André Spicer

ABSTRACT

Despite a rich extant literature, it is unclear what business models are. We assess three dominant conceptions of business models in the academic literature: as transactional structures, value extracting devices, and mechanisms for structuring the organization. To overcome the shortcomings of these approaches, we draw on theories of performativity, social typecasting, and managerial cognition. We propose an alternative conception of business models as performative representations that work in three ways: as narratives that convince, typifications that legitimate, and recipes that guide social action. Rather than actual features of firms, business models are representations that allow managers to articulate and instantiate the value of new technologies.

Technology and Organization: Essays in Honour of Joan Woodward
Research in the Sociology of Organizations, Volume 29, 265–275

ISSN: 0733-558X/doi:10.1108/S0733-558X(2010)0000029020

INTRODUCTION

In her seminal work, Joan Woodward (1965) pointed out that technology shapes the organizational structures and dynamics of control in organizations. While this insight has remained at the center of organizational sociology for many years, it may be due for an overhaul. In particular, one might ask to what extent the results Woodward derived from a study of manufacturing organizations apply to organizations that are heavily reliant on post-industrial technologies such as software, biomedicine, and complex materials science (Zuboff, 1988). New technologies may call for new organizational structures that are inconceivable using Woodward's framework.

One way commentators have sought to capture the link between technology and organization is through the concept of business models. Put simply, business models are "stories that explain how enterprises work" (Magretta, 2002, p. 4). A business model encapsulates the way in which a firm, endowed with a given technology, can successfully configure an organizational structure and its relationships with external stakeholders (Amit & Zott, 2001). For instance, the idea of the business model describes how firms have linked the manufacture of electronic devices with digital distribution technologies as in the case of the Apple iPod (Osterwalder, Pigneur, & Tucci, 2005). In this way, the business model concept appears to offer an attractive tool for determining correspondence between technology, and intraorganizational and extraorganizational structures.

Despite widespread discussions about business models, there is uncertainty about what the concept actually means (George & Bock, 2011). Many accounts of business models are both theoretically imprecise and empirically ambiguous, and they are often normatively inflected. In this short chapter, we argue that business models are not naturalistic entities but representations deployed by business managers as a strategic resource (Phillips, Lawrence, & Hardy, 2004). Drawing on previous work on performativity, social typecasting, and managerial cognition, we conceive of business models as performative representations that articulate and help instantiate the value of a technology. They work by articulating narratives to entice potential constituents, typifying and thereby creating legitimacy for the venture, and providing recipes that instruct practical action.

We aim to contribute to debates on the relationship between technology and organizational structure by suggesting that new technologies have no intrinsic value that can be realized by deploying the "correct" organizational structures. Rather, the value of technologies stems from the ability of entrepreneurs and firms to construct, often ex novo, organizational structures and networks of stakeholders and audiences in ways that allow for value realization. Specifically, the high-technology industries have developed an enormous supply of technologies that are in constant search of value realization opportunities. Here the notion of business models provides a tool for understanding the dynamic process through which actors seek to articulate how value might be extracted from highly uncertain and often ambiguous technologies. Rather than contingency, therefore, we emphasize a constructionist account of the relationship between technology and organization (Orlikowski, this volume).

We begin by reviewing the literature on business models. We claim that these approaches assume that business models describe some underlying reality while they ignore how they are used as performative representation of reality to construct and articulate a particular value around a technology. We conclude by detailing three elements of a preliminary theory of performative representations and their role for structuring the relationship between technology and organization.

THEORIZING BUSINESS MODELS

The concept of business models is widely used. A search of the *Financial Times* archive for the phrase "business model" results in more than 6,000 hits for the period 2004–2009. The concept gained enormous popularity during the Internet boom of the late 1990s and later spread across a wider community of management practitioners and business analysts (Ghaziani & Ventresca, 2005). However, only relatively recently have management researchers turned their attention to this concept (Baden-Fuller & Morgan, 2010). Contributions can be grouped into three conceptions of business models: as transactional structures, value extraction mechanisms, and organizational structuring devices. Below, we summarize each of these approaches.

A first approach conceptualizes business models as *transaction structures*. In this view, business models describe the way firms configure their transactions with groups of stakeholders including customers, suppliers, and vendors (Zott & Amit, 2008). A business model is "the content, structure, and governance of transactions designed so as to create value through the exploitation of business opportunities" (Amit & Zott, 2001, p. 511). For instance, Google's business model generates profit from providing Internet search by organizing transactions between users and advertisers. Differences between transaction structures have led researchers to generate various business model taxonomies. Zott and Amit (2008) argue that there are two generic types of business models – efficiency centered and novelty centered. Bienstock, Gillenson, and Sanders (2002) identify 40 possible business models based on differences in the number of buyers, number of sellers, price mechanism, nature of product offering, and frequency of exchange. Common among these approaches is the assumption that business models, as transaction structures, can be influenced by firms independently from other variables such as strategies, product strategies, or alliance models.

A second approach emphasizes business models as mechanisms for creating and capturing value (Shafer, Smith, & Linder, 2005). At center stage here are the processes and structures through which a firm creates and captures value from a given technology. The business model is a manipulable "focusing device," mediating between technology and economic value creation (Chesbrough & Rosenbloom, 2002). Because technology development is capital-intensive and uncertain, it often results in outputs for which there are no obvious and immediate applications within a given business context. In this situation, business models may help managers decide how to exploit given technological affordances. For instance, IBM has used "open" business models to create value from its technologies by soliciting inputs from external innovators (Chesbrough & Rosenbloom, 2002). Focusing on how value is created and exploited has led researchers to identify various ways of tapping into value streams. For instance, Mahadevan (2000) identified four possible "value streams" in an Internet-based business: virtual communities, reduced transaction costs, exploitation of information asymmetry, and value-added market-making processes.

A third approach treats business models as devices for structuring and designing organizations. Business models are seen as templates for configuring various components within an organization (Winter & Szulanski, 2001). For instance, to implement its "direct" model, Dell had to undertake a significant redesign of its internal processes and relationships with the distribution chain. The business model is the manifestation of how certain organizational variables are configured and the consequences of that configuration on business performance (Casadesus-Masanell & Ricart, 2008). Yip (2004) defines business models as configurations of the following organizational components: a value proposition, the nature of inputs, how inputs are transformed, the nature of outputs, vertical scope, horizontal scope, geographic scope, nature of customers, how to organize, and so on. The central insight from this work is that business models are made up of a series of managerial choices of how to organize components of a firm around a particular technology.

CRITICISMS OF THE BUSINESS MODEL CONCEPT

Existing work on business models is exciting, but it poses some significant problems. First, it is unclear how the concept *fits* with the existing literature on business strategy and organization. Some of the definitions of business models given in the practitioner-oriented literature are so broad that they include nearly every aspect of the business. It is unclear whether the concept can be meaningfully distinguished from other, already established concepts. For instance, "business model" is often used synonymously with "business strategy" even though some authors have attempted to establish the concept as stand-alone theoretical construct (Zott & Amit, 2008). As a result, the business model concept remains polysemic and ambiguous.

A second problem with the existing literature on business models concerns *construct validity*. It is unclear whether the concept refers to something that actually exists. This may be among the reasons why researchers looking for business models often encounter inconsistent empirical signals. Often they find themselves examining what entrepreneurs, investors, or the press claim to be business models. On further investigation, these claims are often weakly linked to what is going on within an organization and play a rhetorical rather than representational role.

A third problem with existing approaches to business models is that they tend to be *normatively* inflected. Many proponents emphasize how thinking about business models can help firms achieve certain goals such as greater innovativeness, creating new revenue streams, or organizational transformation. In the same way that practitioner knowledge is situated and concerned only with fulfilling particular purposes in particular circumstances (Schön, 1983), these contributions detail certain courses of action rather than establishing the general validity of the concept. Furthermore, the "interpretative flexibility" (Bijker, Hughes, & Pinch, 1987) of the concept enables different authors to promote their own versions of the central underlying idea. Hence, the representational quality of the concept becomes secondary to its potential to underpin idea entrepreneurship that often relies on putting old wine into new bottles.

TOWARD A THEORY OF BUSINESS MODELS AS PERFORMATIVE REPRESENTATIONS

To address the conceptual ambiguity, construct validity problems, and normative inflection that haunt most existing accounts of business models, we outline an alternative approach. We suggest that business models can be thought of as performative representations. A business model is a representation in that it is a text that redescribes and reconstructs reality – whether actual or imagined – in a way that is always partial, interested, and intent on persuading (De Cock, 2000). Texts are more durable and intransitive than mere actions and therefore play an important role in infusing change (Phillips et al., 2004). A business model is performative in the sense that it engenders effects through reconstructing the social world in its own image (Callon, 2007). Business models are representations that create material effects such as enrolling buyers and suppliers, persuading investors, and directing employees. We suggest that business models are performative in three ways: as narratives that persuade, as typifications that legitimate, and as recipes that instruct.

First, business models are *narratives* used by promoters of new technology ventures to entice key constituents (Magretta, 2002). Narratives are a genre of text that describes a sequence of events (Bruner, 1991). Narratives comprise a subject searching for an object, a "destinator" (a force determining the subject's destination), and a set of forces furthering or hindering the subject's quest for a desired object (Lounsbury & Glynn, 2001). For a firm to embrace a business model as a narrative then means to construct a representation of how it might succeed in a particular environment.

Existing research in contexts such as corporate failures suggests that people use narratives to infuse ambiguous situations with meaning and persuade sceptical audiences that their account of reality is believable (Brown, 2000). Because of their forward-looking character, business model narratives may be instrumental in inducing expectations among interested constituents about how a business' future might play out (Downing, 2005). Business model narratives may draw on a whole range of linguistic techniques that have been identified in research on narratives in organizations more broadly (Gabriel, 2000). These include the mobilization of fantasy scenarios, using widely known cultural myths, appealing to archetypical figures, constructing a series of episodes, and mobilizing well-known literary tropes such as metaphors. By bringing these components of a story together in a skillful and appealing way, a promoter can craft a new technology as being plausible and appealing to potential constituents such as investors, suppliers, and potential clients.

Second, a business model allows a venture to associate itself with a particular *type* or identity, thereby creating a sense of legitimacy. For a firm, adopting a certain business model means identifying itself with similar firms while dissociating itself from others. In this sense, a business model is an external identity that a firm can assume (Pólos, Hannan, & Carroll, 2002). External identities are directed at audiences that judge whether an organization qualifies as a member of one group or another. These audiences can penalize organizations for deviating from what they consider a valid manifestation of a certain type, or in turn reward them for conforming to a certain type (Zuckerman, 1999).

Such considerations are particularly relevant for firms in new technology contexts characterized by high uncertainty over future performance. Early stage organizations often have legitimacy issues with financial investors that they address through impression management and other symbolic management techniques (Zott & Huy, 2007). Similarly, they may try to woo customers using similar techniques, for instance, by styling themselves as craft beer producers and hence signaling that they are relevant to certain groups of beer consumers (Carroll & Swaminathan, 2000). In this situation, firms may attempt to render themselves identifiable and legitimate by associating themselves with certain business models that form known categories. For instance, an Internet firm might adopt an advertising-centered business model, taking advantage of the existing legitimacy of that model on the basis of success stories such as Google. Because stakeholders recognize this as a legitimate category of organizations, even novel entrants will be granted a legitimacy bonus compared to others sporting an illegitimate business model. This is particularly true for nascent markets where there is little certainty about the value associated with a technology (Sanders & Boivie, 2004). By deploying business models as known categories, they can help firms to obtain legitimacy that in turn may result in real resource flows.

Third, business models provide *recipes* that instruct actors involved with the business what they should do. Managers are often guided in their decision by cognitive frameworks that privilege certain courses of action to the exclusion of others (Tripsas & Gavetti, 2000). Firms tend to adopt "industry recipes" (Spender, 1989) as simplified ways of conducting business and understanding the environment. These recipes are typically adopted by many firms in an industry and provide practical guides to what a firm in a particular industry does. They constitute mental models that codify some key causal relationships assumed to underpin "the business" a firm believes to be in (Porac, Thomas, & Baden-Fuller, 1989). Over time, mental models and strategic choices intertwine to create a stable set of expectations among industry participants (Porac et al., 1989).

But business models are more than just simplified cognitive maps. They often take the form of carefully constructed models, which like an architect's model do not just represent reality but also guide the practice of remaking that reality (Baden-Fuller & Morgan, 2010). An instance of models directing the construction of social reality can be found in economics (Ferraro, Pfeffer, & Sutton, 2005). The Black–Scholes model for pricing financial assets eventually came to shape the markets that they claimed to describe (MacKenzie & Millo, 2003). Business models play a similar role within firms and their ecosystems. Business models tend to be ideal types that may never be instantiated in reality but provide ongoing inspiration for improvement and change. For instance, the ongoing and never-ending efforts to reduce cost at Ryanair, the European budget carrier, are legendary. When Ryanair was at the brink of bankruptcy in the early 1990s, the adoption of the "budget airline" business model provided ongoing guidance for business transformation and eventually became reality (Casadesus-Masanell & Ricart, 2008). However, business models can become locked in when they become entrenched within managers' cognition or even across organizational fields. For instance, Polaroid Corporation failed to successfully enter the market for digital cameras even though it had developed leading edge technology in the digital imaging field (Tripsas & Gavetti, 2000). Senior management was able to develop new beliefs only to the extent that they were consistent with the "razor and blade" business model underlying instant photography. This example illustrates the power of business models in continuously shaping and reinforcing specific ways of doing business.

CONCLUSION

The concept of business models constitutes an important addition to the long debate about technology and organization that Joan Woodward (1965) opened up. Reflections on business models have stimulated debates about the implications of new technologies for organizations and have drawn attention to how firms relate to their ecosystems, in addition to how they are organized. However, many extant accounts of business models view them as naturalist features of firms. In this chapter, we argue that business models are better understood as tools that allow entrepreneurs and managers to imagine and craft organizations adept at drawing value from new technologies. One implication of our analysis is that value is not intrinsic in technologies but has to be realized through suitable and viable configurations of organizational structures and relationships with external actors. The very proliferation of business models in managers' discourse reminds us of the fact that there is no single "best" business model for exploiting any given technology. Choices have to be made as to how technological affordances can be turned into viable organizations. In this process, business models – as texts – assist entrepreneurs and managers by providing narratives designed to convince constituents of the quality of a firm's business, typifications that create a sense of legitimacy around the venture, and recipes that instruct constituents about what exactly they should do.

We believe this approach to business models offers a way of thinking about how new technologies are configured through constructing a warp and weave of narratives, identities, and recipes. Through such performative representations, promoters of new technologies attempt to articulate, instantiate, and eventually extract the potential value of technologies. Following our approach, the study of business models should seek to examine more deeply the narrative work used to convince particular constituents, the processes that underlie the emergence of certain well-recognized and legitimate types, and the conditions under which business models as recipes might or might not direct the activities of constituents.

REFERENCES

Amit, R., & Zott, C. (2001). Value creation in e-business. *Strategic Management Journal, 22*, 493–520.

Baden-Fuller, C., & Morgan, M. S. (2010). Business models. *Long Range Planning*, doi:10.1016/j.lrp.2010.02.005.

Bienstock, C. C., Gillenson, M. L., & Sanders, T. C. (2002). The complete taxonomy of web business models. *Quarterly Journal of Electronic Commerce, 3*, 173–186.

Bijker, W. E., Hughes, T. P., & Pinch, T. J. (1987). *The social construction of technological systems: New directions in the sociology and history of technology*. Cambridge, MA: MIT Press.

Brown, A. D. (2000). Making sense of inquiry sensemaking. *Journal of Management Studies, 37*(1), 45–75.

Bruner, J. (1991). The narrative construction of reality. *Critical Inquiry, 18*(1), 1–21.

Callon, M. (2007). What does it mean to say that economics is performative. In: D. MacKenzie, F. Muniesa & L. Siu (Eds), *Do economists make markets? On the performativity of economics* (pp. 311–357). Princeton: Princeton University Press.

Carroll, G. R., & Swaminathan, A. (2000). Why the microbrewery movement? Organizational dynamics of resource partitioning in the US brewing industry. *American Journal of Sociology, 106*(3), 715–762.

Casadesus-Masanell, R., & Ricart, J. E. (2008). *Strategy vs. business models vs. tactics*. Unpublished manuscript. Harvard Business School, Cambridge.

Chesbrough, H., & Rosenbloom, R. S. (2002). The role of the business model in capturing value from innovation: Evidence from Xerox Corporation's technology spin-off companies. *Industrial & Corporate Change, 11*(3), 529–555.

De Cock, C. (2000). Reflections on fiction, representation, and organization studies: An essay with special reference to the work of Jorge Luis Borges. *Organization Studies, 21*(3), 589–609.

Downing, S. (2005). The social construction of entrepreneurship: Narrative and dramatic processes in the coproduction of organizations and identities. *Entrepreneurship Theory and Practice*, *29*(2), 185–204.

Ferraro, F., Pfeffer, J., & Sutton, R. I. (2005). Economics language and assumptions: How theories can become self-fulfilling. *Academy of Management Review*, *30*(1), 8–24.

Gabriel, Y. (2000). *Storytelling in organizations: Facts, fictions, and fantasies*. Oxford: Oxford University Press.

George, G., & Bock, A. J. (2011). The practice of business models and its implications for entrepreneurship research. *Entrepreneurship Theory and Practice*, *35*(1) (in press).

Ghaziani, A., & Ventresca, M. (2005). Keywords and cultural change: Frame analysis of business model public talk, 1975–2000. *Sociological Forum*, *20*(4), 523–559.

Lounsbury, M., & Glynn, M. A. (2001). Cultural entrepreneurship: Stories, legitimacy, and the acquisition of resources. *Strategic Management Journal*, *22*(6–7), 545–564.

MacKenzie, D., & Millo, Y. (2003). Constructing a market, performing theory: The historical sociology of a financial derivatives exchange. *American Journal of Sociology*, *109*(1), 107–145.

Magretta, J. (2002). Why business models matter. *Harvard Business Review*, *80*(5), 86–92.

Mahadevan, B. (2000). Business models for Internet-based e-commerce. *California Management Review*, *42*(4), 55–69.

Osterwalder, A., Pigneur, Y., & Tucci, C. L. (2005). Clarifying business models: Origins, present, and future of the concept. *Communications of the Association for Information Systems*, *16*, 1–25.

Phillips, N., Lawrence, T. B., & Hardy, C. (2004). Discourse and institutions. *Academy of Management Review*, *29*(4), 635–652.

Pólos, L., Hannan, M. T., & Carroll, G. R. (2002). Foundations of a theory of social forms. *Industrial and Corporate Change*, *11*(1), 85–115.

Porac, J. F., Thomas, H., & Baden-Fuller, C. (1989). Competitive groups as cognitive communities: The case of Scottish knitwear manufacturers. *Journal of Management Studies*, *26*(4), 397–416.

Sanders, W. G., & Boivie, S. (2004). Sorting things out: Valuation of new firms in uncertain markets. *Strategic Management Journal*, *25*(2), 167–186.

Schön, D. A. (1983). *The reflective practitioner: How professionals think in action*. London: Temple Smith.

Shafer, S. M., Smith, H. J., & Linder, J. C. (2005). The power of business models. *Business Horizons*, *48*(3), 199–207.

Spender, J. C. (1989). *Industry recipes: An enquiry into the nature and sources of managerial judgement*. Oxford: Blackwell.

Tripsas, M., & Gavetti, G. (2000). Capabilities, cognition, and inertia: Evidence from digital imaging. *Strategic Management Journal*, *21*(10–11), 1147–1161.

Winter, S. G., & Szulanski, G. (2001). Replication as strategy. *Organization Science*, *12*(6), 730–743.

Woodward, J. (1965). *Industrial organization: Theory and practice*. Oxford: Oxford University Press.

Yip, G. S. (2004). Using strategy to change your business model. *Business Strategy Review*, *15*(2), 17–24.

Zott, C., & Amit, R. (2008). The fit between product market strategy and business model: Implications for firm performance. *Strategic Management Journal*, *29*(1), 1–26.

Zott, C., & Huy, Q. N. (2007). How entrepreneurs use symbolic management to acquire resources. *Administrative Science Quarterly*, *52*(1), 70–105.

Zuboff, S. (1988). *In the age of the smart machine*. New York: Basic Books.

Zuckerman, E. (1999). The categorical imperative: Securities analysts and the illegitimacy discount. *American Journal of Sociology*, *104*(5), 1398–1438.

THE ROLE OF STRUCTURED INTUITION AND ENTREPRENEURIAL OPPORTUNITIES

Gerard George and Adam J. Bock

Leading-edge technology firms present a special challenge to the organizational researcher, exacerbated when novel technologies comprise not just the firm's production output, but also the underlying infrastructure and intermediary outputs not directly linked to the firm's core revenue-generating model. In the IT, communication, and consumer Internet sectors, the firm must maintain and develop sophisticated and evolving capabilities only indirectly connected to the ultimate provision of goods and services into current and future markets.

In the case of pre-market ventures and organizations actively seeking new market opportunities, it is unclear whether the firm's specialized capabilities could be leveraged to identify, assess, and extract value from unfamiliar opportunities. Organizations could "search" for technological solutions or opportunities (Gavetti & Levinthal, 2000; Levinthal, 1997; March, 1991; Rosenkopf & Nerkar, 2001). Whereas most of this rich literature has focused on outcomes of search as well as some organizational or individual attributes such as prior experience (Ahuja & Lampert, 2001; Shane, 2000), it is likely that structure of an organization's knowledge and capabilities could be an enabler or constraint on the nature of entrepreneurial opportunities

Technology and Organization: Essays in Honour of Joan Woodward
Research in the Sociology of Organizations, Volume 29, 277–285

ISSN: 0733-558X/doi:10.1108/S0733-558X(2010)0000029021

perceived, assessed, and exploited (George, Kotha, & Zheng, 2008). As firms develop capabilities that may not be core to the firm's products, these capabilities or processes may also shape the markets or opportunities in which they engage. In this chapter, we suggest that firms "intuit" (verb form of intuition) markets in the face of uncertainty and that research is warranted to assess how firms could be structurally organized to gain value from such a capability.

To begin, we note two specific organizational forms in which *structured intuition* may play an important role. The biotech sector has been heavily studied in various structural- and capabilities-based frameworks; the nature of the business fascinates researchers, in part, because biotech firms operate at the leading edge of life science research, utilize vast sums of venture capital and anticipate termination (preferably by acquizition) before profitability – a measure of success in this sector. The relevant characteristic of biotechnology firms, for our purposes, is the dependence on sophisticated technology throughout the organization: information systems for recording and sharing experimental data, wet lab equipment and supplies requiring extensive training and experience, and the ultimate products that include synthetic viruses and monoclonal antibodies, just as examples. In particular, many, if not most, biotechnology companies must research and develop entirely new technologies that represent only enabling mechanisms or even just verification information regarding the ultimate product. For example, various firms in the transgenic organism market developed retroviruses and genetically modified organisms as enablers and demonstrations of the potential application of transgenic technology for therapeutic manufacturing processes.

In a second example, we consider the virtual structures utilized by many start-up firms in the Web 2.0 social networking space. These organizations, whether driven by a specific *cause* or by strictly financial goals, establish the infrastructure to support multi-modal communication within and between affinity-bound communities. In the end, these sites generally (plan to) generate revenues through linkages to commercial products, whether through traditional web-based advertizing or by selling socio-demographic and utilization pattern data (among other mechanisms), but the technology capabilities and applications that make up the core functionality of the business reside in the communications infrastructure, often spanning multiple modalities (web, mobile, txt, iPod). In fact, the development of the communications infrastructure is a necessary but not sufficient mechanism to determine the firm's revenues because the infrastructure users are, for these firms, not the economic (paying) customers. In other words, even when the infrastructure is established, the firm may not know where or who the final economic market will be. Consequently, firms often develop capabilities that are not core to the business and yet may define how and what markets they would enter at a later point in time.

THE ROLE OF STRUCTURE

Woodward's seminal research linking technology to optimal organizational form presented a contingent theory of managerial structure that, in effect, presented the organizational version of scientific management. Taylorism addressed individual work processes; Woodward's theory addressed organizational structural processes; deviations from optimized processes or systems reduced effectiveness. The very nature of contingency theory, however, relies on the implicit assumption that the production technology of the organization is the primary mechanism by which the firm generates value. In the case of the biotechnology and social networking firms, the underlying production technology and organizational structure are intermediaries to value creation, not production technologies per se.

A critique of organization theory lies in its apparent inability to deal with *change*, such as technological evolution or discontinuity (Woodward, 1980); in addition, while firms may be organically or mechanistically structured to address environmental turbulence or stability (Donaldson, 2001), we have no obvious structural contingency when the market is simply unknown, rather than unstable. In particular, we want to avoid a purely "found" conception of opportunity development dependent entirely on alertness (Kirzner, 1997) or experience (Shane, 2000) without some element of mental processing. This disposition is based partly on recent data suggesting that certain types of firms have advantages in entering entirely new niches (George et al., 2008), but also because an extensive literature on strategic choice suggests that the process of enactment represents a critical step in the managerial decision-making process (Child, 1997). While presumption favors rationality in such enactment, it seems reasonable to consider whether decision-making in the face of significant uncertainty incorporates more than just stepwise rational analysis.

Clearly, there are potential applications for structural contingency theory in the entrepreneurial opportunity identification process exhibited in industry sectors with high-technology dependence and process, but we have no theoretical mechanism to explain the decision process without reverting to randomness, alertness, or pure experience. If these were the key factors, then structural contingency should favor large organizations with extensive slack resources; as we will discuss shortly, research does not support this conclusion (George, 2005; George et al., 2008).

INTUITION

We propose the potential role of *intuition*[1] in opportunity recognition. First, we utilize the definition of intuition developed by Isenman (1997, p. 397), which focuses on "information content ... originally outside of consciousness and beyond voluntary recall, yet [with] the potential to impact thought or action significantly." Important distinctions should be drawn: first, that intuition is not *irrational*, but rather *arational*. Second, we focus on intuition as a *processing mode* and not as "source of *de novo* knowledge" (p. 401). The intuitive process, then, augments conscious thought by accessing the accelerated processing speeds and potentially untapped memory stores of the unconscious, providing two mechanisms for insight: first, identifying commonalities across distinct circumstances, and second, deep pattern identification otherwise hidden by superficial distinctions (p. 399).

Intuition must be distinguished from a number of related but distinct cognitive activities. Creativity is the ability to develop entirely new concepts, ideas, or possibilities, usually without any sort of judgment associated with whether the novelty has inherent value or not. Alternatively, improvization is the process of "making it up as you go along," an active rather than reflective process (Moorman & Miner, 1998). We suggest that intuition may subtly inform creativity and directly impact improvization. Intuition may be a filter for creativity and thus have a positive or negative impact on creative flow, depending on whether the preferred output is measured in "out of the box" characteristics or relevance to the desired goals. On the contrary, intuition likely plays a significant role in improvization, because the process of improvizing requires rapid decision-making with limited information and feedback; intuition could provide deeper processing and information retrieval than the actor perceives in real time.

It should be clear that intuition can play an important role in the strategic enactment of opportunities, in effect enhancing the simulation process utilized to assess likely outcomes. The manager, team, or organization assessing strategic choices, and, in particular, potential market developments, and opportunities, draws on all of the classic characteristics of exploration: experience, knowledge, and intelligence. In some cases, however, the intuitive process is enabled, drawing upon deeper capabilities and information to create surface-level analogies and conclusions otherwise unavailable through the explicit base of data.

Data from the biotechnology sector suggests age-dependent effects on the relationships between the number of "new-to-the-firm" technical initiatives, or *branching*, as well as branching distance from the firm's core, and impact on the firm's technical outcomes. For younger firms, the optimal number of branching is lower, with rapidly decreasing returns for more branching, but with higher relative impact. In addition, younger firms obtain higher impact on outcomes from higher distant branching, suggesting that as firms age, their intuition about new opportunities is best applied to more familiar areas of technical expertise (George et al., 2008).

IMPLICATIONS

Ultimately, structural contingency theory argues that the fit between organizational structure and size, environment, and strategy affect performance (Donaldson, 2001). Woodward's original study of 100 mid-sized manufacturing firms in South Essex could not easily have anticipated the type of environmental or strategic elements that characterize the biotechnology or Web 2.0 firm in 2010. The primary structural element in her study, span of managerial control, may not even be easily measurable in relatively small, virtually operated firms commercializing social networking structures. The simplest explanation applying structural contingency resorts to the broad category of organic structure (Donaldson, 2001), but this conceptualization was designed to apply to firms with relatively well-defined production technologies in a turbulent environment. The addition of intuition to the set of capabilities relevant to the contingency framework offers one mechanism to help assess how firms obtain *fit* in an environment that cannot be classified as turbulent, because the market itself may still be indeterminate.

The implications of intuiting markets cover three broad areas of management. The first considers the role of intuition in identifying potential market opportunities; the second is the role of intuition in the assessment of implementation options and the third is the set of characteristics associated with organizational structure that would support the development and application of intuition as an organizational capability. We assess each of these implications, and then discuss potential future research.

The strategic exploration process is generally described as a feedback loop, in which evaluation, choice, and implementation lead to measurements of effectiveness and renewed evaluation in the new (environmental) context (Child, 1997). Although it could be argued that intuition is relevant in the strategic choice, our focus is on the process itself. The identification of market opportunities and the assessment of implementation options thus both occur in the evaluation stage of strategic exploration. The mechanisms and impact of intuition in these two processes are, however, distinct and noteworthy. In the case of intuiting markets in the evaluation process, we envisage organizations projecting forward to identify where markets may develop or align most closely with the firm's existing or potential capabilities. This is, fundamentally, an exercise in prediction, in which pattern-seeking must consider both the broader market conditions and the specific technological developments that might yield seemingly incongruous results. For example, in our book, *Inventing Entrepreneurs* (George & Bock, 2008), we portray Professor Michael Stonebraker's start-up firm, INGRES. INGRES failed in its intuition that the development of the early relational database market would be determined by open standardization, which occurred when IBM selected a competing Oracle technology.

The use of intuition in the implementation assessment process, however, requires the specific application of knowledge, experience, and percipience about the nature of the firm and its potential to change direction towards a potentially vague or uncertain goal. Here, intuition focuses internally: creating, enacting, and simulating implementation scenarios and projecting outcomes. At small or young firms, it is likely that these activities are embodied within one or only a few individuals, and the success of the intuitive processes is heavily dependent on how effectively those individuals function within the strategic choice context. Anecdotal evidence from the popular press seems to suggest that few firms excel based on the extraordinary intuitive capacity of a unique individual: Jobs at Apple, Branson at Virgin, and Buffett at Berkshire Hathaway. But these appear to be the exceptions rather than the rule.

The mechanisms by which organizational structure may support intuiting markets are the most interesting and the least well understood. The literatures on fostering creativity and improvization within organizations are relatively new (Moorman & Miner, 1998; Im, 2004), and usually couched within the context of product innovation, rather than market assessment or prediction. Arguably, the development of capabilities that intuit markets would be equally or more valuable than the capabilities associated with product development, for example, because accurate market knowledge decreases *uncertainty* whereas effective product development can only decrease the *risk* of product failure *assuming* the market develops as expected.

The challenge for an organization may then not be bounded *rationality*, or information asymmetry, but bounded *knowability*. To summarize Donald Rumsfeld, the former US Defense Secretary, "we don't know what we don't know." The availability of information and the capabilities of management information systems continue to increase dramatically with improvements in data access, storage, and manipulation; while no single solution to so-called information overload exists, organizational structure is a critical determinant of its onset and impact (Eppler, 2004). In fact, it may present the only leverage point for management, because the other key factors (type of information, individual orientation and skills, tasks and processes, and IT deployment) may be partly or wholly fixed. In these scenarios, the differentiating factor, assuming that firms cannot access any one extraordinarily intuitive individual, may be the organizational structure that best leverages the intuitive capabilities of the firm.

This area of structural contingency theory, which links characteristics of the organization to the firm's ability to identify and target novel market opportunities, presents a range of potential future research topics across a spectrum of organizational and management fields. First, capabilities research tools should be applied to distinguish between intuition and absorptive capacity. As most measures of absorptive capacity have focused on the firm's overall *experience* in a given market, it would be beneficial to clarify that intuiting markets presents a capability partly or entirely independent of experience. Within the strategy process field, deeper investigation into precisely when and how intuition is applied in the strategic choice process, and under what circumstances it is most effective, could directly impact our understanding of endogenously driven corporate strategy decision-making.

Management researchers might benefit from prior or newly applied cognitive psychology research on the determinants of individual intuitive capacity – because early stage biotechnology firms tend to have founders or key scientists actively involved in management, there is likely a link between the mindset applied to the scientific process and the effective use of intuition (Isenman, 1997). Social network theory would seem to be a particularly attractive area of research, as the organizational utilization of intuition would seem to incorporate interaction between individuals and groups, and the strength of the relevant ties between those individuals and groups may be closely associated with how intuitively derived observations and conclusions are disseminated, assessed, and selected.

CONCLUSIONS

The role of intuition in the strategic choice process, as an organizational capability potentially influenced by firm structure, presents significant challenges to the management researcher. At the same time, our understanding of strategy process has benefited from analysis of other key socio-psychological functions, including power, authority and creativity, as well as socio-psychological structures such as the informal network. We have long known that organizational decision-making processes have rational, informational and procedural limitations. Assessing the role of intuition, specifically for the market assessment and development process, offers the potential to clarify "new-to-the-firm" opportunity assessment. Preliminary data suggests that organizational characteristics are correlated with the impact of niche entry and technological branching. We encourage further research into structured intuition as an important determinant of success for firms, especially in technology-intensive sectors.

NOTE

1. We do not distinguish between specified individual intuition and the resultant intuition attributed to the organization. The question of whether a firm can act "intuitively" deserves separate attention. Nevertheless, in entrepreneurial organizations, the separation from entrepreneur and firm becomes increasingly blurred.

REFERENCES

Ahuja, G., & Lampert, C. M. (2001). Entrepreneurship in the large corporation: A longitudinal study of how established firms create breakthrough inventions. *Strategic Management Journal*, *22*(6–7), 521–543.

Child, J. (1997). Strategic choice in the analysis of action, structure, organizations and environment: Retrospect and prospect. *Organization Studies*, *18*(1), 43.

Donaldson, L. (2001). *The contingency theory of organizations*. Thousand Oaks, CA: Sage.

Eppler, M. J. (2004). The concept of information overload: A review of literature from organization science, accounting, marketing, MIS, and related disciplines. *The Information Society*, *20*(5), 325.

Gavetti, G., & Levinthal, D. (2000). Looking forward and looking backward: Cognitive and experiential search. *Administrative Science Quarterly*, *45*, 113–137.

George, G. (2005). Slack resources and the performance of privately held firms. *Academy of Management Journal*, *48*(4), 661–676.

George, G., & Bock, A. (2008). *Inventing entrepreneurs: Technology innovators and their entrepreneurial journey*. NY: Prentice Hall Pearson.

George, G., Kotha, R., & Zheng, Y. (2008). Entry into insular domains: A longitudinal study of knowledge structuration and innovation in the biotechnology industry. *Journal of Management Studies*, *45*(8), 1448–1474.

Im, S. (2004). Market orientation, creativity, and new product performance in high-technology firms. *Journal of Marketing*, *68*(2), 114.

Isenman, L. (1997). Toward an understanding of intuition and its importance in scientific endeavor. *Perspectives in Biology and Medicine*, *40*(3), 395–403.

Kirzner, I. M. (1997). Entrepreneurial discovery and the competitive market process: An Austrian approach. *Journal of Economic Literature*, *35*(1), 60–85.

Levinthal, D. A. (1997). Adaptation on rugged landscapes. *Management Science*, *43*(7), 934–950.

March, J. G. (1991). Exploration and exploitation in organizational learning. *Organization Science*, *2*, 71–87.

Moorman, C., & Miner, A. S. (1998). Organizational improvisation and organizational memory. *The Academy of Management Review*, *23*(4), 698–723.

Rosenkopf, L., & Nerkar, A. (2001). Beyond local search: Boundary-spanning, exploration, and impact in the optical disk industry. *Strategic Management Journal*, *22*(4), 287–306.

Shane, S. (2000). Prior knowledge and the discovery of entrepreneurial opportunities. *Organization Science*, *11*(4), 448–469.

Woodward, J. (1980). *Industrial organization: Theory and practice* (2nd ed.). Oxford: Oxford University Press.

THE ORGANIZATION OF TECHNOLOGICAL PLATFORMS

Annabelle Gawer

In 1958, Joan Woodward published a pioneering study of 100 small manufacturing firms in the United Kingdom that showed one could find a significant relationship between firms' performance and their organizational structure, only when one took firms' production technologies into account. Successful firms had adopted organizational structures that were contingent upon the technologies of production that they employed. Woodward's research not only had an enormous impact on the research community of organizational scholars at the time, but the implications of her findings still influence the way we conduct research on organizations today. Of course, she is remembered for having made a persuasive case against the prevailing conventional wisdom, demonstrating that there is no universal best way to organize.[1] But, perhaps more importantly, she put technology "on the map" for organizational theorists and management scholars. In other words, technology became legitimized as an important variable for scholars aiming to develop a finer understanding of firms' performance.

But if Woodward were with us today, what kind of relationship between technology and organization would she find? Let us start by re-examining what Woodward meant by "technology," as the term can mean many different things. A simple meaning is the kind of techniques used to process raw materials into finished products. In this definition, technology is understood as a set of technological processes of production. This meaning is very close to the one Joan Woodward used in her study. When Woodward wrote about

Technology and Organization: Essays in Honour of Joan Woodward
Research in the Sociology of Organizations, Volume 29, 287–296

ISSN: 0733-558X/doi:10.1108/S0733-558X(2010)0000029022

technology, she was really writing about *production technologies*, and given her sample (100 British manufacturing firms), she focused on *manufacturing* technologies. Studying manufacturing firms made a lot of sense in the context of Britain in the late 1950s, as most of the economic activity that created value centered around manufacturing.[2] As she was studying the relationship between organizational design and performance, Joan Woodward considered the various technologies she observed as given (i.e., exogenous) and static.[3] Again, this made sense in the context of her study. In today's globalized business context, however, manufacturing in Europe is not considered the beacon of hope for growth, but rather as something to be salvaged. It is probable that if Woodward were today doing another study on firms' performance, she would probably not focus on manufacturing firms.

In addition, theoretical developments in the fields of economics, innovation and organizations have taught us that the "technology" variable should now be imbued with a richer meaning than Joan Woodward intended. Today's scholars studying the role of technology in organizations and in the economy usually do not limit themselves to seeing technology as "the kind of techniques used to process the raw materials" (even if one takes "raw material" figuratively, meaning "any kind of input"),[4] nor, for the most sophisticated ones, do they see technology as a static or even an exogenous variable (Rosenberg, 2000; Kaplan & Tripsas, 2008). Technology is both dynamic and endogenous. And, in the important case of information and communication technologies, we often find that technology is an input, an output, and a set of processes. This inevitably complicates the relationship between technology and organizations.

In our everyday life and in business, technology has grown more pervasive and fast changing. In particular, the development of information and communication technologies has transformed our business landscape and altered the dynamics of competition and innovation in various industries such as semiconductors, computing, telecommunications, consumer electronics, and their associated service sectors. This technological change has profoundly impacted organizations in these industries as it has altered not only what they produce and sell (e.g., cell phones and computers rather than fridges) but also the ways of designing and producing new goods and services. One of the fundamental changes in production and design processes, seen in particular in information and communication technologies and also in various other high-tech industries, has been the emergence of technological platforms. In the remaining part of this chapter, I shall examine the relationship between technology and organizations in the context of technological industry platforms.

PLATFORMS

Industry platforms are technological building blocks (that can be technologies, products, or services) that act as a foundation on top of which an array of firms, organized in a set of interdependent firms (sometimes called an industry "ecosystem"), develop a set of inter-related products, technologies and services (Gawer, 2009b, 2009c).

The research on industry platforms builds on several distinct literatures, which hitherto had rarely been brought together: the literature on engineering design and product architecture (Ulrich, 1995; Baldwin & Clark, 2000); the organizational literature on modularity (Sanchez & Mahoney, 1996; Schilling, 2000), with the economics literature on standards and network externalities (Katz & Shapiro, 1985; Shapiro & Varian, 1999); and the strategy research on new forms of industry dynamics mixing competition and co-operation (coined as "co-opetition," see Brandenburger & Nalebuff, 1996).[5]

Platforms exist in various industries, and they certainly exist in all high-tech industries. Google, Microsoft Windows, cell phone operating systems, fuel cell automotive engines, and also some genomic technologies are all platforms. Platforms, embedded within industrial ecosystems, have redesigned our industrial landscapes, upset the balance of power between firms, fostered innovation, and raised new questions on competition, innovation, and organization.

Platforms provide an essential, or "core," function to an encompassing system of use. They are subject to "network effects," which tend to dynamically reinforce early-gained advantages such as an installed base of users or the existence of complementary products (Eisenmann, Parker, & Van Alstyne, 2006). These platforms typically emerge in the context of modular industries (Baldwin & Clark, 2000; Baldwin & Woodard, 2009) or industry ecosystems (Iansiti & Levien, 2004). Gawer and Cusumano (2008) indicate that platforms must be "core" to a technological system of use (essential to its function) as well as highly interdependent on other parts of the technological system. The organization of these ecosystems appears to follow a regular structure, with platform leaders acting as "keystone" members of the network of firms that are the platform complementors, with a dense set of interdependencies, both technological and strategic, between the "core" that is the platform and the other parts of the ecosystem/technological system. The complementors themselves occupy a peripheral position in the network, with fewer links between them.

Baldwin and Woodard (2009) indicate that the architecture (or technological organization) of platforms presents observable regularities: The fundamental feature of a *platform architecture*, in their view, is that certain components remain fixed over the life of the platform, while others are allowed to vary in cross-section or change over time. Thus, a platform embodies a set of stable constraints, or design rules, that govern the relationships among components. In particular, fixing the interfaces between components creates specific *thin crossing points* in the network of relationships between the elements of the system (Baldwin, 2008). At these points, the dependencies between the respective components are constrained to obey the interface specification, while other forms of dependency are ruled out. Interfaces in turn establish the boundaries of *modules* – components of a system whose "elements are powerfully connected among themselves and relatively weakly connected to elements in other [components]" (Baldwin & Clark, 2000, p. 63). Because they define points of weak linkage (thin crossing points) in a network of relationships, modular interfaces reduce both co-ordination costs and transaction costs across the module boundary (Baldwin & Clark, 2000; Baldwin, 2008). It follows that the existence of modules and modular interfaces in a large system reduces the costs of splitting design and production across multiple firms (Langlois & Robertson, 1992; Sanchez & Mahoney, 1996). This kind of disaggregation gives rise to *modular clusters* or *business ecosystems* of complementary and competing firms (Baldwin & Clark, 2000; Iansiti & Levien, 2004; Baldwin & Woodard, 2007).

In our work on platforms, Cusumano and I (Gawer & Cusumano, 2002, 2004, 2008) focused on the strategic aspect of platforms and developed the concept of "platform leadership." "Platform leaders" are organizations that manage to successfully establish their product, service, or technology, as an industry platform. As such, they get to a position to drive the technological trajectory of the overall technological and business system of which the platform is a core element as well as derive an architectural advantage from their position in the industry. Industry platform leaders orchestrate firms that do not necessarily buy or sell from each other, but whose combined products, technologies, or services add value to the ecosystem as well as end-users (e.g., West, 2003; Evans, Hagiu, & Schmalensee, 2006; Gawer, 2009b). Platform leaders are highly dependent on innovations developed by the other firms, but, at the same time, take upon themselves to ensure the overall long-term technical integrity of its evolving technology platform (Gawer & Cusumano, 2002). Platform leaders aim to create innovation in complementary products and services, which in turn increase the value of their own product or service, while at the same time they wish to maintain or increase competition among complementors, thereby maintaining their bargaining power over complementors. Platform leadership is therefore always accompanied by some degree of architectural control. Furthermore, the momentum created by the network effects between the platform and its complementary products or services can often erect a barrier to entry from potential platform competitors.

Establishing an industry platform requires not only technical efforts and astute decisions about design and architecture from the platform leader to increase value creation opportunities for the ecosystem participants. It also requires the platform leader to attempt to establish a set of business relationships that are mutually beneficial for ecosystem participants. This often requires the establishment of implicit contracts that structure and shape market relations between the relevant actors (Bresnahan & Greenstein, 1999, Gawer & Cusumano, 2008). While platform leaders will often claim that establishing trust between themselves and complementors is essential to their success, recent research (Perrons, 2009) explores in detail the issue of trust in platform leadership and attempts to separate empirically whether the alignment platform leaders obtain from complementors is due to coercion or due to trust.

THE FOUR LEVERS OF PLATFORM LEADERSHIP

In our initial research on strategies for platform leadership (Gawer & Cusumano, 2002), Cusumano and I suggest that firms who aim to establish their products, technologies, or services as platforms should attempt to orchestrate third-party industry innovation on complements in the context of a coherent set of strategic moves coined "the four levers of platform leadership," which are simply four areas of managerial decisions: (1) firm scope, (2) technology design and intellectual property, (3) external relations with complementors, and (4) internal organization. These four levers need to be used in a *coherent* manner by the platform owner to ensure growth and stability of the platform and to successfully influence the direction of innovation in complementary products by third parties.

In our work, we find that in many platform leaders' organizations, there is a clear separation between two parts of the organization, with a Chinese wall between these two parts. On the one hand, there is a part of the organization in charge of establishing the platform per se, which focuses on establishing collaborative relationships with external complementors. Because of the demand-enhancing network effects that imply that the more valuable complements will be available, the more demand there will be for the platform, it is in the interest of the platform-developing part of the organization to facilitate and encourage innovation on complementary products, technologies and services. To take two examples, the platform-developing part of Microsoft Corporation will try to encourage external firms to develop software that will be compatible with Windows. At Intel Corporation, playing a similar role, there is a group (named the Intel Architecture Lab) that will distribute technologies and share intellectual property with firms that develop complementary products to Intel microprocessors. On the other hand, there are different groups, divisions, or units within the platform leader organization that tends to compete in complementary markets and therefore compete with the firm's own complementors. At Microsoft, such units would be the groups that develop applications such as Microsoft Office, whereas, at Intel, they would be the part of Intel that develops and manufactures motherboards and chipsets. Intel Corporation will give different names to these two parts of the organization units, as they pursue what is called at Intel the respective objectives of "Job 1" (which is to build and sell the platform, that is, the microprocessor) and "Job 2" (which is to compete in complementary markets).

We found that conflicts regularly emerge between these two parts of the organization. At Intel, these two parts had different structures and reward systems, different internal cultures, causing significant tension. At Nokia, another firm we have studied, the platform unit was physically separated from other units with its own special floor only accessible with securitized badge, whereas none of the other units followed this procedure. The respective objectives of these two parts of the organizations could be construed as opposed: to help complementors versus to compete with complementors.

These conflicts seem unavoidable, and further, that perhaps counter-intuitively play a positive role helping a firm to become a platform leader. It seems that this particular form of *internal organization* (two distinct groups separated by a Chinese wall and pursuing what seems to be conflicting objectives) is an empirical regularity for firms attempting to become platform leaders. Moreover, case study evidence indicates that this separation (a form of internal organization) needs to be *observable from the outside* the firm to have an effect on complementors' perception of the likelihood of the platform leader to play fairly with them and not take advantage ex-post of their willingness to invest in co-specialized technologies, products, or services (Gawer & Henderson, 2007). To protect complementors' innovation incentives, it is particularly important for the platform leader to make a credible commitment to complementors that it will not squeeze their margins ex-post (Farrell & Katz, 2000). Conveying such commitment in a credible manner is however difficult for platform leaders because, as the functional boundary between the platform and its complementary products evolves, they are often tempted to enter and compete in complementary markets, which lowers complementors' innovation incentives. Gawer and Henderson (2007) analyze how Intel makes use of its organizational structure, in particular, the separation between the "Job 1" unit (that built the platform) and the "Job 2" units (that built complements to the platform), as well as its management processes, as commitment mechanisms to maintain these incentives.

The study of platforms highlights therefore an intriguing hypothesis: that the *internal organization* of firms (such as platform leaders) and the *external organization* of firms (i.e., the organization of the sector or the ecosystem of firms) are inter-related and mediated by the organization of the platform technology. In particular, the internal organization of firms, when coherent with the organization of the technology, may have an influence on these firms' ability to exert an influence on external firms.

CONCLUSIONS

In conclusion, when examining the organization of technological platforms, one can observe a number of empirical regularities. At the technological level, the architecture of platforms contains a set of stable components while others are allowed to change over time. At the firm level, platform leaders tend to organize internally following a pattern of separation between groups with opposite objectives, with one part of the organization aiming to collaborate with complementors, while the other part competes with complementors. We also observe that the organization of the sector, in particular of the platform ecosystem, seems to follow an established structure, with the platform leader at the core of the network, interacting with a large number of complementors that occupy peripheral positions. Our last observation is that there seems to be a correspondence between the internal organization, the technical organization and the external organization of platforms, leading to the hypothesis that the internal organization plays a crucial role to convey credibly the platform leader's commitment to external complementors and members of its network, and has a positive influence on its likelihood to achieve and maintain a platform leadership role. To summarize, the way platform leaders organize internally influences their ability to exert an organizing influence on the ecosystem they aim to lead, and this is mediated by the way platform firms make design choices on their technology.[6]

Reverting to Joan Woodward, I would like to suggest that this correspondence between the internal organization and the sector-level (or ecosystem) organization, mediated by the organization of the technology, is not only the main message of the four-lever framework (Gawer & Cusumano, 2002), but recalls the idea of contingency. Technological platforms allow us to observe a clear example of a case where there is a fit between internal organization, external organization, and technological organization.

NOTES

1. Woodward's (1958, 1965) findings were a fundamental element of what came to be known as contingency theory.
2. And manufacturing was the vanguard and the hope for the nation as a pathway to growth, in the aftermath of World War II, and people acquiring "things" (cars, washing machines, etc.) in a massive way, together with increased disposable income.
3. Woodward distinguished between three kinds of production technologies: small batch and unit technology; large batch and mass production; and continuous process production. Woodward described the technical complexity of a manufacturing process as the degree of its mechanization – unit technology as the least complex and the continuous process production as the most. She discovered that the relationship between technical complexity and the level of work routine was shaped as an inverse U. Unit and continuous process technologies required non-routine behavior, whereas mass production was better served by mechanical structures characterized by routines and procedures (see Woodward, 1965, 1958).
4. See Perrow in this volume.
5. In particular, Brandenburger and Nalebuff (1996) highlight the importance of "complementors" – developers of complementary products and services – which is a key concept in platforms.
6. The observations and hypotheses formulated in this chapter are exploratory and present rich opportunities for further empirical and theoretical research. The field of platform research is still very young. A vibrant community of researchers is emerging and a new book *Platforms, Markets and Innovation* (Gawer, 2009a) presents leading-edge contributions from 24 top international scholars from 19 universities across Europe, the United States, and Asia, from the disciplines of strategy, organizations, innovation, economics, and knowledge management.

ACKNOWLEDGMENT

Special thanks to Benoit Weil and Nelson Phillips for their helpful comments on this chapter.

REFERENCES

Baldwin, C. Y. (2008). Where do transactions come from? Modularity, transactions, and the boundaries of firms. *Industrial and Corporate Change*, *17*(1), 155–195.

Baldwin, C. Y., & Clark, K. B. (2000). *Design rules: The power of modularity*. Cambridge, MA: MIT Press.

Baldwin, C. Y., & Woodard, C. J. (2007). *Competition in modular clusters*. Working Paper 08-042, December. Harvard Business School, Boston, MA, USA.

Baldwin, C. Y., & Woodard, C. J. (2009). The architecture of platforms: A unified view. In: A. Gawer (Ed.), *Platforms, markets and innovation* (pp. 19–44). Cheltenham, UK; Northampton, MA: Edward Elgar.

Brandenburger, A., & Nalebuff, B. (1996). *Co-opetition: A revolutionary mindset that combines competition and cooperation*. New York: Currency Doubleday.

Bresnahan, T., & Greenstein, S. (1999). Technological competition and the structure of the computer industry. *Journal of Industrial Economics*, *47*, 1–40.

Eisenmann, T., Parker, G., & Van Alstyne, M. (2006). Strategies for two-sided markets. *Harvard Business Review*, *4*(10), 92–101.

Evans, D. S., Hagiu, A., & Schmalensee, R. (2006). *Invisible engines: How software platforms drive innovation and transform industries*. Cambridge, MA: MIT Press.

Farrell, J., & Katz, M. L. (2000). Innovation, rent extraction, and integration in systems markets. *Journal of Industrial Economics*, *97*(4), 413–432.

Gawer, A. (Ed.) (2009a). *Platforms, markets and innovation*. Cheltenham, UK and Northampton, MA, US: Edward Elgar.

Gawer, A. (2009b). In: *Platforms, markets and innovation* (pp. 1–18). Cheltenham, UK; Northampton, MA: Edward Elgar.

Gawer, A. (2009c). In: *Platforms, markets and innovation* (pp. 45–76). Cheltenham, UK; Northampton, MA: Edward Elgar.

Gawer, A., & Cusumano, M. A. (2002). *Platform leadership: How Intel, Microsoft, and Cisco drive industry innovation*. Boston, MA: Harvard Business School Press.

Gawer, A., & Cusumano, M. A. (2004). What does it take to be a platform leader: Some recent lessons from Palm and NTT DoCoMo. *Hitotsubashi Business Review*, *52*, 6–20.

Gawer, A., & Cusumano, M. A. (2008). How companies become platform leaders. *MIT Sloan Management Review*, *49*(2), 28–35.

Gawer, A., & Henderson, R. (2007). Platform owner entry and innovation in complementary markets: Evidence from Intel. *Journal of Economics and Management Strategy*, *16*(1), 1–34.

Iansiti, M., & Levien, R. (2004). *The keystone advantage: What the new dynamics of business ecosystems mean for strategy, innovation, and sustainability*. Boston, MA: Harvard University Press.

Kaplan, S., & Tripsas, M. (2008). Thinking about technology: Applying a cognitive lens to technical change. *Research Policy*, *37*, 780–805.

Katz, M. L., & Shapiro, C. (1985). Network externalities, competition and compatibility. *American Economic Review*, *75*(3), 424–440.

Langlois, R., & Robertson, P. (1992). Networks and innovation in a modular system: Lessons from the microcomputer and stereo component industries. *Research Policy*, *21*, 297–313.

Perrons, R. K. (2009). The open kimono: How Intel balances trust and power to maintain platform leadership. *Research Policy*, *38*(8), 1300–1312, October.

Rosenberg, N. (2000). Schumpeter and the endogeneity of technology: Some American perspectives. The Graz Schumpeter Lectures, 3, Routledge.

Sanchez, R., & Mahoney, J. T. (1996). Modularity, flexibility, and knowledge management in product and organization design. *Strategic Management Journal*, *17*, 63–76.

Schilling, M. A. (2000). Towards a general modular system theory and its application to interfirm product modularity. *Academy of Management Review*, *25*(2), 312–334.

Shapiro, C., & Varian, H. R. (1999). *Information rules: A strategic guide to the network economy*. Boston, MA: Harvard Business School Press.

Ulrich, K. (1995). The role of product architecture in the manufacturing firm. *Research Policy*, *24*(3), 419–440.

West, J. (2003). How open is open enough? Melding proprietary and open source platform strategies. *Research Policy*, *32*, 1259–1285.

Woodward, J. (1958). *Management and technology* (ISBN B0007J8T16). United Kingdom: H. M. Stationary Office.

Woodward, J. (1965). *Industrial organization: Theory and practice* (ISBN 0198741227). United Kingdom: Oxford University Press.